HIGH COURT CASE SUMMARIES

CIVIL PROCEDURE

Keyed to Subrin, Minnow, Brodin, and Main's Casebook on Civil Procedure, 2nd Edition

Memory Graphics by Steve Porter

THOMSON

WEST

Mat #40371062

© 2005 Thomson/West
     610 Opperman Drive
     P.O. Box 64526
     St. Paul, MN 55164–0526
     1–800–328–9352

Printed in the United States of America

ISBN 0–314–16151–1

TEXT IS PRINTED ON 10% POST CONSUMER RECYCLED PAPER

Table of Contents

Alphabetical Table of Cases

CHAPTER ONE

An Introduction to Civil Procedure

United States v. Hall

Instant Facts: Hall (D) entered onto school property to disrupt school activities after notice of a court injunction.

Black Letter Rule: A court sitting in equity may enforce its decisions against all nonparties who have received notice of its orders.

Goldberg v. Kelly

Instant Facts: Kelly (P) and other welfare recipients challenged New York City's (D) policy of terminating welfare benefits without a pre-termination hearing.

Black Letter Rule: Before a state can terminate welfare benefits, it must provide notice of the termination to the recipient and afford him or her an opportunity to be heard.

Mathews, Secretary of Health, Education and Welfare v. Eldridge

Instant Facts: Eldridge's (P) Social Security disability benefits were terminated without a pre-termination hearing after the state determined he was no longer disabled.

Black Letter Rule: Due process does not require a pre-termination evidentiary hearing prior to the termination of benefits unrelated to need when administrative procedures sufficiently afford the recipient an opportunity to challenge the determination.

Boddie v. Connecticut

Instant Facts: Boddie (P), a Connecticut welfare recipient, was unable to obtain a divorce because she could not financially afford the statutory filing fee.

Black Letter Rule: The Due Process Clause of the Fourteenth Amendment prohibits a state from imposing a filing fee upon an indigent litigant seeking a judicial dissolution of marriage.

Lassiter v. Department of Social Services of Durham County, North Carolina

Instant Facts: Lassiter's (D) parental rights were terminated in a civil proceeding brought by the Department of Social Services (P) after a hearing was conducted without the appointment of counsel by the court.

Black Letter Rule: The Due Process Clause of the Fourteenth Amendment requires the appointment of counsel to an indigent person in a civil proceeding only when she faces the loss of physical liberty or the balance of the interests so requires.

United States v. Hall

(*Prosecuting Government*) v. (*Black Activist*)

472 F.2d 261 (5th Cir. 1972)

AN ACTIVIST WAS GUILTY OF CRIMINAL CONTEMPT FOR ENTERING SCHOOL PROPERTY IN VIOLATION OF A COURT ORDER

■ **INSTANT FACTS** Hall (D) entered onto school property to disrupt school activities after notice of a court injunction.

■ **BLACK LETTER RULE** A court sitting in equity may enforce its decisions against all nonparties who have received notice of its orders.

■ **PROCEDURAL BASIS**

Appeal from a judgment of conviction for criminal contempt.

■ **FACTS**

In June 1971, the district court entered a judgment in a separate case requiring the Duval County Florida school board to complete its desegregation of Duval County schools by clustering schools that had previously been predominantly one-race schools. The court retained jurisdiction over the case to make further orders necessary to carry out its judgment. Following the order, a predominantly white school and a predominantly black school were merged to create one desegregated school. Thereafter, the superintendent of schools filed a petition for injunctive relief to restrain all students in the unified school and any person acting independently or in concert with students from interfering in the orderly operation of the school. The petition specifically named Hall (D), a member of a black militant group, as encouraging black students to boycott or otherwise disrupt school activities. The court ordered the injunction, providing that any person with notice who violated the order would be subject to arrest, prosecution, and punishment in criminal contempt. Hall (D) was personally served with the order, though he was not a party to the injunction action or the prior desegregation suit. Four days later, Hall (D) violated the order by entering upon school property to specifically breach the injunction. Hall (D) was arrested and convicted of criminal contempt. Hall (D) appealed the conviction.

■ **ISSUE**

Does a district court have power to punish for criminal contempt a person who, though neither a party nor bearing any legal relationship to a party, violates a court order designed to enforce the court's judgment in a school desegregation case?

■ **DECISION AND RATIONALE**

(Wisdom, J.) Yes. On appeal, Hall (D) argues that he is not bound by the court-ordered injunction because he was neither a party to the prior suit nor acting as a surrogate of a party to that suit. Hall (D) relies on state common law and Rule 65(d) of the Federal Rules of Civil Procedure. While it is true that a court order does not bind a nonparty acting independently of any party named to the suit, such a proposition does not apply when the nonparty's actions disturb the adjudication of the rights and obligations of the original parties. Here, Hall's (D) actions threatened the rights of students to attend an integrated school and the duty of the school district to provide such an educational environment. A court of equity has inherent jurisdiction to preserve the ability to issue orders necessary to enforce its prior judgments. The underlying desegregation order inures to the benefit of the large class of people not initially involved in the original suit. The potential disruption of the court's desegregation order by an indefinable class of persons not a party to the original action requires the court's continuing jurisdiction to effectively enforce the rights and duties adjudged. Rule 65(d) was intended to extend the common-law reach of injunctive relief beyond the parties specifically named, to include others acting in privity with the named parties. It was intended as a codification of the common law, not a limitation upon it. Though a court may not bind all persons by an order for injunctive relief, Hall (D) is bound because he was placed on notice of the order and failed to challenge its application before the court. Under both the common law and Rule 65(d), the court correctly exercised its jurisdiction to enforce its prior desegregation order. Affirmed.

Analysis

Rule 65(d) provides that an injunction is "binding only upon the parties to the action, their officers, agents, servants, employees, and attorneys, and upon those persons in active concert or participation with them who receive actual notice of the order." Thus, a nonparty to the injunction proceeding can be charged with violating the injunction in some circumstances. A distinction must be drawn between violation of the injunction and conduct rising to the level of criminal contempt. While only those classes of persons defined in the rule can be bound by the literal terms of the injunction, one who knowingly and deliberately violates a court order after receiving actual notice of its terms can be charged with criminal contempt notwithstanding his or her relationship to the parties.

CASE VOCABULARY:

CRIMINAL CONTEMPT: An act that obstructs justice or attacks the integrity of the court.

INJUNCTION: A court order commanding or preventing an action.

Goldberg v. Kelly

(*Commissioner of Social Services*) v. (*Federal Aid Recipient*)

397 U.S. 254, 90 S.Ct. 1011 (1970)

WELFARE BENEFITS SERVE IMPORTANT SOCIAL AND GOVERNMENT INTERESTS AND CANNOT BE TERMINATED WITHOUT A HEARING

■ **INSTANT FACTS** Kelly (P) and other welfare recipients challenged New York City's (D) policy of terminating welfare benefits without a pre-termination hearing.

■ **BLACK LETTER RULE** Before a state can terminate welfare benefits, it must provide notice of the termination to the recipient and afford him or her an opportunity to be heard.

■ PROCEDURAL BASIS

Certiorari to review a decision of the district court finding a state procedure unconstitutional.

■ FACTS

New York City residents receiving federal financial assistance under the Aid to Families with Dependent Children (AFDC) law sued the State of New York (D) for terminating their financial benefits without prior notice and a hearing, denying them due process of law. Though there was no procedure for notice and a hearing prior to the termination of aid before the suit, the state subsequently implemented such procedures, which were challenged by the plaintiffs as insufficient. The administrative regulations were changed to require notice prior to the termination of benefits, with such notice containing the reasons for the termination and affording a recipient the right to a post-termination evidentiary hearing to challenge the determination. However, the regulations failed to provide for an evidentiary hearing *before* termination. The plaintiffs claimed the lack of a pre-termination hearing violates the Due Process Clause. The district court agreed, finding that only a pre-termination hearing satisfies due process. Goldberg (D), the New York City Commissioner of Social Services, appealed.

■ ISSUE

Does the termination of public assistance payments to a particular recipient without affording him or her the opportunity for an evidentiary hearing prior to termination deny the recipient of procedural due process in violation of the Due Process Clause of the Fourteenth Amendment?

■ DECISION AND RATIONALE

(Brennan, J.) Yes. The termination of welfare benefits involves state action that adjudicates the important statutory entitlements of persons qualified to receive them. The termination of welfare aid, unlike some other governmental benefits programs, involves the deprivation of the means of obtaining food, clothing, and shelter, for without it the recipient is without independent resources on which to live. Termination of these benefits without notice and an opportunity to be heard beforehand violates the recipients' procedural due process rights. Pre-termination notice and opportunity for a hearing promote important government interests in this context. Welfare helps provide the poor the same opportunities available to those more fortunate. Also, welfare curbs the social malaise resulting from financial frustration and insecurity. Pre-termination evidentiary hearings are important to ensure that these interests are not unjustifiably infringed. Countervailing interests in preserving fiscal and administrative resources do not outweigh the interests in maintaining welfare benefits when appropriate, for the state may reduce this burden by implementing a procedure for timely pre-termination hearings when requested. Although due process requires a pre-termination hearing, this hearing need not resemble a judicial proceeding. So long as the pre-termination hearing reasonably produces an initial determination of the validity of the state's grounds for discontinuing the recipient's payments in order to protect the recipient from an erroneous termination of his or her benefits, the hearing meets due process requirements. The hearings must afford only the minimum procedural safeguards, designed to the particular needs of welfare recipients, and limited to the controversy at issue. Accordingly, before a state may terminate welfare benefits, it must provide adequate notice of the termination with the reasons for termination and an evidentiary hearing at which the recipient may confront witnesses and present evidence supporting the case. Affirmed.

■ DISSENT

(Black, J.) The United States has become too much of a welfare state, taxing affluent citizens for the benefit of those less fortunate. Those receiving welfare benefits have been selected by state welfare officials according to criteria establishing their eligibility. Undoubtedly, some error occurs in the course of identifying welfare eligibility. The Court's decision requires that the states, upon discovering such errors, continue to pay these undeserving recipients from state funds until a pre-termination hearing can be completed. The Due Process Clause does not, however, provide such broad protection. Just as when a private individual cannot be compelled to pay an undeserving recipient money under a prior understanding, the Due Process Clause cannot compel the payment of public money to undeserving private recipients until a determination of ineligibility, including administrative hearings, judicial hearings, and potential appeals, is final. If such a system is desired in this country, it should not be founded on constitutional principles, but left to Congress to direct in its legislative capacity.

Analysis

Goldberg v. Kelly culminated a strong debate over the nature of interests involved in the newly designed social welfare programs of the 1960s. While the Court ultimately concluded that welfare recipients are entitled to procedural protections from deprivation of the statutory entitlements for which they are eligible, no substantive rights were guaranteed to the recipients. Proponents of substantive rights sought to guarantee every American a minimum income, the right to jobs, and other rights.

■ CASE VOCABULARY

PROCEDURAL DUE PROCESS: The minimal requirements of notice and a hearing guaranteed by the Due Process Clauses of the Fifth and Fourteenth Amendments, especially if the deprivation of a significant life, liberty, or property interest may occur.

Mathews, Secretary of Health, Education and Welfare v. Eldridge

(*Secretary of Health, Education and Welfare*) v. (*Social Security Recipient*)

424 U.S. 319, 96 S.Ct. 893 (1976)

STATE ADMINISTRATIVE PROCEDURES FOR DETERMINING INELIGIBILITY FOR SOCIAL SECURITY DISABILITY BENEFITS SATISFY DUE PROCESS

■ **INSTANT FACTS** Eldridge's (P) Social Security disability benefits were terminated without a pre-termination hearing after the state determined he was no longer disabled.

■ **BLACK LETTER RULE** Due process does not require a pre-termination evidentiary hearing prior to the termination of benefits unrelated to need when administrative procedures sufficiently afford the recipient an opportunity to challenge the determination.

■ **PROCEDURAL BASIS**

Certiorari to review a decision of the court of appeals requiring a pre-termination hearing before Social Security benefits are withheld.

■ **FACTS**

Eldridge (P) was awarded Social Security benefits based on a complete disability for which such benefits are available. Four years later, he received a questionnaire from the state agency charged with administering the program to monitor his medical condition. In completing the questionnaire, Eldridge (P) indicated that his condition had not improved and identified the physicians who had recently treated his condition. The state obtained reports from his physician and a psychiatric consultant and informed Eldridge (P) by letter that on the basis of the reports it had concluded that he was no longer disabled and was ineligible for continuing Social Security benefits. The letter provided a statement of reasons for the proposed termination and informed Eldridge (P) that he could request reasonable time to obtain additional information to support his disability. In response, Eldridge (P) claimed the state already had sufficient information on his disability and disputed one characterization of his medical condition. The state made its final determination, which was accepted by the Social Security Administration. When notifying Eldridge (P) of his ineligibility, the Social Security Administration advised him that he could seek reconsideration within six months. In lieu of reconsideration, Eldridge (P) filed suit against the Secretary of Health, Education and Welfare (D), challenging the constitutionality of the administrative procedures for terminating his benefits without providing him with a pre-termination hearing. After the district court ruled on the defendant's motion to dismiss, the court of appeals determined that a pre-termination hearing was required under *Goldberg v. Kelly*. The Secretary of Health, Education and Welfare (D) appealed.

■ **ISSUE**

Does the Due Process Clause of the Fifth Amendment require that, prior to the termination of Social Security disability benefit payments, the recipient be afforded an opportunity for an evidentiary hearing?

■ **DECISION AND RATIONALE**

(Powell, J.) No. Due process is a flexible concept that generally provides a person the opportunity to be heard at a meaningful time and in a meaningful manner before he or she is deprived of a property interest. The Secretary (D) argues that the existing administrative procedures satisfy this requirement. The existing procedures require the state to investigate the recipient's disability through consultation with physicians and a non-medical person trained in disability evaluation, as well as steady contact with the recipient. Thereafter, the state informs the recipient whenever its initial evaluation differs from the recipient's assessment, providing the basis for the state's evaluation and affording the recipient an opportunity to review the evidence in the case file and provide additional evidence. Once a final determination is made and accepted by the Social Security Administration, the recipient is informed of the decision in writing and advised that de novo reconsideration is available upon request. Upon a request for reconsideration, the recipient has the right to an evidentiary hearing before an administrative law judge. Benefit termination is enforced two months after the month during which the recipient ceases to be disabled.

To determine whether these procedures provide the recipient with due process, the private and governmental interests affected must be reviewed. Just as in *Goldberg*, the recipient's interest at stake here is only the uninterrupted receipt of benefits, for he is entitled to full retroactive benefits should he prevail. Unlike the welfare benefits at issue in *Goldberg*, however, Social Security benefits are not based on need, for access to other private financial sources or government programs does not affect the recipient's eligibility. Eldridge (P) is less likely to be left without means of survival by the loss of disability benefits than a welfare recipient whose benefits are terminated would be. Additionally, the administrative procedures at issue are based not on the subjective views of a caseworker, but on the objective evidence provided by unbiased medical professionals treating the recipient. A pre-termination hearing is less likely to contribute additional evidence that would render such objective evidence unreliable or unfair. Finally, the procedures afford the terminated recipient full access to all evidence reviewed to determine his eligibility and an opportunity to bring forth additional evidence before he stops receiving benefits. The recipient's private interests are sufficiently safeguarded by the existing procedures.

The minor burden on Eldridge's (P) private interests must be considered in light of the public interests at stake. A constitutionally required pre-termination hearing would require continuing benefits to an undeserving recipient until the completion of the administrative and judicial processes. Because the likelihood that the state erred in its objective determination is minimal, the public cost of such a requirement outweighs the private and public interests in ensuring a just decision is made. The ultimate public interest, however, lies in the desire to preserve administrative action without judicial-type procedures. Administrative agencies operate without the complexities of strict rules of procedure, trial, and review in order to provide a swift decision. Evidentiary hearings are not an effective method of administrative decision-making and are not required as long as administrative procedures are narrowly tailored to afford those affected with a meaningful opportunity to present their case. As the existing procedures provide such a safeguard, they comply with due process. A pre-termination evidentiary hearing is not required. Reversed.

■ DISSENT

(Brennan, J.) The Court's decision presumes recipients of disability benefits have no financial need for the benefits in order to assure a means of survival without a detailed examination of the specific needs of the recipient. The legislative determination that benefits are to be afforded without consideration of need, however, leads to the opposite presumption—that the recipient in fact does need benefits to survive. Here, Eldridge (P) lost his home and family furniture following the termination of his benefits. The availability of other government benefits, should the need surface, provides no justification for the Court's holding.

Analysis:

Following *Goldberg v. Kelly*, the Court considered many due process challenges to established administrative procedures governing federal assistance programs. In an effort to delineate the limits of *Goldberg*, the Court's three-part analysis sets forth several criteria a court must consider to determine whether due process is offended: a court must consider (1) the private interests at stake, (2) the government's interests, and (3) the risk that the procedures used will lead to erroneous decisions. Critics of the *Eldridge* factors argue that the Court gives too much deference to the decisions of district court judges to reach a conclusion based not on constitutional notions of due process, but rather on the utilitarian value of the procedures in maximizing social welfare.

CASE VOCABULARY

PROCEDURAL DUE PROCESS: The minimal requirements of notice and a hearing guaranteed by the Due Process Clauses of the Fifth and Fourteenth Amendments, especially if the deprivation of a significant life, liberty, or property interest may occur.

Boddie v. Connecticut

(Welfare Recipient) v. *(State Government)*

401 U.S. 371, 91 S.Ct. 780 (1971)

A STATE MUST ENSURE COURT ACCESS TO ALL INDIGENT LITIGANTS SEEKING A DIVORCE

■ **INSTANT FACTS** Boddie (P), a Connecticut welfare recipient, was unable to obtain a divorce because she could not financially afford the statutory filing fee.

■ **BLACK LETTER RULE** The Due Process Clause of the Fourteenth Amendment prohibits a state from imposing a filing fee upon an indigent litigant seeking a judicial dissolution of marriage.

■ **PROCEDURAL BASIS**

Certiorari to review the constitutionality of a state statute.

■ **FACTS**

Boddie (P) was a welfare recipient who sought to file for divorce in a Connecticut court. Connecticut requires payment of a $40 filing fee, and a small fee for service of process is required to commence any action. Unable to afford the fees, Boddie (P) was unable to file for divorce. Boddie (P) filed suit on behalf of herself and all others similarly situated, claiming the state filing fee requirement deprived her access to the courts in violation of the Due Process Clause of the Fourteenth Amendment. The district court granted the state's (D) motion to dismiss. Boddie (P) appealed.

■ **ISSUE**

Does due process prohibit a state from denying, solely because of inability to pay, access to its courts to individuals who seek judicial dissolution of their marriages?

■ **DECISION AND RATIONALE**

(Harlan, J.) Yes. The Due Process Clauses of the Fifth and Fourteenth Amendments serve as a guide to the court system in ensuring that all individuals are not deprived of life, liberty, or property. Due process challenges typically involve the rights of defendants, for court action can rarely deprive a plaintiff of interests in life, liberty, or property because sufficient alternative avenues of relief often exist. However, the marital relationship is a fundamental aspect of life over which the states extend considerable regulation. Dissolution of a marriage can be achieved only through resort to the judicial process. Accordingly, a plaintiff's right to access to the courts presents the same due process concerns often faced by defendants who must necessarily resort to the courts because of the election of the opposing party. Due process requires, at a minimum, that those forced to settle their differences through the courts be afforded a meaningful opportunity to be heard. The state's (D) interest in preventing frivolous lawsuits and ensuring the allocation of resources is substantial. However, a statute that requires a fee to gain access to the courts as the only available avenue of relief violates the Due Process Clause when the litigant sufficiently demonstrates that by reason of her indigency, she is unable to obtain a legal divorce. While due process has been violated in this instance, the Court declines to find an absolute constitutional right to access to the courts in all circumstances not involving the judicial adjustment of a fundamental human relationship. Reversed.

■ DISSENT

(Black, J.) Without specific constitutional regulation, the institution of marriage, and therefore divorce, lies exclusively within the powers of the states because it is of peculiar importance to the people of the states. The Court's decision, however, extends so little respect to the power of the state so as to deprive it of charging even a nominal fee in the exercise of its power. While due process has been afforded to indigent criminal defendants who would otherwise be unable to appeal convictions because of their indigency, civil actions do not command such protections. A criminal defendant is entitled to relief from court-imposed filing fees because she is thrust into the system by the actions of the government, who stands both as arbiter and opponent. In the civil system, the government does not compel a party's participation, but merely provides a neutral forum for her to resolve her differences. Because of these important distinctions, the strict requirements of the Due Process Clause should not be imposed upon a state in a civil action as they are in criminal matters.

Analysis

Federal rules of civil and appellate procedure now address proceedings involving indigent litigants. In general, a party may proceed *in forma pauperis* upon a timely application to the court establishing indigency. If the court is satisfied that the party is truly indigent, certain court fees and costs will be waived to ensure the party's constitutional access to the court. Once established at the trial level, the party may continue to proceed *in forma pauperis* while any appeals remain pending.

■ CASE VOCABULARY

PROCEDURAL DUE PROCESS: The minimal requirements of notice and a hearing guaranteed by the Due Process Clauses of the Fifth and Fourteenth Amendments, especially if the deprivation of a significant life, liberty, or property interest may occur.

IN FORMA PAUPERIS: In the manner of an indigent who is permitted to disregard filing fees and court costs.

Lassiter v. Department of Social Services of Durham County, North Carolina

(Mother) v. *(Department of Social Services)*
452 U.S. 18, 101 S.Ct. 2153 (1981)

AN INDIGENT PARENT IS NOT ENTITLED TO APPOINTED COUNSEL PRIOR TO THE TERMINATION OF PARENTAL RIGHTS

■ **INSTANT FACTS:** Lassiter's (D) parental rights were terminated in a civil proceeding brought by the Department of Social Services (P) after a hearing was conducted without the appointment of counsel by the court.

■ **BLACK LETTER RULE** The Due Process Clause of the Fourteenth Amendment requires the appointment of counsel to an indigent person in a civil proceeding only when she faces the loss of physical liberty or the balance of the interests so requires.

■ **PROCEDURAL BASIS**

Certiorari to review a decision of the North Carolina Court of Appeals affirming the trial court's decision terminating the defendant's parental rights.

■ **FACTS**

After a hearing, a North Carolina court declared Lassiter's (D) son neglected due to her failure to provide him with necessary medical care and ordered the child transferred to the custody of the Department of Social Services (P). The next year, Lassiter (P) was convicted of first-degree murder and began serving a twenty-five-to forty-year sentence. Two years later, the Department of Social Services petitioned the court to terminate Lassiter's (D) parental rights because she failed to remain involved in the child's life and effectively abandoned him. Lassiter (D) was served with the petition and notice of the hearing while in prison, but failed to inform the attorney retained for her in the criminal matter of the hearing. At the Department's (P) request, Lassiter (P) was brought from prison to the hearing. At the beginning of the hearing, the court considered whether the hearing should be postponed to afford Lassiter (D) additional time in which to consult with an attorney. Finding that Lassiter (P) had ample time to retain counsel prior to the hearing, the court proceeded with the hearing. At no time did Lassiter (D) claim she was indigent or request the appointment of counsel. After the Department (P) offered witness testimony demonstrating Lassiter's (D) lack of involvement in the child's life, Lassiter (D) was permitted to cross-examine the witnesses and offer testimony on her own behalf. After the close of the evidence, the court found that Lassiter (D) had not contacted the Department (P) since custody was transferred and willfully failed to maintain concern or responsibility for her son's welfare, and it therefore terminated her parental rights. Lassiter (D) appealed, arguing that because she was indigent, the Due Process Clause of the Fourteenth Amendment required the assistance of counsel provided by the state. The North Carolina Court of Appeals affirmed. After the Supreme Court of North Carolina denied her petition for discretionary review, Lassiter (D) appealed to the United States Supreme Court.

■ **ISSUE**

Does the Due Process Clause of the Fourteenth Amendment require the appointment of counsel to an indigent defendant in a proceeding for the termination of her parental rights?

■ **DECISION AND RATIONALE**

(Stewart, J.) No. Due process is not a static concept, but rather a flexible requirement embodying fundamental fairness under particular circumstances. To determine what is fundamentally fair, the court must consider both the relevant precedents and the interests that are at stake. While the Sixth Amendment may require the appointment of counsel to criminal defendants who cannot afford an attorney, the Fourteenth Amendment similarly applies to a civil litigant who may face institutionalization or other deprivation of personal freedom upon the outcome of the case. Fundamental fairness has thus been determined to require the appointment of counsel to an indigent litigant when, if she loses, she may be deprived of her physical liberty. Under *Mathews v. Eldridge*, a court must in all other cases consider the private interests at stake, the government's interests, and the risk that the procedures used will lead to erroneous decisions to determine whether a procedure violates due process. These three elements must be weighed and applied against the presumption that due process will be violated absent the appointment of counsel only when, if the litigant loses, her personal freedom will be sacrificed.

A person's parental interests are undoubtedly among the most vital private interests, which require substantial protection. If the state succeeds in a parental-rights-termination suit, it not only infringes upon this interest, but ends it. The state has a similarly important interest in ensuring the health and welfare of the child. These interests are often shared with the parent, for both ordinarily seek the utmost protection of a child's welfare. When a state seeks to terminate parental interests, however, the state's interests and the parent's interests diverge. The state's interest is in achieving the termination and expending the least amount of economical and judicial resources necessary. As important as this interest is, it must necessarily yield to the parental interest in providing for the child. The question remains whether the procedure established for the termination of parental rights risks erroneous decisions. While the North Carolina procedure limits those who may seek the termination of parental rights, requires a detailed factual basis for a termination, and demands that the parent be afforded notice and an opportunity to be heard, the risk of erroneous decisions is sufficiently high without representation by counsel. Termination proceedings often require expert or medical evidence to support the state's case. Parents, many of whom may possess little education, are not likely to be sufficiently able to understand such evidence in order to formulate a meaningful response. Without the assistance of counsel in this regard, the risk of an erroneous judgment is substantial.

Because due process requires a particularized analysis of the three *Mathews v. Eldridge* factors to determine whether they rebut the presumption that a litigant is entitled to the appointment of counsel only when her personal freedom is at risk, the trial court is best suited to make such a decision, subject to appellate review. Here, no expert witnesses were offered at trial nor were complicated points of law at issue. While Lassiter (D) failed to completely present her defense and some hearsay evidence was admitted, the presence of counsel would not have changed the outcome. The weight of the evidence supported the court's finding that Lassiter (D) had failed to maintain a meaningful relationship with the child, such that the absence of the assistance of counsel could be deemed fundamentally unfair. Affirmed.

■ **DISSENT**

(Blackmun, J.) Because the parent's unique interest in maintaining the care and custody of her child is of utmost importance and the state's interests at stake pale in comparison, due process requires the appointment of counsel in a termination proceeding. On numerous occasions, the Court has considered under which circumstances the appointment of counsel is required. In each instance, the Court has held that due process necessarily varies according to the private interests at stake and the nature of the proceedings. Implicit in these decisions is the assertion that as the personal interests heighten, the importance of the assistance of counsel increases to ensure fundamental fairness. Evaluating the three factors considered by the majority, due process requires the appointment of counsel in termination proceedings. The personal interest in retaining the custody and companionship of one's child is one of the most fundamental and vital interests an individual possesses. The loss of this interest is just as critical to the individual as the loss of personal freedom. The Court's perceived presumption that physical confinement comprises the limits of deprivation insensitively ignores the crucial significance of other rights, including the right to care for one's child.

When the personal interests at stake are so vital as those at issue here, fundamental fairness requires that every procedural protection be afforded to the parent. Additionally, just as in a criminal proceeding, a termination proceeding presents an adversarial challenge to a person's individual rights, initiated by the state and against the litigant's will. The risk of erroneous decisions is at least as great in a termination proceeding as in a criminal proceeding, during which the assistance of counsel is required. Without the assistance of counsel, a parent who has successfully resurrected her life to the satisfaction of the state may be incapable of so proving, whether due to intimidation, inarticulateness, or confusion. This problem similarly diminishes the state's legitimate interests in protecting the well-being of children, for the best interests of the child may be to remain in the care or custody of his or her mother, rather than in the custody of the state or foster parents. While the majority's evaluation of these three factors is substantially similar, it chooses an illogical conclusion that due process does not require the appointment of counsel in such cases, resorting instead to a case-by-case approach wrought with danger. In this case, the trial court failed to consider whether better alternatives to the termination of Lassiter's (D) rights existed, such as whether custody of the child would be better given to his grandmother than the state. This result is due in large part to Lassiter's (D) inability to present a defense without the assistance of counsel. If due process requires concessions to an indigent person seeking access to the court to obtain a divorce, as in *Boddie v. Connecticut*, due process similarly requires the appointment of counsel to an indigent person facing the sad consequence of losing her parental rights.

Analysis:

Since *Lassiter* was decided, most states have enacted statutes directly addressing the availability of counsel to an indigent parent in a termination proceeding. While some statutes specifically require the appointment of counsel, others leave such an appointment to the discretion of the trial judge. When discretionary, a judge must take *Lassiter*'s case-by-case approach to determine whether due process requires the appointment under the circumstances.

CHAPTER TWO

Remedies and Stakes

Fuentes v. Shevin

Instant Facts: Fuentes's (P) property was seized after a creditor obtained a writ of replevin under a Florida statute.

Black Letter Rule: Due process requires notice and an opportunity to be heard at a meaningful time and in a meaningful manner before the deprivation of an important life, liberty, or property interest.

American Hospital Supply Corp. v. Hospital Products Ltd.

Instant Facts: American Hospital Supply Corp. (P) obtained a preliminary injunction against Hospital Products Ltd. (D) to prevent the defendant from continuing to breach a contract between the parties.

Black Letter Rule: A preliminary injunction may be issued when the risk of irreparable harm to the plaintiff if the injunction is denied outweighs the risk of irreparable harm to the defendant if it is granted.

Walgreen Co. v. Sara Creek Property Co.

Instant Facts: Walgreen's (P) obtained a court injunction against Sara Creek Property Co. (D) to prevent the lease of space in the defendant's shopping mall in violation of Walgreen's (P) lease.

Black Letter Rule: A permanent injunction is appropriate in a breach of contract case when the benefits of the injunction outweigh the costs associated with calculating actual damages.

Carey v. Piphus

Instant Facts: Students were suspended for violating school rules without affording them an opportunity to be heard.

Black Letter Rule: A denial of due process is actionable for nominal damages even without proof of actual injury, but actual injury must be proven in order for compensatory damages to be awarded.

Marek v. Chesney

Instant Facts: Following judgment for the plaintiff, Chesney (P) sought recovery of costs and attorney's fees incurred after he rejected the defendants' settlement offer.

Black Letter Rule: Rule 68 of the Federal Rules of Civil Procedure permits the recovery of attorney's fees as a part of the costs of litigation if so provided by the underlying substantive statute governing the action.

City of Riverside v. Rivera

Instant Facts: The plaintiffs' were awarded $245,256.75 in attorney's fees following a civil rights trial in which they recovered $66,700 in compensatory and punitive damages.

Black Letter Rule: Under 42 U.S.C. § 1988, an attorney's fee award, for reasonable hours expended at a reasonable hourly rate, is reasonable though it exceeds the ultimate monetary recovery at trial.

Walker v. City of Birmingham

Instant Facts: Black protesters organized public marches in blatant violation of a court injunction enforcing a city parade ordinance requiring a permit for public demonstrations.

Black Letter Rule: Civil disobedience of an unchallenged unconstitutional statute or court order exposes the offenders to contempt liability.

Fuentes v. Shevin

(*Consumer*) v. (*Unknown State Representative*)

407 U.S. 67, 92 S.Ct. 1983 (1972)

STATE STATUTES PERMITTING A WRIT OF REPLEVIN WITHOUT NOTICE TO THE POSSESSOR OF PROPERTY VIOLATE DUE PROCESS

■ **INSTANT FACTS:** Fuentes's (P) property was seized after a creditor obtained a writ of replevin under a Florida statute.

■ **BLACK LETTER RULE:** Due process requires notice and an opportunity to be heard at a meaningful time and in a meaningful manner before the deprivation of an important life, liberty, or property interest.

■ **PROCEDURAL BASIS**

Certiorari to review decisions of two district courts denying due process challenges to state prejudgment replevin statutes.

■ **FACTS**

Fuentes (P) purchased a gas stove and service policy from Firestone Tire and Rubber Company under a sales contract calling for periodic monthly payments. A few months later, she purchased a stereo from Firestone under a similar contract. Under the contracts, Firestone maintained ownership of the goods until Fuentes (P) made all payments due under the contracts. After some time, a dispute arose over the servicing of the stove, and Fuentes (P) refused to continue her monthly payments on both the stove and the stereo. Firestone sued Fuentes (P) in small claims court for repossession of both items and simultaneously obtained a writ of replevin ordering the sheriff to seize the property. Under Florida law, a party need only complete a form requesting a writ of replevin upon the filing of a civil complaint to have the sheriff seize property allegedly wrongfully detained. The next day, a deputy sheriff arrived at Fuentes' (P) house and seized the stove and stereo. Fuentes (P) thereafter filed suit challenging the constitutionally of Florida's prejudgment replevin statute on due process grounds. The district court held that the statute did not violate due process because the items seized were not necessities. Fuentes (P) appealed. The United States Supreme Court consolidated her appeal with a similar suit contesting Pennsylvania's prejudgment replevin statute.

■ **ISSUE**

Does a state prejudgment replevin statute permitting the issuance of an ex parte writ of replevin without prior notice and an opportunity to be heard violate the Due Process Clause of the Fourteenth Amendment?

■ **DECISION AND RATIONALE**

(Stewart, J.) Yes. The Florida statute allows a person to obtain a writ of replevin without any convincing showing of entitlement to the property. The statute authorizes a court clerk to issue the writ upon the completion of an application concurrent with the filing of a complaint for repossession and the posting of a bond. The writ is issued without notice to the party in possession of the property and without an opportunity to be heard on his or her valid possessory claims. The only hearing afforded to a defendant is after the property seizure has occurred and during the course of the suit for repossession. Similarly,

Pennsylvania's statute affords a post-seizure hearing if initiated by the defendant. Procedural due process requires that a party whose property rights are affected be entitled to notice and an opportunity to be heard at a meaningful time and a meaningful manner. The right to be heard not only ensures fair treatment throughout the judicial process, but also protects the individual's right to the use and enjoyment of his or her property against arbitrary deprivations. If this right is to be enforced, it must be afforded at a time when such deprivations may still be prevented.

The statutes at issue violate due process. They permit a party to obtain a writ of replevin by posting a bond, merely alleging a right to the property. While the preliminary steps provide some protection, they do not satisfy due process by providing the right to be heard before the property deprivation. Though the property at issue may be nonessential, the deprivation may be only temporary, and the possessor may not have full title to the property, the right to the use and enjoyment of the property has been established, requiring due process before any property seizure. Under "extraordinary situations," notice and an opportunity to be heard can be postponed when the seizure is directly necessary to further an important government interest requiring prompt action initiated by a government official. But the state replevin statutes do not fall into this unique category, for the writs are sought by private individuals for private purposes. No governmental interest is implicated requiring the suspension of the possessor's due process rights. The Florida and Pennsylvania statutes violate the Due Process Clause by permitting the deprivation of property interests without notice and an opportunity to be heard. Vacated and remanded.

Analysis

The important factor invalidating the Florida and Pennsylvania replevin statutes was the lack of court involvement in the granting of the writ. Shortly after *Fuentes* was decided, the Supreme Court upheld a similar Louisiana statute permitting the recovery of goods purchased under an installment sales contract upon an application and posting of a bond without notice and an opportunity for a hearing to the possessor. Unlike the statutes in *Fuentes*, however, the statute required the application to be made to the court, which ensures that a sufficient factual basis exists before the writ is issued.

■ CASE VOCABULARY

PROCEDURAL DUE PROCESS: The minimal requirements of notice and a hearing guaranteed by the Due Process Clause of the Fifth and Fourteenth Amendments, especially if the deprivation of significant life, liberty, or property interest may occur.

REPLEVIN: An action for the repossession of personal property wrongfully taken or detained by the defendant, whereby the plaintiff gives security for and holds the property until the court decides who owns it.

American Hospital Supply Corp. v. Hospital Products Ltd.

(*Distributor*) v. (*Supplier*)

780 F.2d 589 (7th Cir. 1986)

WHEN IRREPARABLE HARM MAY BE SUFFERED, TEMPORARY INJUNCTION SHOULD ISSUE

■ **INSTANT FACTS** American Hospital Supply Corp. (P) obtained a preliminary injunction against Hospital Products Ltd. (D) to prevent the defendant from continuing to breach a contract between the parties.

■ **BLACK LETTER RULE:** A preliminary injunction may be issued when the risk of irreparable harm to the plaintiff if the injunction is denied outweighs the risk of irreparable harm to the defendant if it is granted.

■ PROCEDURAL BASIS

Appeal from a district court order granting a preliminary injunction.

■ FACTS

Hospital Products Ltd. (D), a manufacturer of reusable surgical stapling systems that had filed for reorganization in bankruptcy at the time of the suit, entered into a supply contract with American Hospital Supply Corp. (P) as the plaintiff's exclusive distributor of its stapling systems in the United States. The contract extended initially for three years, with automatic one-year renewals unless the plaintiff notified the defendant at least ninety days prior to the end of the three-year period that it wished to terminate the contract. Exactly ninety days before the three-year contract expired, the defendant hand-delivered a letter to the plaintiff demanding to know whether it wished to terminate the contract. The plaintiff responded, that day, that since it was not terminating the contract, it was renewed for one additional year. The next day, the defendant informed the plaintiff that it had considered the contract terminated and thereafter informed the plaintiff's dealers that the plaintiff was no longer authorized to distribute its products. American Hospital (P) sued Hospital Products (D) for breach of contract and obtained a preliminary injunction forbidding the defendant from further breaching the contract and requiring the defendant to inform the plaintiff's dealers that the plaintiff remains an authorized distributor. Hospital Products (D) appealed.

■ ISSUE

Did the trial court err in granting the plaintiff a preliminary injunction against the defendant?

■ DECISION AND RATIONALE

(Posner, J.) No. Because the record is incomplete, the risk of error in granting or denying a preliminary injunction is substantial and the effects of the error often irreparable. If a preliminary injunction is granted when relief should not have been afforded, the defendant suffers irreparable harm while it is in effect, and if the preliminary injunction is denied to one to whom relief should have been afforded, he or she suffers irreparable harm by the denial. The costs of error can be minimized however, by weighing the harm to the plaintiff if the injunction is denied, multiplied by the likelihood of the plaintiff's success at trial, against the harm to the defendant if the injunction is granted, multiplied by the likelihood that the plaintiff will not succeed at trial. Like the well-established formula for determining negligence, these factors can be reduced to a simple formula: If $P \times H_p > (1-P) \times H_d$, injunctive relief should be granted.

This formula embodies the four factors traditionally considered by a court in determining whether an injunction should be granted. These factors serve to provide the court a basis for determining which course of action minimizes the risk of error in its decision.

Applying these four factors here, the court's decision to grant the preliminary injunction produces the least risk of error. In determining the extent of irreparable harm to the plaintiff, the focus must be on whether the plaintiff will be damaged in the future if the injunction is not granted, for past damages are actionable under a breach of contract suit for money damages. Looking to the future, although the plaintiff was able to replace the defendant's product offering with a suitable alternative, the defendant's letter to the plaintiff's dealers may have damaged the goodwill between the plaintiff and those dealers by the suddenness and urgency of the termination. While goodwill may be considered as a potential harm to the plaintiff, it is speculative and may have been cured by the defendant's retraction. The greater risk of harm to the plaintiff lies in its unsold inventory obtained from the defendant. The plaintiff obtained the inventory in part as security on loans extended to the defendant and also by purchasing more inventory than needed because the defendant requested financial assistance. It is not unlikely that the plaintiff's dealers will refuse to purchase the plaintiff's surgical stapling systems for fear of future litigation over the purchase. While this harm is not typically irreparable, the defendant's insolvency suggests the plaintiff may be otherwise unable to dispose of the excess inventory if not able to sell it to its dealers. While the exact amount of damages incurred by the plaintiff is uncertain, it is substantial and irreparable.

The harm presented to the defendant is the consequence of insolvency resulting from an extension of the supply contract for an additional year. The continuing financial loss faced by the defendant and its shareholders, if permitted through trial, may require the conversion of the defendant's bankruptcy reorganization into liquidation, reducing the value of the defendant's assets at auction or to a subsequent purchaser. While these substantial costs must be considered, they are insufficient to conclude that the preliminary injunction here was in error. The costs to nonparties similarly must be considered. The costs to the hospital dealers purchasing the defendant's products, however, are not significant. If the injunction were denied, the dealers would continue to have access to the defendant's products, though directly from the defendant rather than through the plaintiff as the defendant's distributor. Because the risk of irreparable harm to the plaintiff if the injunction is denied outweighs the risk of irreparable harm to the defendant if it were granted, the district court correctly granted the preliminary injunction. Affirmed.

■ DISSENT

(Swygert, J.) The court's effort to quantify the four factors that must be considered in deciding whether to issue injunctive relief possesses only limited value. Derived from well-founded tort principles, the court's formula for weighing the considerations for equitable relief ignores the obvious distinctions between cases sounding in tort and those brought in equity. In tort, the judgment must be definite, while equitable relief must be flexible to sufficiently address the issues that arise. The variables established by the court in its formula are incapable of numerical calculation, for the probability of success on the merits cannot be determined with such precision. The court offers no insight as to how courts should value each variable. Judges must determine the propriety of injunctive relief not on the basis of any quantifiable data, but on their own judgment. The court's formula inappropriately quantifies a qualitative judgment.

Analysis

The mathematical formula devised by the court for determining the appropriateness of a preliminary injunction appears not to account for several traditional factors necessary for a preliminary injunction, raising the question of whether it altered the traditional findings necessary to obtain the preliminary injunction. The Seventh Circuit Court of Appeals has since acknowledged that no formula can include all the factors necessary to the determination, instead requiring a party to first demonstrate that he has no adequate remedy at law, that he is reasonably likely to prevail on the merits, and that the injunction would not harm the public interest. Only then should the court balance the irreparable harms under Judge Posner's mathematical formula.

■ CASE VOCABULARY

PRELIMINARY INJUNCTION: A temporary injunction issued before or during trial to prevent an irreparable injury from occurring before the court has a chance to decide the case.

Walgreen Co. v. Sara Creek Property Co.

(*Tenant*) v. (*Landlord*)

966 F.2d 273 (7th Cir. 1992)

PERMANENT INJUNCTIONS ARE AVAILABLE IN BREACH OF CONTRACT CASES

■ **INSTANT FACTS:** Walgreen's (P) obtained a court injunction against Sara Creek Property Co. (D) to prevent the lease of space in the defendant's shopping mall in violation of Walgreen's (P) lease.

■ **BLACK LETTER RULE:** A permanent injunction is appropriate in a breach of contract case when the benefits of the injunction outweigh the costs associated with calculating actual damages.

■ PROCEDURAL BASIS

Appeal from a district court injunction against the defendant.

■ FACTS

Walgreen Co. (P) operated a pharmacy under a lease with Sara Creek Property Co. (D) in the defendant's mall. The lease provided that the defendant would not lease space in the mall to any tenant who operates a pharmacy or a store containing a pharmacy. Fearful that its largest tenant was about to close its store, Sara Creek (D) informed Walgreen's (D) that it intended to buy out that tenant and lease the space to a large discount store containing a pharmacy. The new tenant was expected to offer cheaper prices for its pharmaceutical products than Walgreen's (P) offered and would be located within a short distance from Walgreen's (P) store entrance. Walgreen's (P) filed suit against Sara Creek (D) and the new tenant for breach of contract and sought an injunction against Sara Creek (D) to stop the intended lease. After an evidentiary hearing, the court found a breach of Walgreen's (P) lease and entered a permanent injunction to prevent the lease to the new tenant until the expiration of Walgreen's (P) lease. Sara Creek (D) appealed, arguing that a breach of contract does not permit injunctive relief when monetary damages are an adequate remedy.

■ ISSUE

In a breach of contract action, is a permanent injunction an available remedy?

■ DECISION AND RATIONALE

(Posner, J.) Yes. In breach of contract cases, money damages are the traditionally appropriate remedy available to a plaintiff, for some breaches may be calculated to relieve a party from performance by paying the other party the benefit of its bargain. Yet, injunctive relief can be issued when a plaintiff meets its burden of persuasion that damages are an inadequate remedy. When a permanent injunction is sought, rather than a temporary injunction, the irreparable harm to the plaintiff if the injunction is not issued is irrelevant, for irreparable means the harm will not be cured by the entry of a final judgment. With a permanent injunction, the injunction itself is the final judgment, not a subsequent judgment on the merits of the case. Irreparable harm is not synonymous with an inadequate remedy at law.

Injunctive relief in lieu of monetary damages relieves the court of the burden of determining the harm resulting from the defendant's conduct and places it on the parties. The costs and benefits include the monetary losses of the plaintiff, the price for dissolving the injunction, the cost of private negotiation, the cost of preparation for litigation, and the cost of diminished accuracy of the results. Further, the amount of damages is better determined by the free market for the goods involved, not the government. Considering the costs and benefits of injunctive relief, the court must determine whether they weigh more favorably toward granting the injunction or not. Here, Walgreen's (P) cost of determining damages would be substantial given the need to project sales revenue and the cost of business over the ten years remaining on the lease and comparing them to the projected loss of business due to the competing pharmacy's presence in the shopping mall. While costs are not always as complicated and costly to ascertain, they are substantial and burdensome in this case. The only cost of issuing the injunction is that costs may be created by the continuing negotiation between the parties to dissolve the injunction. While this cost may be so substantial as to require denial of the injunction, there is no evidence that the costs will have a disparate economic effect on the parties. Having reasonably considered the costs and benefits of the permanent injunction, the court's order is affirmed.

Analysis

Generally, a breach of contract carries no assessment of fault or blame, for damages are awarded to place the "innocent" contractor in a position preserving the benefit of its bargain by proving the measure of damages suffered by the breach. Commentators suggest the substitution of a permanent injunction for damages for breach unjustifiably relieves the plaintiff of the burden of proving the extent of damages merely because it would be too costly or demanding to calculate accurately. If the plaintiff is unable to present proof of damages, they argue, he or she fails to carry a necessary element of the cause of action, requiring dismissal or a judgment for the defendant.

■ CASE VOCABULARY

PERMANENT INJUNCTION: An injunction granted after a final hearing on the merits.

Carey v. Piphus

(School District Representative) v. (Student)
435 U.S. 247, 98 S.Ct. 1042 (1978)

NO PROOF OF INJURY FROM A DUE PROCESS VIOLATION PRECLUDES COMPENSATORY DAMAGES

■ **INSTANT FACTS:** Students were suspended for violating school rules without affording them an opportunity to be heard.

■ **BLACK LETTER RULE:** A denial of due process is actionable for nominal damages even without proof of actual injury, but actual injury must be proven in order for compensatory damages to be awarded.

■ **PROCEDURAL BASIS**

Certiorari to review a decision of the Seventh Circuit Court of Appeals reversing a district court order dismissing the plaintiffs' complaints.

■ **FACTS**

Piphus (P) was a student in a Chicago high school when he was seen by the school principal passing what appeared to be a marijuana cigarette to another student. Upon confronting the students and detecting the odor of marijuana, the principal directed that the students be suspended for twenty days, the usual punishment for violation of the school's drug policy. After notice of the suspension was given to Piphus's (P) mother, two meetings were arranged to explain the purpose for the suspension without discussion of whether Piphus (P) had in fact been smoking marijuana. Thereafter, Piphus (P), through his mother, filed suit against the school district under 42 U.S.C. § 1983 seeking actual and punitive damages for suspending him without due process under the Fourteenth Amendment.

In a separate incident, Brisco (P), a sixth-grade student in Chicago, came to school wearing one small earring. The year before, the school had instituted a rule prohibiting the wearing of earrings by male students to control gang activity threatening the school. After being asked to remove the earring, Brisco (P) refused. After notifying Brisco's (P) mother that he would be suspended for twenty days if he did not remove the earring, Brisco's (P) mother supported her son's position, and Brisco (P) was suspended. Brisco (P), through his mother, sued the school district under 42 U.S.C. § 1983 seeking declaratory and injunctive relief, as well as compensatory and punitive damages for violation of his due process rights. After the two cases were consolidated for trial, the district court held that both suspensions occurred without affording the students due process. Nonetheless, the court declined to award the plaintiffs damages because they failed to submit proof of the extent of their actual injuries. The court further acknowledged that both the plaintiffs were entitled to declaratory relief, but it failed to enter such an order, dismissing the complaints instead. The Seventh Circuit Court of Appeals reversed and remanded because the court erred in not ordering the declaratory relief it acknowledged was appropriate. The Court of Appeals further held that the plaintiffs were entitled to substantial compensatory damages even if the suspensions were justified and without proof of actual injury caused by the due process violation. The school district appealed.

■ **ISSUE**

In an action under § 1983 for due process violations, must a plaintiff prove that he was actually injured by the violation before he may recover substantial "nonpunitive" damages?

■ DECISION AND RATIONALE

(Powell, J.) Yes. The legislative history of 42 U.S.C. § 1983 indicates that the statute was enacted to create "a species of tort liability" against a person acting under color of law who violates the "rights, privileges, or immunities" granted to another. The damages corresponding with this unique tort liability are no different than damages applicable to common-law torts. Damages are designed to compensate persons for injuries caused by the actions of another. There is nothing in the legislative history to imply that the traditional concept of damages should not apply under the statute nor that such damages were intended to serve a more deterrent purpose than compensatory damages. When the violation of a constitutional right under § 1983 closely mirrors the interests protected under the common law of torts, traditional compensatory damages rules, including proximate cause and actual injury, will apply. Where the constitutional rights are not analogous to the interests at stake in a common law tort, damages must be evaluated in an alternative manner that fairly compensates the plaintiff for his actual injury.

Injuries to constitutional rights must not go uncompensated merely because the common law recognizes no analogous cause of action. Due process seeks not to prevent the deprivation of life, liberty, or property interests, but rather the unjustified or mistaken deprivation of such interests. Here, the court of appeals remanded the case to determine whether the students would have been suspended even if a prior hearing were held, relieving any due process concerns because no damages were caused. While the court of appeals is correct on this point, its further holding that the plaintiffs could recover substantial damages if due process has been violated, even if the suspensions were justified and they fail to prove actual injury resulting from the violations, must be reversed. Just as with other torts, actual damage is an element that must be proven, not presumed, to support recovery. Unlike defamation per se, which presumes damages to exist upon the commission of the act, due process violations are not inherently likely to cause significant emotional and mental distress. When such distress results from a due process violation, its proof will usually be easily demonstrated by evidence supporting a damages award. Without such proof, substantial compensatory damages are unavailable. The right to due process, however, is a fundamental right guaranteed by the Constitution and recognized by society. Inasmuch as the right has been violated, though no actual injury has been caused, the plaintiff may recover damages in a nominal amount to redress the minor infringement upon this right. Reversed and remanded.

Analysis

While *Carey* generally ensures a plaintiff a remedy for the violation of civil rights, pursuing a § 1983 action without any actual injuries may cause the plaintiff more in attorney's fees and costs than he or she will recover in nominal damages. Under Rule 68 and 42 U.S.C. § 1988, a plaintiff may shift the burden of these costs to the defendant if he or she prevails, but a savvy defendant may offer a nominal settlement amount shortly after the suit is filed to effectively shield itself from absorbing the plaintiff's fees and costs.

■ CASE VOCABULARY

COMPENSATORY DAMAGES: Damages sufficient in amount to indemnify the injured person for the loss suffered.

INJUNCTION: A court order commanding or preventing an action.

NOMINAL DAMAGES: A trifling sum awarded when a legal injury is suffered but when there is no substantial loss or injury to be compensated.

PUNITIVE DAMAGES: Damages awarded in addition to actual damages when the defendant acted with recklessness, malice, or deceit.

Marek v. Chesny

(Police Officer) v. *(Decedent's Father)*

473 U.S. 1, 105 S.Ct. 3012 (1985)

THE PLAINTIFF COULD NOT RECOVER POST–SETTLEMENT–OFFER COSTS AND FEES WHEN THE RECOVERY AT TRIAL WAS LESS THAN THE OFFER

■ **INSTANT FACTS:** Following judgment for the plaintiff, Chesney (P) sought recovery of costs and attorney's fees incurred after he rejected the defendants' settlement offer.

■ **BLACK LETTER RULE:** Rule 68 of the Federal Rules of Civil Procedure permits the recovery of attorney's fees as a part of the costs of litigation if so provided by the underlying substantive statute governing the action.

■ PROCEDURAL BASIS

Certiorari to review a decision of the Seventh Circuit Court of Appeals reversing a district court order denying the plaintiff's request for post-offer costs.

■ FACTS

Chesney's (P) son was shot and killed by Marek (D) and two other police officers responding to a report of a domestic disturbance. Chesney (P) sued the defendants in federal court under 42 U.S.C. § 1983 and under state tort law. Before trial, the defendants offered to settle the case for $100,000, which offer Chesney (P) refused. Following trial, Chesney (P) was awarded $5000 on his wrongful death claim, $52,000 for § 1983 violations, and $3000 in punitive damages. Chesney (P) then filed a petition with the court under 42 U.S.C. § 1988 to require the defendants to pay over $170,000 in costs and attorney's fees incurred both before and after the settlement offer. The defendants opposed the request, arguing that Rule 68 of the Federal Rules of Civil Procedure requires the plaintiff to bear his own costs and fees incurred after rejecting a settlement offer that exceeds the plaintiff's recovery at trial. The district court agreed and denied the plaintiff's request for post-offer costs and fees. After the parties agreed to payment of pre-offer costs and fees, the plaintiff appealed the denial of post-offer costs and fees. The Seventh Circuit Court of Appeals reversed, holding that Rule 68 cannot be linked with the fee-shifting provisions of 42 U.S.C. § 1988 because it would deprive civil rights plaintiffs of a meaningful choice when considering the adequacy of a settlement offer. The defendants appealed.

■ ISSUE

Must attorney's fees incurred by a plaintiff subsequent to an offer of settlement under Rule 68 of the Federal Rules of Civil Procedure be paid by the defendant under 42 U.S.C. § 1988, when the plaintiff ultimately recovers a judgment for less than the offer?

■ DECISION AND RATIONALE

(Burger, C.J.) No. Under the American Rule, each party is generally required to bear his own costs of litigation, including attorney's fees. Rule 68 and 42 U.S.C. § 1988, however, shift this burden to the unsuccessful party in litigation under certain circumstances. Rule 68 is designed to encourage settlement of claims and avoid litigation, prompting both parties to evaluate the risks and costs of litigation and balance them against the likelihood of success at trial. Similarly, 42 U.S.C. § 1988,

---

permitting a court to award reasonable attorney's fees to a prevailing civil rights litigant, ensures a civil rights plaintiff will not be financially deterred from holding the defendants responsible for civil rights violations. While Rule 68 permits the recovery of costs, it does not define the term or specifically provide for an award of attorney's fees. However, at the time of its adoption, numerous federal fee-shifting statutes existed addressing both costs and attorney's fees. Because of the importance of the term "costs" to Rule 68, the reasonable inference to be drawn from the failure to distinguish attorney's fees from other costs is that the authors intended Rule 68 to apply to all costs, including attorney's fees, that are recoverable under the underlying statutes governing the merits of the case. Here, § 1988 specifically permits a prevailing party to recover attorney's fees "as a part of the costs." Since Congress expressly provided so by statute, attorney's fees are recoverable as costs under Rule 68. This construction is the only means of giving effect to both Rule 68 and § 1988 and does not frustrate the goal of ensuring civil rights plaintiffs' access to justice, for it merely requires a plaintiff to evaluate the risks of litigation in light of the offer, just as in any civil case. Together, Rule 68 and § 1988 combine to encourage plaintiffs to bring meritorious civil rights suits, but also settle those claims upon receipt of a reasonable settlement offer. Reversed.

■ DISSENT

(Brennan, J.) The Court's decision to include attorney's fees within the meaning of the term "costs" as used in Rule 68 creates variations in the application of the numerous federal fee-shifting statutes because of the precise language chosen in a particular statute. Congress and the Judicial Conference of the United States have launched strenuous attacks on Rule 68 in an effort to bring attorney's fees within its scope. These attacks indicate the legislative viewpoint that federal statutes speaking only in terms of attorney's fees are not to be inexplicably incorporated within Rule 68's meaning of "costs." While the plain meaning of Rule 68 addresses only costs and § 1988 specifically provides that attorney's fees are a component of costs, the Court must look beyond the implication of the statutory words to reach the legislative intent of their meaning. "Costs," as it is used in Rule 68, must be considered only to mean those taxable costs traditionally allowed at common law. This is so because nowhere in the historical treatment of the Federal Rules is it insinuated that costs should vary in application depending on the language of the substantive statute at issue. Further, the Federal Rules provide that costs may be taxed by the court clerk, suggesting "costs" is limited to only those charges readily determinable from the records of the court. Likewise, elsewhere in the Federal Rules, attorney's fees are given separate treatment when the rule is intended to cover both costs and fees. Finally, words expressed in the Federal Rules must be construed in favor of a consistent application, as the drafters could not have intended different results from Rule 68 in the absence of qualifying language.

Using the Court's approach, Rule 68, when applied along with Rule 54(d), would require an unsuccessful civil rights plaintiff to pay the defendant's attorney's fees and costs, which directly conflicts with § 1988. The Court's decision impermissibly brings the explicit language of federal fee-shifting statutes within the requirements of Rule 68, which runs contrary to the legislative intent of those statutes and results in the inconsistent application of the rule. With specific reference to § 1988, the Court's decision conflicts with the congressional policies underlying the statute. Section 1988 requires that attorney's fees be reasonable, considering various factors such as the number of hours expended and the hourly rate charged, and permitting the court to be sensitive of the complexities of the merits. Rule 68, on the other hand, contains no such provision. It strips the court of all discretion by requiring the shifting of costs incurred after a settlement is rejected. Rule 68 pressures a plaintiff to accept a low offer early in litigation for fear of bearing all their fees even if later discovery would indicate a stronger case than they first contemplated. Because Rule 68 permits a defendant to make subsequent offers, the inclusion of attorney's fees within the rule encourages the defendants to gradually increase their unacceptable settlement offers in an effort to further cut off the plaintiff's right to recover fees under § 1988 should he or she prevail.

Analysis

While Rule 68, on its face, applies to both plaintiffs and defendants, the interpretation of § 1988 has been that plaintiffs are not responsible for the costs and attorney's fees incurred by the defendant absent certain circumstances. Though a defendant may succeed entirely on the merits of the case, the policy of § 1988 of promoting civil rights plaintiffs' access to justice requires the defendant to bear its own costs in defending legitimate, though unsuccessful, claims. This conclusion is often supported by the fact that the defendant controls its own conduct and has committed at least some act that gives rise to potential liability, though none was imposed.

■ **CASE VOCABULARY**

AMERICAN RULE: The general policy that all litigants must bear their own attorney's fees, including the prevailing party.

City of Riverside v. Rivera

(*Municipality*) v. (*Civil Rights Plaintiffs*)
477 U.S. 561, 106 S.Ct. 2686 (1986)

AN AWARD OF $245,256 IN ATTORNEYS' FEES WAS NOT UNREASONABLE EVEN THOUGH THE PLAINTIFFS' TOTAL RECOVERY WAS ONLY $66,700

■ **INSTANT FACTS:** The plaintiffs' were awarded $245,256.75 in attorney's fees following a civil rights trial in which they recovered $66,700 in compensatory and punitive damages.

■ **BLACK LETTER RULE:** Under 42 U.S.C. § 1988, an attorney's fee award, for reasonable hours expended at a reasonable hourly rate, is reasonable though it exceeds the ultimate monetary recovery at trial.

■ **PROCEDURAL BASIS**

Certiorari to review a decision of the Ninth Circuit Court of Appeals affirming a trial court's attorney's fee award.

■ **FACTS**

Eight Chicano persons were arrested while attending a party at the home of Rivera (P) when unidentified police officers employed by the City of Riverside (D) entered without a warrant and broke up the party with tear gas and unnecessary force. Rivera (P) and the persons arrested sued the City of Riverside (D) and thirty individual officers under several federal civil right statutes, alleging violations of their First, Fourth, and Fourteenth Amendment rights. After the court granted summary judgment to seventeen individual defendants, the plaintiffs obtained thirty-seven verdicts against the remaining defendants for § 1983 violations, false arrest and imprisonment, and negligence. The plaintiffs' total monetary recovery was $66,700 in compensatory and punitive damages. Additionally, the plaintiffs received $245,456.25 in attorney's fees under 42 U.S.C. § 1988, though no multiplier for the high quality of the attorneys' efforts was applied. The attorney's fees award was based on 1946.75 hours at an hourly rate of $125, plus time expended by law clerks. The City of Riverside (D) appealed the attorney's fee award to the Ninth Circuit Court of Appeals, which affirmed the award. On appeal to the United States Supreme Court, the decision was vacated and remanded for further consideration in light of *Hensley v. Eckerhart*, decided by the Supreme Court in 1983. On remand, the district court reexamined the record and conducted additional hearings, again concluding that the attorney's fee award was appropriate. The defendants again appealed to the Ninth Circuit Court of Appeals, which rejected the defendant's argument that the award was unreasonable because it grossly exceeded the plaintiffs' recovery at trial. The defendants again appealed to the United States Supreme Court.

■ **ISSUE**

Is an award of attorney's fees under 42 U.S.C. § 1988 per se unreasonable within the meaning of the statute if it exceeds the amount of damages recovered by a plaintiff in the underlying civil rights action?

■ **DECISION AND RATIONALE**

(Brennan, J.) No. The Civil Rights Attorney's Fees Awards Act, 42 U.S.C. § 1988, permits a court to award reasonable attorney's fees to a prevailing party in a civil rights action, but fails to define what reasonable is. In *Hensley v. Eckerhart*, the Supreme Court set forth guidelines for determining the reasonableness of an attorney's fee award under § 1988. Among the considerations is the product of "the number of hours reasonably expended on the litigation multiplied by a reasonable hourly rate." Comprised of two components of reasonableness, this ultimate "lodestar" is presumed to be reasonable.

In applying this standard, the district court carefully reviewed the facts to determine that the hours expended were reasonable, and counsel, though young, displayed excellent performances in representing their clients to justify payment at legal rates determined by the market. Though the plaintiffs failed to prevail on every claim presented in their cause of action, this was so because the plaintiffs were unable at the outset of the litigation to determine which of the named officers had committed the violations charged. Under such circumstances, a downward adjustment of the attorney's fees incurred is not required. Similarly, the award need not be reduced because it exceeds the amount of damages ultimately recovered by the plaintiffs. The amount of the monetary award does not determine the extent of success of the action, for the size of the award resulted from juror reluctance to impose a large financial burden on police officers and the plaintiffs' modest explanation of the injuries caused. The fact that the lodestar exceeds the plaintiffs' monetary recovery does not render the lodestar unreasonable. While the size of the recovery is relevant to the reasonableness of the lodestar, it is but one of many factors to consider. A civil rights action is more than a private tort action, for it vindicates civil and constitutional rights that are difficult to evaluate in monetary terms. Congress enacted § 1988 to provide civil rights plaintiffs access to the courts to protect their rights without the risk of bearing significant attorney's fees that they could not otherwise afford. Limiting fee awards to a proportionate share of the plaintiffs' recovery would result in private attorneys declining to invest the time and effort in civil rights actions in which minimal monetary damages are frequently recovered. Affirmed.

■ CONCURRENCE

(Powell, J.) The fee award should be affirmed not because of *Hensley v. Eckerhart*, but because the findings made by the district court were not clearly erroneous as required for reversal of such an award. While some conclusory opinions are presented in the court's findings, they are primarily supported by objective facts in favor of the award. Because the legislative history of § 1988 does not support a rule that fee awards must be proportionate to the monetary recovery, the court's findings should not be disturbed.

■ DISSENT

(Burger, C.J.) The plaintiffs' attorneys were young and inexperienced, graduating from law school just years before this civil rights action was brought. An award valuing their inexperienced legal services at the prevailing market rate of $125 per hour constitutes an abuse of discretion, particularly since the Court has vacated and remanded the award on a prior occasion. The excessive fee award sanctioned by the Court serves only to further public disdain over the legal profession.

■ DISSENT

(Rehnquist, J.) The complaint in this matter included 256 claims against more than thirty separate defendants. Prior to trial, over half of the defendants had been dismissed and the plaintiffs' claims for injunctive and declaratory relief were abandoned. The plaintiffs also dropped their allegations that the defendants acted with discriminatory intent. At trial, recovery was ultimately achieved from only seven of the original the plaintiffs. It is an inescapable conclusion that the majority of the 1946.75 hours expended on this case were unnecessary and unreasonable in light of traditional billing practices of the legal profession and fundamental notions of reasonableness embodied in § 1988.

Analysis

The potential of a disproportionate fee award serves as a valuable deterrent against the conduct of a defendant and provides an incentive to settle even though the defendant feels its position is strong on the merits. Even when the defendant perceives its actual liability is only minimal, the threat of paying a plaintiff's attorney's fees will promote settlement discussions, for the cost of defending the plaintiff's civil rights claims may be grossly in excess of its actual liability. The reasonableness requirement of § 1988 serves as a check, however, against an award of attorney's fees not reasonably necessary to prosecute the plaintiff's claims.

Walker v. City of Birmingham

(*Civil Rights Activist*) v. (*Municipality*)

388 U.S. 307, 87 S.Ct. 1824 (1967)

EVEN ALLEGEDLY UNCONSTITUTIONAL RULES MUST BE FOLLOWED

■ **INSTANT FACTS:** Black protesters organized public marches in blatant violation of a court injunction enforcing a city parade ordinance requiring a permit for public demonstrations.

■ **BLACK LETTER RULE:** Civil disobedience of an unchallenged unconstitutional statute or court order exposes the offenders to contempt liability.

■ PROCEDURAL BASIS

Certiorari to review a decision of the Alabama Supreme Court affirming a court contempt order.

■ FACTS

In 1963, the City of Birmingham, Alabama, (P) filed a complaint in state court seeking injunctive relief against Walker (D) and others alleged to sponsor or encourage "sit-ins", "kneel-ins", street protests and other activities designed to breach the peace. The complaint alleged the activities threatened the "lives, safety, peace, tranquility, and general welfare" of the people of Birmingham and that there was no adequate remedy at law. The court granted a temporary injunction requiring a permit to organize mass protests, citing a city ordinance. Walker (D) and others were served with the writ of injunction and shortly thereafter held a press conference expressing their intention to disobey the order as an exercise of government tyranny, threatening mob activity to overcome the judicial favoritism afforded local police. Later that evening, Walker (D) participated in a meeting to organize a public march the following day. The next day, fifty to sixty people participated in a public parade in which the participants engaged in "clapping, and hollering, and whooping." That night, some of the defendants participated in another meeting to organize a march to the jail on Easter Sunday. Organized by one of the petitioners, 1500 to 2000 protesters walked side-by-side down a public sidewalk. Violence erupted when members of the on-looking crowd threw rocks, injuring a news reporter and damaging a police motorcycle. The following day, city officials applied to the court for an order to show cause why the defendants should not be held in contempt of court for violating the injunction. The defendants appeared in court to challenge the constitutionality of the injunction and the city parade ordinance as vague, overbroad, and in violation of the First Amendment. The court declined to address the defendants' constitutional objections and found them in contempt, sentencing them to five days in jail and a fine. The Alabama Supreme Court affirmed without considering the constitutional objections.

■ ISSUE

Could the defendants violate the court injunction and the Birmingham parade ordinance based on their alleged unconstitutionality?

■ DECISION AND RATIONALE

(Stewart, J.) No. The court unquestionably had jurisdiction over the defendants and the subject matter involved after the issuance of its injunction. Unregulated public demonstrations threaten the free movement of traffic and threaten to create public disorder, both of which are legitimate government concerns. The First and Fourteenth Amendments do not protect that speech arising from disorderly protests occurring on public streets or highways. While the city parade ordinance implicates several constitutional concerns, the defendants failed to raise those concerns through a proper application to the state courts for their review. Instead, the terms of the injunction clearly put the defendants on notice of its terms, which they blatantly disobeyed. Without an application for review by the court, the ordinance is not unconstitutional on its face. Likewise, the injunction itself raises concerns of constitutionality, but the defendants similarly failed to petition the court for modification or dissolution of the injunction in light of these concerns. Had the defendants applied for a permit and been denied, their claims of arbitrary and discriminatory application could have been considered by the court upon a motion for dissolution of the injunction. Without such action, however, the defendants' claims must fail. Civil disobedience cannot be upheld by the court when legal recourse remains available to the defendants. Affirmed.

■ DISSENT

(Warren, C.J.) While the Court agrees that the ordinance is unconstitutional and was unconstitutionally applied as to the defendants, it permits the enforcement of the ordinance merely because it was incorporated into a court-ordered injunction. The defendants had tried in the past to obtain the necessary permit to voice their concerns over the deprivation of civil rights, leading them to the logical conclusion that further attempts to secure a permit would be fruitless. Convinced of this fact, the defendants took matters into their own hands to spread their message to their followers, resulting in the injunction at issue. Upon receiving notice of the injunction, the defendants chose to disobey it, believing its manifestly unconstitutional terms carried no legal effect. They did not seek to avoid justice by fleeing the jurisdiction or avoiding the court. Instead, they appeared in court to defend their actions and test the constitutionality of the injunction and the underlying ordinance. In doing so, they were in the same position as one who violates a criminal statute and raises a constitutional defense during his prosecution. So long as the defendant is willing to accept the penalties for violating the statute, his actions do not arise to contempt. The city parade ordinance is unconstitutional on its face by permitting city officials the absolute discretion over the grant or denial of a permit, and its constitutionality is compounded when those officials exercise that discretion in a discriminatory manner.

■ DISSENT

(Douglas, J.) The defendants did not blatantly disobey the city ordinance by organizing a protest without a permit. On numerous prior occasions, they sought the necessary permit but were denied one. Believing further efforts to be futile, they exercised their right to challenge the constitutionality of the ordinance through civil disobedience. The right to defy an unconstitutional statute cannot be destroyed merely because a judge issues an ex parte order enjoining the right. Fear of riots or civil disobedience cannot serve as the basis for court action resulting in the deprivation of constitutional rights.

Analysis

Walker gained national attention because of the political setting in which it arose and the notoriety of several of the individuals involved. Among those arrested and charged with contempt in *Walker* was Dr. Martin Luther King, Jr. Dr. King's belief in civil disobedience as a means of challenging oppression by the government spawned considerable debate over the actions of law enforcement and the government throughout the country. While the Court has never recognized that blatant disregard of court orders and statutory requirements may be sanctioned by the law, the efforts of Dr. King and others gained substantial societal support.

■ CASE VOCABULARY

CIVIL DISOBEDIENCE: A deliberate but nonviolent act of lawbreaking to call attention to a particular law or set of laws of questionable legitimacy or morality.

CONTEMPT: Conduct that defies the authority or dignity of a court or legislature. Because such conduct interferes with the administration of justice, it is punishable, usually by fine or imprisonment.

CHAPTER THREE

Thinking Like a Trial Lawyer, Pleadings, and Simple Joinder

Texas Dep't of Community Affairs v. Burdine

Instant Facts: Burdine (P), who was not promoted and ultimately fired by the Texas Department of Community Affairs (D), brought an action against the defendant, claiming its actions were based on sexual discrimination in violation of federal law.

Black Letter Rule: Once an employee has proven a prima facie case of employment discrimination, an employer has the burden of producing evidence of legitimate nondiscriminatory reasons for the challenged employment decision.

Dioguardi v. Durning

Instant Facts: Dioguardi's (P) complaint that some of his imported bottles of tonics disappeared and that others were improperly sold at auction was dismissed for failure to state facts sufficient to constitute a cause of action.

Black Letter Rule: A complaint need only include a short and plain statement of the claim showing that the plaintiff is entitled to relief.

Conley v. Gibson

Instant Facts: Black employees brought a class action against a union and its officers for not representing them or protecting their labor contract job and seniority rights.

Black Letter Rule: A complaint should not be dismissed for failure to state a claim unless it appears beyond doubt that the plaintiff can prove no set of supporting facts that would entitle him or her to relief.

Leatherman v. Tarrant County Narcotics Intelligence and Coordination Unit I

Instant Facts: Citizens subjected to beatings and whose pets were killed during the execution of search warrants brought a civil rights action, which was dismissed for failure to plead sufficient detail to establish an official unlawful municipal policy.

Black Letter Rule: To plead a successful civil rights claim under § 1983, a plaintiff must meet a heightened pleading standard that requires detailed allegations that a municipality engaged in a policy for which it can be held responsible.

Leatherman v. Tarrant County Narcotics Intelligence and Coordination Unit II

Instant Facts: Citizens subjected to beatings and whose pets were killed during the execution of search warrants by a municipal law enforcement agency brought a civil rights action, which was dismissed for failure to plead sufficient detail to establish an official unlawful municipal policy.

Black Letter Rule: A heightened pleading standard does not apply to § 1983 actions against municipalities.

Bower v. Weisman

Instant Facts: Bower's (P) complaint alleged that Weisman (D) breached agreements to provide her with assets and financial security after their personal and business relationship was terminated; Weisman moved to dismiss the complaint.

Black Letter Rule: Detailed pleadings will result in dismissal if the alleged facts do not correspond to the cause of action.

Henry v. Daytop Village, Inc.

Instant Facts: Henry (P), a black female who was discharged for misrepresenting her husband's medical claims, denied any misrepresentation and alternatively claimed that white male employees were not discharged for similar misconduct.

Black Letter Rule: A plaintiff may plead two or more alternative statements of a claim, regardless of consistency.

DM II, Ltd. v. Hospital Corp. of America

Instant Facts: Members of a hospital partnership sued other partnership members for wrongfully competing against the partnership.

Black Letter Rule: Under Georgia law, members of a partnership may sue other members of the partnership for breach of fiduciary duty to the partnership, and the partnership is not an indispensable party to the action.

Doe v. United Services Life Ins. Co.

Instant Facts: In order to avoid being incorrectly identified publicly as homosexual, Doe (P), a heterosexual, sought permission to proceed anonymously to challenge United Services Life Insurance Company's (D) practices related to suspected homosexual applicants.

Black Letter Rule: In rare cases, a plaintiff may proceed anonymously if necessary to protect privacy concerns.

Greenbaum v. United States

Instant Facts: Greenbaum (P) fell and was injured on Post Office (D) property while picking up his paycheck.

Black Letter Rule: A fact that is denied for lack of knowledge or information may be deemed admitted if the matter is one to which the party has, or with reasonable investigation should have, knowledge or information.

Controlled Environment Sys. v. Sun Process Co., Inc.

Instant Facts: Not stated.

Black Letter Rule: An answer that a party is without personal knowledge sufficient to admit or deny allegations is inadequate.

Gomez v. Toledo

Instant Facts: Gomez (P), a police officer, was discharged by Toledo (D), the Superintendent of Police in Puerto Rico, after giving sworn statements and testifying that other police officers had offered false evidence.

Black Letter Rule: A public official's qualified immunity is an affirmative defense that must be pleaded by the defendant.

Singletary v. Pennsylvania Dep't of Corrections

Instant Facts: Dorothy Singletary (P), the mother of a prisoner who committed suicide, attempted to amend her § 1983 complaint against the Pennsylvania Department of Corrections (D), its prison, and some of its officials, to add a previously unnamed staff psychologist after the statute of limitations had run.

Black Letter Rule: Under Rule 15(c)(3), an amended complaint relates back for a newly identified party only if the party had timely notice of the action.

Christopher v. Duffy

Instant Facts: The mother of a child who allegedly died from complications from lead poisoning sought to amend her complaint to add paint manufacturers and a paint trade association, six years after bringing the action.

Black Letter Rule: Under the law of Massachusetts, an amendment to a complaint will be denied if it will cause undue prejudice to an opponent.

Progress Federal Savings Bank v. National West Lenders Association, Inc.

Instant Facts: Three months after it was granted summary judgment dismissing all claims, National West (D) moved for sanctions against Progress Federal (P) for filing a groundless lawsuit.

Black Letter Rule: A motion for Rule 11 sanctions must be filed before a judge rejects the offending contention in order to permit the allegedly offending party to withdraw or appropriately correct the contention.

Kedra v. City of Philadelphia

Instant Facts: Several members of the Kedra (P) family sued several police officers, police supervisors, and the City of Philadelphia (D) for injuries and civil rights violations related to abusive police actions occurring over a fifteen-month period.

Black Letter Rule: Multiple parties may be joined in the same case if some of the claims by or against each party arise out of reasonably related events and contain common factual or legal questions.

Banque Indosuez v. Trifinery

Instant Facts: Trifinery (D) asserts that it has a valid counterclaim to set off the amount it owes on a promissory note to Banque Indosuez (P), but Banque Indosuez (P) asserts that the counterclaim is barred by provisions in the note disallowing counterclaims.

Black Letter Rule: A contractual agreement between the parties that precludes bringing a permissive counterclaim is enforceable.

Gross v. Hanover Ins. Co.

Instant Facts: Gross (P) sought insurance proceeds from Hanover (D) for jewels stolen while consigned to the Rizzos; Hanover (D) sought to implead the Rizzos as third-party defendants.

Black Letter Rule: Third-party defendants who may be liable to an insurer for payments on a claim against an insurance policy may be impleaded under Rule 14(a).

Texas Dep't of Community Affairs v. Burdine

(Employer) v. *(Employee Claiming Sex Discrimination)*
450 U.S. 248, 101 S.Ct. 1089 (1981)

AN EMPLOYER HAS THE BURDEN OF PRODUCING EVIDENCE OF NONDISCRIMINATORY REASONS FOR ITS EMPLOYMENT DECISIONS

■ **INSTANT FACTS** Burdine (P), who was not promoted and ultimately fired by the Texas Department of Community Affairs (D), brought an action against the defendant, claiming its actions were based on sexual discrimination in violation of federal law.

■ **BLACK LETTER RULE** Once an employee has proven a prima facie case of employment discrimination, an employer has the burden of producing evidence of legitimate nondiscriminatory reasons for the challenged employment decision.

■ **PROCEDURAL BASIS**

Certiorari to review a Fifth Circuit decision affirming in part and reversing in part a trial court decision in favor of the defendant employer.

■ **FACTS**

Burdine (P), a female employee of the Texas Department of Community Affairs (TDCA) (D), applied for the position of her resigning supervisor. The federal agency funding TDCA (D) threatened to terminate funding because of inefficiencies in the department. TDCA (D) convinced the agency to continue funding, provided it reformed the division, including filling the vacant supervisory position and reorganizing the division staff. TDCA (D) hired a male employee from another division for the supervisory position and discharged three employees, including Burdine (P). TDCA (D) later rehired Burdine (P) in another division and subsequently promoted her. Burdine (P) claimed that the failure to promote her to the supervisory position and her later termination were based on sex discrimination in violation of Title VII. The trial court rejected her claim, noting that the federal agency required the employment moves, the hiring was based on a nondiscriminatory evaluation of the applicants' relative qualifications, and the three employees were fired because they did not work well together. The Fifth Circuit affirmed the hiring decision based on the trial court's implicit finding that the person hired was more qualified than Burdine (P), but reversed the firing decision, finding that TDCA (D) had not carried its burden of proving by a preponderance of the evidence that legitimate nondiscriminatory reasons existed for the termination and that the persons hired or promoted were better qualified than Burdine (P).

■ **ISSUE**

Once an employee has proven a prima facie case of employment discrimination, must an employer prove by a preponderance of the evidence legitimate nondiscriminatory reasons for the challenged employment actions?

■ **DECISION AND RATIONALE**

(Powell, J.) No. The plaintiff must establish a prima facie case of employment discrimination in promotion by proving by a preponderance of the evidence that the plaintiff was qualified for the

---

position, but was rejected under circumstances that gave rise to an inference of unlawful discrimination. Once the employee shows a prima facie case of employment discrimination, the burden shifts to the employer to articulate a legitimate nondiscriminatory reason for the challenged employment action. The employee then has the opportunity to prove by a preponderance of the evidence that the articulated reason was a pretext for discrimination. The defendant's evidence need only raise a genuine issue of fact as to whether it discriminated against the plaintiff. The plaintiff has the ultimate burden of persuasion, and must demonstrate that the explanation was not the true reason for the employment decision. This burden may be carried either directly, by persuading the court that a discriminatory reason more likely motivated the employer, or indirectly, by showing that the employer's explanation is not credible. The court of appeals placed the burden of persuasion for a nondiscriminatory reason for the employment actions on the employer, but an employer need only meet its burden of producing admissible evidence that would allow the trier of fact to conclude that the employment decision had not been motivated by discrimination. The court of appeals also erred by requiring the employer to prove objectively that the person hired was more qualified than plaintiff. Such a standard would require an employer to hire a female or minority whenever that applicant's objective qualifications were equal to those of a white male. This preference would violate Title VII, which does not require preferential treatment for minorities or women. Vacated.

Analysis:

Burdine's allocation of burdens does not unduly hinder plaintiffs. The defendant's explanation must be clear and reasonably specific, and although the defendant does not formally bear the burden of persuasion, it will normally attempt to prove a factual basis for its explanation. *Burdine* provides a clearly articulated explanation of the elements of a prima facia case for employment discrimination under Title VII of the Civil Rights Act of 1964. Upon producing sufficient evidence of a prima facia case, a reasonable jury is entitled to find for the plaintiff absent rebuttal evidence by the defendant. *Burdine* also clearly distinguishes between burdens of production and burdens of persuasion at various stages of a proceeding, while emphasizing that the ultimate burden of persuading the court that an employer intentionally discriminated on the basis of an unlawful factor remains with the plaintiff.

■ CASE VOCABULARY

BURDEN OF PERSUASION: A party's duty to convince the fact-finder to view the facts in a way that favors that party.

BURDEN OF PRODUCTION: A party's duty to introduce enough evidence on an issue to have that issue decided by the fact-finder, rather than decided against the party in a peremptory ruling such as a summary judgment or a directed verdict.

BURDEN OF PROOF: A party's duty to prove a disputed assertion or charge. The burden of proof includes both the burden of persuasion and the burden of production.

Dioguardi v. Durning

(Tonic Importer) v. *(Customs Official)*
139 F.2d 774 (2d Cir. 1944)

ONLY A SHORT AND PLAIN STATEMENT OF THE CLAIM IS REQUIRED IN A COMPLAINT

■ **INSTANT FACTS** Dioguardi's (P) complaint that some of his imported bottles of tonics disappeared and that others were improperly sold at auction was dismissed for failure to state facts sufficient to constitute a cause of action.

■ **BLACK LETTER RULE** A complaint need only include a short and plain statement of the claim showing that the plaintiff is entitled to relief.

■ **PROCEDURAL BASIS**

Appeal from the trial court's dismissal of the plaintiff's complaint on a motion to dismiss.

■ **FACTS**

Dioguardi (P) brought suit against Durning (D), the Collector of Customs for the Port of New York, related to the plaintiff's attempts to import merchandise from Italy. His "home drawn" complaint alleged, among other claims inadequately stated, that some of his merchandise was sold at "public custom" for "my price of $110, and not of his price of $120," and that three weeks before the sale, two cases disappeared. From other allegations, it appears that the merchandise was in Durning's (D) possession while Dioguardi (P) had a dispute with his consignor in Italy, and that Durning (D) subsequently sold the items at auction after holding them for a year. The initial complaint was dismissed, with leave to amend. An amended complaint expanded upon the allegations, including a statement that it wasn't "so easy to do away with two cases" but the defendants, being protected, "take this chance." This complaint was also dismissed.

■ **ISSUE**

Must a complaint state detailed facts sufficient to constitute a cause of action?

■ **DECISION AND RATIONALE**

(Clark, J.) No. Rule 8(a) of the Federal Rules of Civil Procedure requires only that there be "a short and plain statement of the claim showing that the pleader is entitled to relief." The District Court did not explain why it concluded that no claim had been stated upon which relief could be granted. Despite how inarticulately the plaintiff drafted the complaint, it does disclose the plaintiff's claims that the collector had converted or otherwise done away with two cases of tonic and that the remaining merchandise was improperly sold at public auction. The defendant could have responded with a motion for summary judgment, but he did not, and the plaintiff is entitled to his day in court.

Analysis:

Dioguardi, written by the principal draftsman of the original Federal Rules of Civil Procedure after his appointment to the Second Circuit Court of Appeals, liberally reads Rule 8(a). This result is consistent with the fundamental basis of the Rules that emphasizes that notice is the only essential function of

---

pleading. In essence, this view takes the position that liberal pleading rules promote access to the courts, even if some non-meritorious claims reach trial. A liberal reading of the pleading rules is particularly appropriate with a pro se plaintiff, and the *Dioguardi* court goes out of its way to find a claim in the complaint, even attempting to define the statutory provisions under which the plaintiff might be able to proceed.

■ CASE VOCABULARY

PRO SE: For oneself; on one's own behalf; without a lawyer.

Conley v. Gibson

(*Black Employees*) v. (*Union Officers*)
355 U.S. 41, 78 S.Ct. 99 (1957)

DISMISSAL IS APPROPRIATE ONLY IF NO SET OF FACTS CAN SUPPORT A CLAIM

■ **INSTANT FACTS** Black employees brought a class action against a union and its officers for not representing them or protecting their labor contract job and seniority rights.

■ **BLACK LETTER RULE** A complaint should not be dismissed for failure to state a claim unless it appears beyond doubt that the plaintiff can prove no set of supporting facts that would entitle him or her to relief.

■ **PROCEDURAL BASIS**

Certiorari to review a dismissal of the complaint.

■ **FACTS**

Conley and other black employees (P) brought a class action against a union, its local, and its officers, alleging federal Railway Labor Act violations. The complaint alleged that the plaintiffs were employees of the Texas and New Orleans Railroad in Houston and members of Local 28 of the Brotherhood of Railway and Steamship Clerks. A collective bargaining contract between the railroad and the union gave the members seniority and job rights. The railroad purported to abolish the jobs of the black employees, but, in reality, white employees filled most of the jobs and the few black employees hired back lost seniority. Despite the plaintiffs' requests, the union did not protect them against the discharges and refused to give them protection comparable to that given to white employees, thereby violating the union's duty of fair representation under the Railway Labor Act. Gibson and other union officers (D) moved to dismiss on the grounds that the National Railroad Adjustment Board had exclusive jurisdiction over the claims, that the railroad had not been joined as an indispensable party, and that the complaint failed to state a claim upon which relief could be granted. The trial court dismissed on the exclusive jurisdiction ground and the Fifth Circuit Court of Appeals affirmed.

■ **ISSUE**

Should a complaint be dismissed for failure to state a claim upon which relief may be granted only if the plaintiff cannot prove a set of facts that would entitle him or her to relief?

■ **DECISION AND RATIONALE**

(Black, J.) Yes. A complaint should be dismissed only if there is no doubt that the plaintiff cannot prove a set of facts entitling him to relief. Here, the complaint alleged that the plaintiffs were wrongfully discharged by the railroad and that the union refused to protect their jobs or to help them with their grievances because they were black. If proven, these allegations constitute a manifest breach of the union's statutory duty to represent fairly and without discrimination all bargaining unit members. Once a bargaining agent undertakes to represent a bargaining unit, it must represent in good faith and without discrimination all employees in the unit. The Federal Rules of Civil Procedure do not require a complaint to set forth specific facts to support general allegations of discrimination; the rules require only a "short and plain statement of the claim" that will give the defendant fair notice of the claim and the grounds upon which it rests. Following the simple guide of Rule 8(f) that "all pleadings shall be so construed as to do substantial justice," the complaint adequately sets forth a claim and gives the defendants fair notice of its basis. Pleading is not a game of skill in which one misstep of counsel may be decisive. Reversed.

Analysis:

Conley is the leading case on pleading requirements under the Federal Rules of Civil Procedure. In *Conley*, the Supreme Court clearly demonstrates the liberality with which the Federal Rules of Civil Procedure approach pleading. The Court rejects two distinct arguments raised by the defendants: that no cause of action exists under the Railway Labor Act and that the complaint contains insufficient factual detail. In reaching its conclusion, the Court also dismissed the defendants' contention that the National Railroad Adjustment Board had exclusive jurisdiction and that the railroad was an indispensable party.

■ CASE VOCABULARY

CLASS ACTION: A lawsuit in which a single person or a small group of people represents the interests of a larger group.

Leatherman v. Tarrant County Narcotics Intelligence and Coordination Unit

(Search Warrant Subjects) v. *(Municipal Law Enforcement Agency)*

954 F.2d 1054 (5th Cir. 1992)

SECTION 1983 ACTIONS AGAINST MUNICIPAL DEFENDANTS REQUIRE DETAILED PLEADINGS

■ **INSTANT FACTS** Citizens subjected to beatings and whose pets were killed during the execution of search warrants brought a civil rights action, which was dismissed for failure to plead sufficient detail to establish an official unlawful municipal policy.

■ **BLACK LETTER RULE** To plead a successful civil rights claim under § 1983, a plaintiff must meet a heightened pleading standard that requires detailed allegations that a municipality engaged in a policy for which it can be held responsible.

■ **PROCEDURAL BASIS**

Appeal from the trial court's dismissal of the complaint against the defendants.

■ **FACTS**

Leatherman (P) and other plaintiffs brought a § 1983 civil rights action against certain municipalities, their law enforcement agency, and certain municipal officials in their official capacity following the execution of two search warrants. Police officers stopped Leatherman (P) and her son in their vehicle, threatened them, informed them that police officers were searching their home, and told them that officers had killed their two dogs. When Leatherman (P) returned home, she found that both dogs had been killed and that police officers had found nothing relevant to the search warrant. Another plaintiff alleged that police officers searched the residence of Andert, a sixty-four-year-old man, pursuant to a narcotics search warrant while Andert and his family mourned his wife's death. The police beat Andert, inflicting injuries, and forced family members at gunpoint to lie on the floor, insulting and threatening them for over an hour. Nothing related to narcotics violations was found. The initial and amended complaints set forth factual details related to the search warrants' executions, the police officers' actions, and the injuries suffered. The amended complaint generally alleged that the municipalities failed to formulate and implement adequate policies to train their officers on the proper manner of executing search warrants and responding to family dogs. The allegations were "boilerplate," alleging no details to support the assertion that the municipalities had adopted policies, customs, or practices condoning the officers' conduct. On the municipalities' motion, the trial court dismissed the complaint on the grounds that the plaintiffs had failed to meet the heightened pleading standard requiring them to allege that the municipality had adopted a policy or custom condoning the police conduct or that the failure to adequately train the officers amounted to a deliberate indifference to the plaintiffs' civil rights.

■ **ISSUE**

Must the plaintiffs in a § 1983 civil rights action against a municipality plead with particularity facts sufficient to establish an unlawful municipal policy or custom, under a heightened pleading standard?

■ DECISION AND RATIONALE

(Goldberg, J.) Yes. In all § 1983 civil rights actions against municipalities, a heightened pleading standard applies, requiring plaintiffs to allege detailed facts establishing the existence of an unlawful municipal practice, policy or custom. In § 1983 actions involving state actors in their individual capacities, the Fifth Circuit Court of Appeals imposes a heightened pleading standard, requiring the complaint to state with factual detail the basis for the claim, which necessarily includes why the official does not have immunity. This heightened pleading standard has been extended to municipalities. Although municipalities have no immunity, the standard reduces litigation costs for municipalities by requiring plaintiffs' attorneys to inquire into the underlying facts before bringing an action. In the present case, no allegation indicates a pattern of similar conduct that would demonstrate inadequate training and show the existence of an official policy as required for municipal liability under § 1983. Because the plaintiffs were not prepared to allege specific facts to meet the heightened pleading standard, the lower court's dismissal of the complaint, without notice to the plaintiffs that the court intended to do so *sua sponte*, was harmless error. Affirmed.

Analysis:

The Fifth Circuit Court of Appeals is essentially trying to revive fact pleading for actions that it does not favor because of the heavy burden they place on the federal courts. It is also attempting to reduce litigation costs for municipalities by imposing stricter pleading standards on plaintiffs bringing § 1983 civil rights cases. To the extent that it has done so with respect to actions against state officials, its heightened pleading standard applies. On subsequent appeal of this case, the Supreme Court rejected this method of weeding out frivolous litigation in the context of municipal defendants, but in its aftermath, other methods of requiring plaintiffs to produce more specific pleadings arose.

■ CASE VOCABULARY

BOILERPLATE: Ready-made or all-purpose language that will fit in a variety of documents.

IMMUNITY: Any exemption from a duty, liability, or service of process; especially, such an exemption granted to a public official.

SUA SPONTE: On its own motion.

Leatherman v. Tarrant County Narcotics Intelligence and Coordination Unit

(*Search Warrant Subjects*) v. (*Municipal Law Enforcement Agency*)
507 U.S. 163, 113 S.Ct. 1160 (1993)

SUPREME COURT RULES SECTION 1983 ACTIONS AGAINST MUNICIPAL DEFENDANTS DO NOT REQUIRE MORE DETAILED PLEADINGS

■ **INSTANT FACTS** Citizens subjected to beatings and whose pets were killed during the execution of search warrants by a municipal law enforcement agency brought a civil rights action, which was dismissed for failure to plead sufficient detail to establish an official unlawful municipal policy.

■ **BLACK LETTER RULE** A heightened pleading standard does not apply to § 1983 actions against municipalities.

■ **PROCEDURAL BASIS**

Certiorari to review the Fifth Circuit's affirmance of the trial court's dismissal of the complaint against the defendants.

■ **FACTS**

Leatherman (P) and other plaintiffs brought a § 1983 civil rights action against certain municipalities, their law enforcement agency, and certain municipal officials in their official capacity following the execution of two search warrants. Police officers stopped Leatherman (P) and her son in their vehicle, threatened them, informed them that police officers were searching their home, and told them that officers had killed their two dogs. When Leatherman (P) returned home, she found that both dogs had been killed and that police officers had found nothing relevant to the search warrant, but had lounged around the premises, apparently celebrating. The other plaintiff alleged that police officers searched the residence of Andert, a sixty-four-year-old man, pursuant to a narcotics search warrant while Andert and his family mourned his wife's death. The police allegedly beat Andert, inflicting injuries, and forced family members at gunpoint to lie on the floor, insulting and threatening them for over an hour. Nothing related to narcotics was found. The initial and amended complaints set forth factual details related to the search warrants' execution, the police officers' actions, and the injuries suffered. The amended complaint generally alleged that the municipalities failed to formulate and implement an adequate policy to train its officers on the proper manner of executing search warrants and responding to family dogs. The allegations were "boilerplate," including no details to support the assertion that the municipalities had adopted policies, customs, or practices condoning the officers' conduct. On the municipalities' motion, the trial court dismissed the complaint on the grounds that the plaintiffs had failed to meet the heightened pleading standard requiring them to allege facts that the municipality had adopted a policy or custom condoning the police conduct or that the failure to adequately train the officers amounted to a deliberate indifference to the plaintiffs' civil rights. The Fifth Circuit affirmed.

■ **ISSUE**

In a § 1983 civil rights action against a municipality, must plaintiffs plead with particularity facts sufficient to establish an unlawful municipal policy or custom, under a heightened pleading standard?

■ DECISION AND RATIONALE

(Rehnquist, C.J.) No. The heightened pleading standard required by the Fifth Circuit cannot be squared with the notice pleading required by Rule 8(a)(2), which requires that a complaint include only a "short and plain statement of the claim showing that the pleader is entitled to relief." Rule 9(b), which requires further particularity only in cases of fraud and mistake, does not reference § 1983 actions against municipalities. If the rules were rewritten today, they might specifically list § 1983 actions against municipalities, which were authorized after the original rules were adopted. However, only an amendment to the rules, not judicial interpretation, may change them. Absent an amendment, summary judgment and control over discovery must be used to weed out unmeritorious claims. Reversed.

Analysis:

The Supreme Court has continued to enforce the liberal pleading provisions of Rule 8(a), except in cases of fraud or mistake or when specific federal statutes impose a different pleading standard. The *Leatherman* reasoning would appear to preclude heightened pleading standards in all but those cases specifically enumerated in Rule 9(b). Following that same reasoning, in *Swierkiewicz v. Sorema, N.A.*, 534 U.S. 506 (2002), the Supreme Court held that heightened pleading is permitted in federal court only if prescribed by a specific rule or a federal statute, and it rejected heightened pleading for claims under Title VII or the Age Discrimination in Employment Act. However, after *Leatherman*, the Supreme Court has suggested that a reply required under Rule 7 and a motion for a more definite statement under Rule 12(e) can be used to require a plaintiff to provide more specificity about a claim that a police officer has acted with a wrongful motive, regardless of whether the defendant claims an immunity defense. *See Crawford-El v. Britton*, 523 U.S. 574 (1998).

■ CASE VOCABULARY

EXPRESSIO UNIUS EST EXCLUSIO ALTERIUS: A canon of construction holding that to express or include one thing implies the exclusion of the other, or of the alternative.

Bower v. Weisman

(*Plaintiff Business Associate*) v. (*Defendant Business Associate*)

639 F.Supp. 532 (S.D.N.Y. 1986)

PLEADED FACTS THAT ARE INCONSISTENT WITH THE CLAIM RAISED WILL RESULT IN DISMISSAL

■ **INSTANT FACTS** Bower's (P) complaint alleged that Weisman (D) breached agreements to provide her with assets and financial security after their personal and business relationship was terminated; Weisman moved to dismiss the complaint.

■ **BLACK LETTER RULE** Detailed pleadings will result in dismissal if the alleged facts do not correspond to the cause of action.

■ PROCEDURAL BASIS

Hearing on the defendants' motion for a more definite statement and motions to dismiss for failure to state fraud with particularity and failure to state a claim upon which relief may be granted.

■ FACTS

Bower (P) and Weisman (D) terminated a fifteen-year personal and business relationship. Bower (P) alleged that Weisman (D) had, in various agreements, promised her assets and financial support even if the relationship ended, provided she remained unmarried and did not leave the United States. Bower (P) claimed that a final agreement, dated a few days before their relationship ended, gave her a home; substantial trusts for her and her daughter; payment of living expenses; and rent-free use of a townhouse, among other things. Bower (P) claimed that Weisman (D) reneged on the agreement and attempted to coerce her to leave the townhouse, and she further alleged that Weisman's (D) agents entered the townhouse, removed artwork, changed the locks, and posted guards in the lobby. The complaint set forth seven claims, and Weisman (D) brought various motions against the complaint, including a motion to dismiss for a more definite statement and motions to dismiss for failure to state fraud with particularity and failure to state a claim upon which relief may be granted.

■ ISSUE

Is dismissal appropriate if a detailed complaint does not allege facts that correspond to the cause of action?

■ DECISION AND RATIONALE

(Sweet, J.) Generally, yes. Pursuant to Rule 12(e), a motion for a more definite statement will be granted if the pleading is "so vague and ambiguous that a party cannot reasonably be required to frame a responsive pleading." Bower's (P) complaint clearly identifies the offending acts, traces the initial agreement and subsequent modifications, and identifies the specific provisions that Weisman (D) allegedly violated. Therefore, Weisman (D) has fair notice of the claims against him, can formulate a responsive pleading, and the motion for a more definite statement is denied. However, the complaint fails to identify which of the three defendants are being referred to in each of the claims. Because Weisman (D) cannot respond to claims for which he is not identified as the individual defendant, the motion for a more definite statement is granted in that respect.

Rule 9(b) provides that in all fraud or mistake allegations, the circumstances constituting the fraud or mistake must be stated with particularity. A well-pleaded claim typically includes the time, place, and content of the misrepresentation; the facts misrepresented; and the nature of the detrimental reliance. Because Bower's (P) complaint does not contain the required detail for the defendant to effectively respond, the motion is granted with leave to replead.

A motion to dismiss for failure to state a claim upon which relief may be granted is disfavored and seldom granted. The complaint must be reviewed in the light most favorable to the plaintiff to determine whether the claims state any basis for relief. Regarding the trespass claim, Bower's (P) complaint alleged all necessary elements to sustain a cause of action. Therefore, the motion to dismiss the trespass claim is denied. In its false imprisonment claim, the complaint alleges that Bower was unable to enter and exit her premises freely and therefore was a prisoner, but other allegations in the complaint indicate that she was allowed to enter and leave without restraint. Therefore, the false imprisonment claim is dismissed with leave to replead. In her intentional infliction of emotional distress claim, Bower (P) included each of the necessary elements, and it is up to the trier of fact to determine whether the defendant's actions were outrageous. Therefore, the motion to dismiss that claim is denied. In the private nuisance claim, the complaint fatally contains no allegation that the property was reduced in value. Thus, the claim of a private nuisance is dismissed with leave to replead. Motions denied in part and granted in part.

Analysis:

Bower demonstrates another manner in which a complaint may be dismissed for failure to state a claim upon which relief may be granted. Dismissal may be appropriate if the complaint sets forth a known cause of action, but alleges facts that, even if true, are inconsistent with or otherwise defeat the stated cause of action. The court will analyze the factual allegations in detail by setting them against the relevant claim's elements to determine if the claim can stand, assuming all the factual allegations are true.

■ CASE VOCABULARY

FALSE IMPRISONMENT: A restraint of a person in a bounded area without justification or consent.

INTENTIONAL INFLICTION OF EMOTIONAL DISTRESS: The tort of intentionally or recklessly causing another person severe emotional distress through one's extreme or outrageous acts.

PRIVATE NUISANCE: A condition that interferes with a person's enjoyment of property, but does not involve a trespass.

Henry v. Daytop Village, Inc.

(*Discharged Employee*) v. (*Employer*)

42 F.3d 89 (2d Cir. 1994)

ALTERNATIVE OR INCONSISTENT THEORIES IN PLEADINGS DO NOT REQUIRE DISMISSAL

■ **INSTANT FACTS** Henry (P), a black female who was discharged for misrepresenting her husband's medical claims, denied any misrepresentation and alternatively claimed that white male employees were not discharged for similar misconduct.

■ **BLACK LETTER RULE** A plaintiff may plead two or more alternative statements of a claim, regardless of consistency.

■ **PROCEDURAL BASIS**

Appeal from a grant of summary judgment in favor of the defendant.

■ **FACTS**

Henry (P), a black female, and her spouse were covered under the medical insurance plan offered by her employer, Daytop Village (D). Her husband's claims were covered to the extent they were not covered by his insurance. Over a number of years, Henry (P) obtained reimbursement for her husband's medical expenses under Daytop Village's (D) insurance plan. An investigation revealed that Henry (P) had been overpaid $760.35 for her husband's medical expenses as a result of duplicative claims. Her supervisor confronted her with the company's findings, an argument ensued, and Henry (P) was fired for employee misconduct. Henry (P) filed suit, claiming she was unlawfully terminated under Title VII on the basis of sex and race. She argued that she had not misrepresented her husband's medical coverage and that Daytop Village's (D) misconduct accusations were a pretext for firing her. As an alternate theory, she argued that white male employees had received more lenient sanctions for similar misconduct. Daytop Village (D) moved for summary judgment, asserting that Henry's (P) allegations related to similarly situated white male employees were a constructive admission of her conduct and inconsistent with her claims that she had not committed misconduct. The lower court granted summary judgment in favor of the defendant.

■ **ISSUE**

May a plaintiff plead two or more alternative statements of a claim, even if they are inconsistent?

■ **DECISION AND RATIONALE**

(Cabranes, J.) Yes. Pursuant to Rule 8(e)(2) of the Federal Rules of Civil Procedure, a plaintiff may plead two or more statements of a claim, even within the same count, regardless of consistency. Henry (P) did not admit misconduct when she claimed disparate treatment. Rather, she claimed that regardless of whether she was guilty of misconduct, she was treated more harshly than similarly situated white male employees. The actual fact of misconduct is immaterial to the claim that white male employees who were accused of misconduct were treated differently. Also, even if Henry (P) conceded misconduct for one claim, she did not concede misconduct with respect to her other distinct claim that she was falsely accused of violating the disciplinary code in order to fire her as a pretext for sex and race discrimination. Although the common law imposed strict rules on inconsistent allegations, the federal rules sought to liberate pleaders from the inhibiting effect of technical consistency, especially in the context of civil rights claims, in which complex questions of parties' intent may sometimes justify raising multiple, inconsistent claims.

Analysis:

Contrast this case with *Bower v. Weisman*, 639 F.Supp. 532 (S.D.N.Y. 1986), in which the facts as alleged in support of the claim were found to be inconsistent with the claim of false imprisonment. There, inconsistent facts or theories were not alleged; rather, the facts as alleged did not support the asserted claim. By contrast, in *Henry* the alternative and hypothetical theories were set forth as such in the pleadings, and the inconsistencies between the claims did not result in dismissal. If a party proceeds in good faith to plead alternative factual and legal theories under Rule 8(e), an attorney will meet his or her obligations under Rule 11 in signing the pleadings.

■ CASE VOCABULARY

MATERIAL FACT: A fact that is significant or essential to the issue or matter at hand.

PRIMA FACIE CASE: The establishment of a legally required rebuttable presumption; a party's production of enough evidence to allow the fact-trier to infer the fact at issue and rule in the party's favor.

DM II, Ltd. v. Hospital Corp. of America

(*Plaintiff Partners*) v. (*Defendant Partners*)
130 F.R.D. 469 (N.D. Ga. 1989)

THE PARTNERSHIP IS NOT AN INDISPENSABLE PARTY TO AN ACTION BETWEEN PARTNERS

■ **INSTANT FACTS** Members of a hospital partnership sued other partnership members for wrongfully competing against the partnership.

■ **BLACK LETTER RULE** Under Georgia law, members of a partnership may sue other members of the partnership for breach of fiduciary duty to the partnership, and the partnership is not an indispensable party to the action.

■ **PROCEDURAL BASIS**

Hearing on the defendants' motion to dismiss under Fed. R. Civ. P. 17(a) for failure to prosecute on behalf of the real party in interest (the partnership).

■ **FACTS**

DM II (P) and other Georgia corporations brought an action against Hospital Corporation of America (D) and another Tennessee corporation for breach of fiduciary duties in relation to a hospital in Columbus, Georgia. The plaintiffs allege that the hospital is owned and operated by a partnership in which the plaintiffs and the defendants are partners, that the partnership relationship imposed fiduciary duties on all partners, and that the defendant partners had breached those duties by establishing a competing hospital. The plaintiffs seek an accounting of all profits earned by the defendants at the partnership's expense and the imposition of a constructive trust on the profits. The defendants moved to dismiss for failure to prosecute the action in the name of the real party in interest, claiming that under substantive Georgia law, the plaintiffs' claims belong to the partnership and must be brought by the partnership or by each partner in a single action. The plaintiffs contend that the claims belong to each partner and may be brought either jointly or individually.

■ **ISSUE**

Is the partnership the real party in interest in an action for breach of fiduciary duty against partnership members?

■ **DECISION AND RATIONALE**

(Forrester, J.) No. As a threshold matter, pursuant to Georgia law, the partnership exists among the plaintiffs and the defendants for the ownership and operation of the hospital. Rule 17(a) requires that every action must be prosecuted in the name of the party that, by the controlling substantive law, has the right sought to be enforced. Under the Georgia Partnership Act, each partner is required to account to the partnership for any profits obtained without the consent of other partners from any transaction associated with the conduct of the partnership or its property. The plaintiffs' action seeking an accounting for profits derived by the defendants through wrongful competition with the partnership business is an action for breach of fiduciary duty closely akin to the action permitted under the Georgia Partnership Act. The Act also gives any partner the right to bring this action independent of the partnership. Therefore, pursuant to Georgia substantive law, each partner is a real party in interest and dismissal is not required for that reason.

Analysis:

Rule 17(a) requires that the plaintiff be a person with a substantive right to be enforced. Therefore, in diversity cases, one must look to state law to determine who that person is. Note that because members of the partnership were both Georgia and Tennessee corporations, including the partnership as a plaintiff would have destroyed diversity jurisdiction. Note also that Rule 17(a) does not cover defendants.

■ CASE VOCABULARY

CONSTRUCTIVE TRUST: A trust imposed by a court on equitable grounds against one who has obtained property by wrongdoing, thereby preventing the wrongful holder from being unjustly enriched.

EQUITABLE REMEDY: A nonmonetary remedy, such as an injunction or specific performance, obtained when monetary damages cannot adequately redress the injury.

REAL PARTY IN INTEREST: A person entitled under the substantive law to enforce the right sued upon and who generally, but not necessarily, benefits from the action's final outcome.

Doe v. United Services Life Ins. Co.

(Pseudonym of Life Insurance Applicant) v. *(Insurance Company)*

123 F.R.D. 437 (S.D.N.Y. 1988)

PLAINTIFFS MAY PROCEED ANONYMOUSLY IF NECESSARY TO PROTECT PRIVACY

■ **INSTANT FACTS** In order to avoid being incorrectly identified publicly as homosexual, Doe (P), a heterosexual, sought permission to proceed anonymously to challenge United Services Life Insurance Company's (D) practices related to suspected homosexual applicants.

■ **BLACK LETTER RULE** In rare cases, a plaintiff may proceed anonymously if necessary to protect privacy concerns.

■ **PROCEDURAL BASIS**

A plaintiff sought leave to prosecute an action under a pseudonym, and United Services (D) moved to dismiss for failure to identify the plaintiff under Rule 10(a).

■ **FACTS**

Doe (P) applied to United Services (D) for a life insurance policy on Doe's life. As part of the application process, United Services (D) interviewed Doe and gave him a physical examination. Doe (P) alleges that United Services (D) takes extra precautions in processing homosexuals' applications, which precautions were applied to Doe (P) because he is a single male living with another male. Because Doe (P) admitted to being arrested for public intoxication and his blood test revealed enzymes often associated with alcohol abuse, United Services (D) imposed a surcharge on Doe's (P) premium. Doe (P) alleges, and United Services (D) concedes, that Doe (P) is heterosexual. Doe (P) originally brought his action in New York state court. He obtained an *ex parte* order authorizing service of the complaint under the name of John Doe. His motion to proceed under a pseudonym was pending when United Services (D) removed the action to federal court. United Services (D) moved to dismiss in federal court.

■ **ISSUE**

May a plaintiff proceed anonymously to protect strong privacy concerns?

■ **DECISION AND RATIONALE**

(Sweet, J.) Yes. A plaintiff may proceed anonymously if necessary to protect strong privacy interests. Generally, the public has a legitimate interest in knowing the identity of the parties to a lawsuit. However, under special circumstances, including protection of privacy interests, courts have permitted parties to use fictitious names. Here, Doe (P) might be identified as homosexual, even though he is not. Doe (P) contends he is bringing suit to eliminate unfair insurance practices and vindicate rights of homosexuals, and he is represented by counsel identified with homosexual rights groups. Significantly, United Services (D) will not be prejudiced, because it knows Doe's (P) true identity, will have full discovery rights, and will be barred only from publicly disclosing Doe's identity. Plaintiff's motion granted and defendants' motion denied.

Analysis:

Implicit in the court's decision is the general judicial reluctance to permit plaintiffs to proceed anonymously because of the presumption of openness that attaches to American judicial proceedings. Only when exceptional circumstances exist, such as a threat of violence or a substantial invasion of privacy, do courts permit parties to proceed anonymously. Although there is no express provision in the Federal Rules of Civil Procedure for proceeding anonymously, some courts have held that, if plaintiff files a complaint without permission to proceed anonymously, the court lacks jurisdiction over the party. Note that the court rejects any argument that anonymity is required to protect a party's professional or economic life, which in this case involved Doe's employment as a law clerk to a federal judge.

■ CASE VOCABULARY

EX PARTE ORDER: An order made by the court upon the application of one party to an action without notice to the other.

MOOTNESS DOCTRINE: The principle that American courts will not decide moot cases—that is, cases in which there is no longer any actual controversy.

REMOVAL: The transfer of an action from state to federal court.

Greenbaum v. United States

(Injured Post Office Employee) v. *(Federal Government)*

360 F.Supp. 784 (E.D. Pa. 1973)

TIMELY INVESTIGATION IS REQUIRED TO PROPERLY RESPOND TO A COMPLAINT

■ **INSTANT FACTS** Greenbaum (P) fell and was injured on Post Office (D) property while picking up his paycheck.

■ **BLACK LETTER RULE** A fact that is denied for lack of knowledge or information may be deemed admitted if the matter is one to which the party has, or with reasonable investigation should have, knowledge or information.

■ PROCEDURAL BASIS

Hearing on a post-trial motion to dismiss for lack of subject matter jurisdiction.

■ FACTS

On his day off on March 1, 1968, Greenbaum (P) fell as he crossed the Post Office (D) parking lot in order to enter the building through the employee entrance. Greenbaum (P) filed his claim against the Post Office under the Federal Tort Claims Act, 28 U.S.C.A. § 2671, on May 17, 1968 and brought suit on May 9, 1969. Greenbaum (P) claimed that he was a business invitee on the premises to buy stamps, never claiming he was injured while on duty. At trial, it was established that one reason he was on the premises was to pick up his paycheck. In its answer to the complaint, the Post Office (D) stated that it lacked sufficient knowledge or information to admit or deny the allegation that Greenbaum (P) was a business invitee. The Post Office (D) did not commence discovery until the eve of trial in February 1973. During trial preparation, the Post Office (D) located reports prepared by a Post Office supervisor at the time of the accident that indicated Greenbaum (P) was on the premises to pick up his paycheck. Following trial, the Post Office (D) moved for dismissal for lack of subject matter jurisdiction, asserting that the Federal Employees Compensation Act (FECA), 5 U.S.C.A. § 8101 *et seq.*, provided Greenbaum's (P) exclusive remedy. Under FECA, a covered employee's only remedy is certain compensation for disability resulting from personal injuries sustained while performing duties. The Secretary of Labor's decision regarding the compensation is final and not reviewable by a court. The courts have not decided whether an employee injured on the way to pick up his paycheck is covered by FECA. The Post Office (D) moved to dismiss or to hold the action in abeyance until the Secretary of Labor decided the issue.

■ ISSUE

Does failure to exert reasonable diligence to obtain knowledge of the facts mean those facts will be deemed admitted if they are denied in a responsive pleading for lack of knowledge or information?

■ DECISION AND RATIONALE

(Huyett, J.) Yes. A party has a duty to exercise reasonable effort to obtain knowledge of a fact. If a party pleads that it lacks knowledge or information to admit or deny a fact, the fact may be deemed admitted if the party fails to exercise reasonable care to investigate. Mere delay in challenging jurisdiction does not waive the right to raise a defense under Rule 12(h)(3). However, highly relevant and available documents in the Post Office's (D) possession would have given rise to the FECA defense if the Post

Office (D) had examined them in a timely fashion. The long delay in discovering this information was inexcusable. Only when the demand for damages was increased did the Post Office (D) take this case seriously and discover the elementary facts required to challenge jurisdiction. A fact that is denied for lack of knowledge or information will be deemed admitted if the matter is one to which the party has knowledge or information. Therefore, the Post Office (D) will be held to an admission that Greenbaum (P) was a business invitee. Motion denied.

Analysis:

This case demonstrates the court's refusal to accept the phrase "without knowledge or information sufficient to form a belief" in Rule 8(b) as an excuse to avoid making a reasonable inquiry before admitting or denying allegations. Note that Rule 11 sets forth the requirement that an attorney must certify (by "signing, filing, submitting or later advocating") that a pleading is to the "best of his knowledge, information and belief, formed after an inquiry reasonable under the circumstances," and that it contains factual and legal theories that are supportable and warranted. Detailed representations covered in the certification are set forth in the Rule, and sanctions for violating the certification are at the court's discretion. *See Progress Federal Savings Bank v. Lenders Association, Inc. and NatWest Home Mortgage Corp.,* 1996 WL 57942 (E.D. Pa. Feb. 12, 1996).

■ CASE VOCABULARY

BUSINESS INVITEE: A person who is invited or permitted to enter or remain on another's land for a purpose directly or indirectly connected with the landowner's or possessor's business dealings.

Controlled Environment Sys. v. Sun Process Co., Inc.

(Answering Plaintiff) v. *(Moving Defendant)*
173 F.R.D. 509 (N.D. Ill. 1997)

LACK OF INFORMATION SUFFICIENT TO FORM A BELIEF IS REQUIRED TO NEITHER ADMIT OR DENY AN ALLEGATION

■ **INSTANT FACTS** Not stated.

■ **BLACK LETTER RULE** An answer that a party is without personal knowledge sufficient to admit or deny allegations is inadequate.

■ **PROCEDURAL BASIS**

Hearing on the defendant's motion to strike portions of the plaintiff's answer to a counterclaim.

■ **FACTS**

Not stated.

■ **ISSUE**

Is an answer that a party lacks sufficient personal knowledge of allegations to admit or deny them adequate to avoid a motion to strike?

■ **DECISION AND RATIONALE**

(Shadur, J.) No. Rule 8(b) requires more than lack of sufficient knowledge to avoid a motion to strike. A party may lack knowledge but still have enough information to form a belief. Therefore, Rule 8(b) requires a disclaimer regarding both lack of knowledge and information before a party is entitled to plead that it neither admits nor denies the allegations. Here, Controlled Environment Systems (P) must representation both its lack of knowledge and its lack of information sufficient to form a belief regarding the allegations, if it can do so in good faith, in order to form an adequate answer to the counterclaim. Motion to strike granted.

Analysis:

In this case, no allegation was made in the answer with respect to information sufficient to form a belief. However, if a party has information that leads to a belief that the allegation may be false, but it is uncertain, the party may answer that it denies the allegation upon information and belief. Although not a direct denial, and thus not expressly authorized by Rule 8(b), such denials on information and belief are permitted. *See* Charles A. Wright & Arthur R. Miller, 5 *Federal Practice and Procedure* § 1263.

■ **CASE VOCABULARY**

MOTION TO STRIKE: A party's request that the court delete insufficient defenses or immaterial, redundant, impertinent, or scandalous statements from an opponent's pleading.

Gomez v. Toledo

(Discharged Police Officer) v. *(Police Supervisor)*
446 U.S. 635, 100 S.Ct. 1920 (1980)

QUALIFIED IMMUNITY IS AN AFFIRMATIVE DEFENSE

■ **INSTANT FACTS** Gomez (P), a police officer, was discharged by Toledo (D), the Superintendent of Police in Puerto Rico, after giving sworn statements and testifying that other police officers had offered false evidence.

■ **BLACK LETTER RULE** A public official's qualified immunity is an affirmative defense that must be pleaded by the defendant.

■ **PROCEDURAL BASIS**

Certiorari to review a court of appeals' judgment affirming dismissal of the complaint.

■ **FACTS**

Gomez (P), a police officer in Puerto Rico, submitted a sworn statement to his supervisor that two agents had offered false evidence for use in a criminal case under their investigation. Gomez (P) was immediately transferred to a job without any investigative duties. An investigation of Gomez's (P) claims found them to be true. Gomez (P) was subsequently subpoenaed to testify in the criminal case arising out of the evidence he had claimed to be false. Appearing as a defense witness, Gomez (P) testified the evidence was false. The next month, Toledo (D), the Puerto Rico Police Superintendent, brought criminal charges against Gomez (P), alleging unlawful wiretapping of the two agents. Toledo (D) suspended Gomez (P) and later discharged him without a hearing. The criminal charges were dismissed for lack of probable cause. Gomez's (P) discharge was revoked on administrative review, and he was reinstated with back pay. Gomez (P) brought this § 1983 action for damages for violation of his due process rights and defamation. The District Court dismissed the complaint for failure to state a claim upon which relief may be granted because the complaint did not allege that Toledo's (D) acts were motivated by bad faith. The First Circuit Court of Appeals affirmed the dismissal.

■ **ISSUE**

Must a plaintiff plead that a public official acted in bad faith in order to state a claim in a § 1983 action?

■ **DECISION AND RATIONALE**

(Marshall, J.) No. Section 1983 requires only two allegations in order to state a cause of action: an allegation that some person has deprived the plaintiff of a federal right and an allegation that the person who has deprived him or her of that right acted under color of state law. The qualified immunity available to a public official is not relevant to the plaintiff's cause of action; rather, it is a defense available to the official in question. Because it is a defense, the burden of pleading qualified immunity rests with the defendant. An official pleading qualified immunity must plead that his or her conduct was justified by an objectively reasonable belief that it was lawful. There is no reason for a plaintiff to anticipate a qualified immunity defense by pleading that the defendant acted in bad faith. Moreover, whether immunity has been established depends on facts within the defendant's knowledge and control. The existence of reasonable grounds for the belief, coupled with good faith, provide the basis for qualified immunity for officials for acts performed in the course of official conduct. Both objective and subjective good faith are required, and subjective good faith frequently turns on facts known only to the defendant. Reversed.

■ CONCURRENCE

(Rehnquist, J.) The Court leaves open the burden of persuasion issue with respect to the qualified immunity defense and decides only the issue of the burden of pleading.

Analysis:

Gomez involves the issue of who has the burden of pleading an affirmative defense. Unlike the Circuit Court in *Leatherman,* 954 F.2d 1054 (5th Cir. 1992), the Supreme Court is not imposing a heightened standard of pleading on any of the parties. However, even though the plaintiff is not required to plead the allegations necessary to overcome a defendant's claim of immunity as a result of *Gomez,* plaintiffs must be prepared to address the immunity issues because they are often decided early in the litigation and may be determinative.

■ CASE VOCABULARY

BURDEN OF ALLEGATION/PLEADING: A party's duty to plead a matter in order for that matter to be heard in the lawsuit.

Singletary v. Pennsylvania Dep't of Corrections

(Deceased Prisoner's Mother) v. *(Corrections Department)*

266 F.3d 186 (3d Cir. 2001)

TIMELY NOTICE IS REQUIRED FOR AN AMENDED COMPLAINT TO "RELATE BACK"

■ **INSTANT FACTS** Dorothy Singletary (P), the mother of a prisoner who committed suicide, attempted to amend her § 1983 complaint against the Pennsylvania Department of Corrections (D), its prison, and some of its officials, to add a previously unnamed staff psychologist after the statute of limitations had run.

■ **BLACK LETTER RULE** Under Rule 15(c)(3), an amended complaint relates back for a newly identified party only if the party had timely notice of the action.

■ **PROCEDURAL BASIS**

Appeal of the grant of summary judgment for the defendants and denial of leave to amend the complaint to add a defendant.

■ **FACTS**

Edward Singletary, who had been convicted of rape, was serving a sentence in prisons run by the Pennsylvania Department of Corrections (D). While in prison, Edward was under observation and care for actions that indicated possible mental illness. Edward committed suicide by hanging himself in his cell. In the days immediately before the suicide, a psychiatrist and Regan, a prison psychological service specialist, interviewed Edward and evaluated his mental state. Based on this evaluation, neither Regan nor the psychiatrist ordered suicide precautions for Edward. Dorothy Singletary (P), Edward's mother, brought a § 1983 action against the Pennsylvania Department of Corrections (D), the prison, the prison superintendent, and "Unknown Corrections Officers," alleging cruel and unusual punishment in violation of the Eighth Amendment and state law claims for wrongful death. The trial court dismissed the federal claims against the Department of Corrections (D) and the prison, but denied the motion to dismiss with respect to the pendent state claims. Following discovery, all defendants moved for summary judgment. More than two years after the suicide, Singletary (P) moved to amend her complaint by adding Regan as a defendant. The summary judgment motions were granted as to all defendants, the plaintiff was denied leave to amend the complaint, and all state law claims were dismissed. Singletary (P) did not appeal the grant of summary judgment to the Department of Corrections (D) or the prison, and her appeal of the summary judgment in favor of the prison superintendent was denied for lack of any plain merit because there was no evidence that he exhibited any deliberate indifference to Edward's medical needs. The remaining issue on appeal was the denial of Singletary's (P) motion to amend her complaint to add Regan.

■ **ISSUE**

Did the added defendant have timely notice of the action, so that an amended complaint would relate back under Rule 15(c)(3) to the original complaint?

■ DECISION AND RATIONALE

(Becker, C.J.) No. Regan did not have notice, within the meaning of Rule 15(c)(3), because he did not share an attorney with an original defendant and because he did not have an identity of interest with any originally named defendant. The applicable statute of limitations period is two years, which expired on the day the plaintiff filed the original complaint. Singletary (P) filed the motion to add Regan as a defendant almost two years after the statute of limitations had expired. Therefore, the statute of limitations problem is avoided only if the proposed amendment relates back to the original complaint. The court must resolve three issues in the plaintiff's favor for her proposed amendment to relate back: (1) whether Regan received timely notice that the action had been filed; (2) whether the notice Regan received was sufficient to avoid prejudice in maintaining his defense; and (3) whether Regan knew or should have known in a timely manner that, but for a mistake, he would have been named as a party in the original complaint. "Timely notice" is within 120 days of the filing of the original summons and complaint, and notice may be deemed to have occurred if the party has some reason to expect his potential involvement as a defendant because he hears of the litigation through some informal means. Singletary (P) claims Regan had constructive notice because he shared an attorney with the other defendants and had an identity of interest with an original defendant. A single state attorney represented all original defendants, including Regan, at later stages of the action. However, this attorney did not become the defendants' and Regan's attorney until well after the relevant 120-day period had run, and the attorney representing the original defendants during the 120-day period did not represented Regan. Therefore, notice under this theory cannot be imputed to Regan. Similarly, although an identity of interest between an original defendant and a newly named defendant can impute notice, Regan was a staff-level employee with no administrative or supervisory authority who was not high enough in the prison hierarchy to conclude that his interests were identical to the prison's interests. Therefore, the lower court's denial of the motion to amend the complaint to add Regan is affirmed. Because the absence of notice means that the motion to amend the complaint was properly denied, the court does not need to address the question under Rule 15(c)(3)(B) of whether, but for a mistake concerning the identity of the proper party, the newly added party should have known the action would be brought against him. However, the court sets forth an analysis of the issue nevertheless, because it believes that the law as applied by other Courts of Appeals incorrectly interprets the rule. Also, in a footnote, the court states that an amendment to a "John Doe" complaint by later substituting a specific, named defendant should relate back to the original complaint. Particularly in § 1983 actions, plaintiffs do not know the names of specific officials until after substantial discovery has been completed. There is no reason to require plaintiffs to complete discovery before the statute of limitations has run in order to identify defendants. Affirmed.

Analysis:

Even if the plaintiff had been able to satisfy the requirements of Rule 15(c)(3), there is some question as to whether she could have met the requirements of Rule 15(a), which require that when a party moves to amend a pleading she must meet the "justice so requires" standard. Note also the unusual extent to which the Third Circuit sets forth in dicta its reasons for disagreeing with the other courts of appeals on the issue of interpreting Rule 15(c)(3)(B). Its advocacy of explicit language for changing the Rule is also unusual.

■ CASE VOCABULARY

CONSTRUCTIVE NOTICE: Notice arising by presumption of law from the existence of facts and circumstances that a party had a duty to take notice of, such as a registered deed or a pending lawsuit; notice presumed by law to have been acquired by a person and thus imputed to that person.

PENDENT JURISDICTION: A court's jurisdiction to hear and determine a claim over which it would not otherwise have jurisdiction, based on the claim's arising from the same transaction or occurrence as another claim that is properly before the court.

RELATION BACK: The doctrine that an act done at a later time is considered to have occurred at an earlier time; for example, in federal civil procedure, an amended pleading relates back, for purposes of the statute of limitations, to the time when the original pleading was filed.

Christopher v. Duffy

(Mother of Child Victim) v. *(Lead Paint Remover)*
28 Mass. App. Ct. 780 (1990)

UNDUE PREJUDICE TO AN OPPONENT CAN PRECLUDE AN AMENDMENT TO A PLEADING

■ **INSTANT FACTS** The mother of a child who allegedly died from complications from lead poisoning sought to amend her complaint to add paint manufacturers and a paint trade association, six years after bringing the action.

■ **BLACK LETTER RULE** Under Massachusetts law, an amendment to a complaint will be denied if it will cause undue prejudice to an opponent.

■ **PROCEDURAL BASIS**

Appeal by the plaintiff from a denial of a motion to amend the complaint.

■ **FACTS**

Janette Christopher, a young child, was diagnosed with lead poisoning in June 1981. Duffy (D) was hired to "delead" the apartment in which Janette and her family lived. He allegedly performed his task improperly and increased the lead exposure in the apartment. In July 1981, Janette was hospitalized for lead poisoning. Shortly after she was released from the hospital, she died of pneumonia that she contracted in the hospital and was unable to resist because of her lead poisoning. Mary Christopher (P), Janette's mother, commenced this action in May 1982 against several defendants, including the property owners and Duffy (D) (named in the original complaint as "John Doe"). The complaint alleged wrongful death, negligence, and violations of various statutes, including lead-poisoning prevention statutes. In January 1987, Christopher (P) settled with several defendants, but not Duffy (D), who had not been served with the complaint. Duffy (D) later died. In November 1987, Christopher (P), as administrator of Janette's estate, moved to amend her complaint to drop all defendants except Duffy (D) and to add five paint manufacturers, a paint trade association, and several theories of liability, including negligence in product design, failure to give warning, breach of warranty, and conspiracy to conceal the hazards of lead paint from the public. The trial court denied the plaintiff's motion to amend on the ground that the new defendants would be prejudiced by having to respond to the delayed claims.

■ **ISSUE**

Will an amendment made six years after an action was commenced cause undue prejudice to the newly added parties?

■ **DECISION AND RATIONALE**

(Kaplan, J.) Yes. An amendment generally will be allowed unless a good reason appears for denying it. An amendment that adds new parties and new theories to remedy the injury relates back to the original complaint. The court must decide whether the amendment will unduly prejudice an opposing party. Delay may add substantially to the prejudice. Here, the proposed new defendants, previously unconnected with the case, were served six years after the cause of action arose to defend a complex lead poisoning case, requiring extensive discovery and documentation of causal links. Duffy (D), a significant actor in the chain of events, is dead. Conditions of the premises and the identity of the company that supplied the paint have been obscured by time. The policies behind extinguishing claims after the limitations period has run weigh against granting an amendment adding new parties. The trial court did not abuse its discretion in finding prejudice and denying the amendment. Affirmed.

Analysis:

The court contrasts this case of adding new parties previously unconnected to the case with the more common case of adding a new theory of liability applicable to an existing party. Prejudice is far less likely if the amendment adds only a new theory of liability. Note that the Massachusetts Rule of Civil Procedure 15(c) is more lenient than Federal Rule 15(c) on the issue of relation back, because an amendment, including one adding a new party, arising out of the "conduct, transaction, or occurrence" set forth in the original pleading relates back to the original pleading.

■ CASE VOCABULARY

ADMINISTRATOR: A person appointed by the court to manage the assets and liabilities of an intestate decedent.

INTERLOCUTORY APPEAL: An appeal that occurs before the trial court's final ruling on the entire case.

INTESTATE: Of or relating to a person who has died without a valid will.

Progress Federal Savings Bank v. National West Lenders Association, Inc.

(Alleged Fraud Victim) v. *(Defendant Moving for Sanctions)*

1996 WL 57942 (E.D. Pa. Feb. 12, 1996)

A MOTION FOR SANCTIONS MUST BE TIMELY FILED

■ **INSTANT FACTS** Three months after it was granted summary judgment dismissing all claims, National West (D) moved for sanctions against Progress Federal (P) for filing a groundless lawsuit.

■ **BLACK LETTER RULE** A motion for Rule 11 sanctions must be filed before a judge rejects the offending contention in order to permit the allegedly offending party to withdraw or appropriately correct the contention.

■ **PROCEDURAL BASIS**

On the defendant's motion for Rule 11 sanctions and the plaintiff's motion to strike the defendant's motion.

■ **FACTS**

Progress Federal (P) sued National West (D) for fraud, misrepresentation, intentional interference with contractual relations, and civil conspiracy. The fraud and misrepresentation claims were dismissed for failure to state a claim upon which relief could be granted. Five months later, the court granted National West's (D) motion for summary judgment on the remaining claims. Three months later, National West (D) served Progress Federal (P) with a motion for Rule 11 sanctions. Twenty-one days later, National West (D) filed its motion for sanctions with the court.

■ **ISSUE**

Is a defendant's motion for Rule 11 sanctions timely if it is filed three months after the court granted the defendant's motion for summary judgment?

■ **DECISION AND RATIONALE**

(Yohn, J.) No. A party cannot delay filing its Rule 11 motion until the conclusion of a case because the opposing party would have no opportunity to withdraw or correct the offending contention. The purpose of Rule 11 is to deter groundless proceedings and abusive litigation practices. The purpose of the "safe harbor" notice, which requires a twenty-one-day formal notice to the other party before filing a Rule 11 motion with the court, is to give the opposing party an opportunity to withdraw or to correct the challenged matter. Once summary judgment was granted to National West (D), Progress Federal (P) had nothing to correct or withdraw.

The three arguments for exceptions to the "safe harbor" provision are rejected. First, assuming that Progress Federal (P) asked National West (D) to delay filing the Rule 11 motion until after the court had ruled on summary judgment, that would not constitute estoppel, because, even if the allegation is true, neither the court nor the parties can change the rule's requirements. Second, National West (D) argues that Progress Federal (P) would not have withdrawn its papers even if served with a timely motion, so the "safe harbor" rule should not apply. However, speculation on what a party might not have done is

---

not sanctioned by the Rule 11 test. Finally, National West (D) argues that, because the court acted on the motion for summary judgment in nineteen days, it did not have time to file a timely motion for sanctions. However, this argument fails because National West (D) did not file its motion until three months after summary judgment was granted. Motions denied.

Analysis:

Note that the court states that the "safe harbor" provisions do not apply when the court, rather than a party, initiates a consideration of sanctions. The Notes to the rules encourage courts, in imposing sanctions, to consider whatever corrective action has been taken in response to its order to show cause. The court observes that the purpose of both the "safe harbor" provision on party motions and the court's considerations on show cause orders is to address and correct abuses as they occur. Interestingly, the court treats Progress Federal's (P) motion to strike National West's (D) Rule 11 motion as a brief in opposition to the Rule 11 sanction motion, because the rules to do not permit the filing of a motion to strike a motion.

■ CASE VOCABULARY

ESTOPPEL: A bar that prevents one from asserting a claim or right that contradicts what one has said or done before or what has been legally established as true.

SAFE HARBOR: A provision (as in a statute or regulation) that affords protection from liability or penalty.

SANCTION: A penalty or coercive measure that results from failure to comply with a law, rule, or order.

Kedra v. City of Philadelphia

(Police Abuse Victim) v. *(Police Officer Employer)*

454 F.Supp. 652 (E.D. Pa. 1978)

RELATED CLAIMS AND PARTIES MAY BE JOINED

■ **INSTANT FACTS** Several members of the Kedra (P) family sued several police officers, police supervisors, and the City of Philadelphia (D) for injuries and civil rights violations related to abusive police actions occurring over a fifteen-month period.

■ **BLACK LETTER RULE** Multiple parties may be joined in the same case if some of the claims by or against each party arise out of reasonably related events and contain common factual or legal questions.

■ **PROCEDURAL BASIS**

On defendants' motion to dismiss for improper joinder of parties.

■ **FACTS**

The plaintiffs are Delores Kedra (P), her eight children, and the husband (Rozanski) of one of her daughters, Elizabeth. Defendants are the City of Philadelphia (D), five police department officials, six police detectives, a police lieutenant, six police officers, and unidentified police officers. The City of Philadelphia (D) employed all of the individual defendants at relevant times. The plaintiffs allege that the individual defendants acted separately and in concert, under color of state law, and sued them individually and in their official capacity. The complaint alleged that three of the plaintiffs were arrested without probable cause, taken to police headquarters, interrogated for seventeen hours and beaten severely, suffering serious injuries. Meanwhile, police removed Elizabeth from her home and took her to police headquarters, where she was detained and questioned for seventeen hours, shown her husband after he had been beaten, and threatened with arrest in order to coerce a false statement from her. Delores Kedra (P), who went to police headquarters to obtain the release of the others, was forcibly detained for nine hours and coerced into signing a release permitting a search of her home. Later, two officers went to the Kedra home and attempted to remove Rozanski from the home, but the door was shut and locked. With the aid of additional officers, but without a warrant or probable cause, the officers broke down the door and entered the house with weapons in hand. They searched the house and physically assaulted four of the plaintiffs. Four plaintiffs were taken to the police station and detained for twenty-four hours. They were repeatedly denied requests for counsel. Rozanski was charged with murder, burglary, and receiving stolen goods, while two other plaintiffs were charged with assault and battery, harboring a fugitive, and resisting arrest. All three were later acquitted of all charges. The complaint, which alleged that a similar pattern of abuse continued over a fifteen-month period, sets forth claims of violations of federal civil rights and state constitutional rights, and numerous state law claims such as false arrest, false imprisonment, assault and battery. All defendants have moved for dismissal on various procedural and substantive grounds, including improper joinder of parties under Rule 20(a).

■ ISSUE

Do reasonably related events that arise over a period of time, but contain common factual or legal questions, arise out of "the same transaction, occurrence, or series of transactions or occurrences" within the meaning of Rule 20(a)?

■ DECISION AND RATIONALE

(Luongo, J.) Yes. The allegations relate to a "systematic pattern" of police abuse over an extended time period; this pattern means the events over fifteen months are reasonably related for purposes of joinder under Rule 20(a). Common factual and legal questions are present in this case; the similarity of claims against all defendants means there are common issues. Unification of claims in a single action is more convenient, less expensive, and less time-consuming for the parties and the court. Therefore, Rule 20(a) permits liberal joinder of parties and claims that are reasonably related, and absolute identity of events is not required. Joinder permitted.

Analysis:

The court separately considered the issue of whether all claims and defendants would be addressed in a single trial. Under Rule 20(b), trials may be separated as necessary to prevent prejudice to the parties. Although this court recognized that prejudice might occur, it decided to wait until discovery was completed and the case was ready for trial before determining whether a separate trial was required. Note that, although joinder may be proper under Rule 20(a), issues such as subject matter jurisdiction, personal jurisdiction, venue, notice, issue preclusion, and litigation strategy may either compel or prevent joinder of all possible parties.

■ CASE VOCABULARY

PERMISSIVE JOINDER: The optional joinder of parties if (1) their claims or the claims asserted against them are asserted jointly, severally, or in respect of the same transaction or occurrence, and (2) any legal or factual question common to all of them will arise.

Banque Indosuez v. Trifinery

(Creditor) v. *(Debtor)*

817 F.Supp. 386 (S.D.N.Y. 1993)

A PERMISSIVE COUNTERCLAIM CAN BE WAIVED BY CONTRACTUAL AGREEMENT BETWEEN THE PARTIES

■ **INSTANT FACTS** Trifinery (D) asserts that it has a valid counterclaim to set off the amount it owes on a promissory note to Banque Indosuez (P), but Banque Indosuez (P) asserts that the counterclaim is barred by provisions in the note disallowing counterclaims.

■ **BLACK LETTER RULE** A contractual agreement between the parties that precludes bringing a permissive counterclaim is enforceable.

■ **PROCEDURAL BASIS**

Hearing on the plaintiff's motion for partial summary judgment.

■ **FACTS**

Banque Indosuez (P) brought an action for payment on a promissory note, requiring Trifinery (D) to pay it $1,404,420. Banque Indosuez (P) moved for partial summary judgment on the entire amount of the note. Trifinery (D) had paid Banque Indosuez (P) $963,183.36, claiming a set-off of $461,236.44. Trifinery (D) did not deny liability, but contended summary judgment was inappropriate because of its claim for set-off. A clause in the promissory note provided that Trifinery (D) waived any right to interpose a counterclaim or set-off in any action on the note.

■ **ISSUE**

Is a contractual waiver of a right to interpose a permissible counterclaim enforceable?

■ **DECISION AND RATIONALE**

(Haight, J.) Yes. If the counterclaim is permissive, a contractual agreement waiving the right to assert a counterclaim is enforceable, and the defendant would be required to bring its set-off claims in another action. On the other hand, if the counterclaim is compulsory, it would be unfair to enforce the waiver clause because failure to raise a compulsory counterclaim bars a subsequent action on the claim in either state or federal court. Trifinery (D) claims that the counterclaim is compulsory and that any contractual provision to waive compulsory counterclaims is unenforceable. The relevant factors in determining whether a counterclaim is compulsory are whether the issues of fact and law raised by the claim and the counterclaim are largely the same, whether res judicata bars a subsequent suit on the defendant's claims, whether substantially the same evidence supports or refutes the plaintiff's claim and the defendant's counterclaims, and whether any logical relationship exists between the claim and the counterclaim. Banque Indosuez's (P) claim is for payment on a promissory note, and Trifinery's (D) counterclaim is that Banque Indosuez (P) negligently delayed the processing and delivery of letters of credit. These claims present a number of different factual and legal issues. Also, res judicata would not bar the defendant's subsequent claim, and the fact that the claims arise out of the same business relationship is inadequate to make the claim compulsory. Counterclaim dismissed without prejudice and motion for partial summary judgment granted.

Analysis:

Under New York law, contractual waivers of counterclaims, set-offs, and affirmative defenses are enforceable as not against public policy and all counterclaims are permissive. A finding that the counterclaim was compulsory under the federal rules would have meant that Banque Indosuez (P) would have been barred by res judicata from bringing the action in either state or federal court. This sets up the possibility that, by bringing an action in federal court where a counterclaim is compulsory, a defendant could be barred from ever asserting the counterclaim if the contractual waiver provision were enforced. Courts are reluctant to permit the choice of state or federal court to determine the subsequent outcome of the litigation; therefore, federal courts refuse to enforce a contractual waiver of a compulsory counterclaim.

■ **CASE VOCABULARY**

COMPULSORY COUNTERCLAIM: A counterclaim that must be asserted to be cognizable, usually because it relates to the opposing party's claim and arises out of the same subject matter. If a defendant fails to assert a compulsory counterclaim in the original action, that claim may not be brought in a later, separate action (with some exceptions).

COUNTERCLAIM: A claim for relief asserted against an opposing party after an original claim has been made; especially, a defendant's claim in opposition to or as a setoff against the plaintiff's claim.

PERMISSIVE COUNTERCLAIM: A counterclaim that need not be asserted to be cognizable, usually because it does not arise out of the same subject matter as the opposing party's claim or involves third parties over which the court does not have jurisdiction. Permissive counterclaims may be brought in a later, separate action.

Gross v. Hanover Ins. Co.

(Insured) v. *(Insurance Company)*
138 F.R.D. 53 (S.D.N.Y. 1991)

THIRD–PARTY IMPLEADER PRACTICE INCLUDES SUBROGATION CLAIMS

■ **INSTANT FACTS** Gross (P) sought insurance proceeds from Hanover (D) for jewels stolen while consigned to the Rizzos; Hanover (D) sought to implead the Rizzos as third-party defendants.

■ **BLACK LETTER RULE** Third-party defendants who may be liable to an insurer for payments on a claim against an insurance policy may be impleaded under Rule 14(a).

■ PROCEDURAL BASIS

Hearing on the defendant's motion to implead third-party defendants.

■ FACTS

Gross (P) consigned to and kept diamonds and emeralds at 3–R Jewelers, a retail store that was owned by Anthony Rizzo and employed Anthony's brother, Joseph Rizzo. Gross (P) alleged that the jewels were stolen from 3–R and made a claim under Hanover's (D) insurance policy for coverage. Hanover (D) moved to implead the Rizzos, alleging that Joseph set up the store for a "theft." Hanover (D) alleged that Joseph, who had a cocaine habit, permitted someone to enter the store and take the jewels. The proposed third-party complaint sought to implead Joseph and Anthony on the ground that they would be liable to Hanover (D) if Hanover (D) were found liable to Gross (P). The proposed third-party complaint alleged that Joseph was negligent in handling the jewels; that Joseph was liable for conversion of the jewels; and that Anthony negligently hired, retained, and supervised Joseph.

■ ISSUE

May a defendant implead persons who are allegedly responsible for the plaintiff's claim?

■ DECISION AND RATIONALE

(Leisure, J.) Yes. A court has considerable discretion in deciding whether to permit a third-party complaint. The purpose of Rule 14(a) is judicial efficiency by eliminating the need for a defendant to bring a separate action against a third individual who may be liable to the defendant for all or part of the plaintiff's claim. A court must balance the benefits of efficiency against the potential prejudice to the plaintiff and third-party defendants. Here, the relevant events arose out of the same core set of facts, so efficiency would be served by having all claims heard in the same action. The court, which rejects Gross's (P) argument that Hanover's (D) claims are speculative, notes that it is not clear that the plaintiff can attack the merits of proposed third-party claims at this stage of the proceeding. The court also asserts that Rule 14(a) expressly addresses third-party defendants who "may be liable," so certainty is not required, and that subrogation claims are within third-party impleader practice under New York and federal law. Gross's (P) argument that Hanover (D) was dilatory in bringing the motion and that Gross (P) would be prejudiced by increased discovery also fails because any prejudice to Gross (P) is outweighed by the benefits of permitting impleader. There is also no evidence that Hanover (D) sought to delay the proceedings by bringing its motion. Motion granted.

Analysis:

The court has great discretion in determining whether a defendant may implead persons who are allegedly responsible for the plaintiff's claim. However, three conditions must be met to implead a new party: (1) the new third-party defendant must not already be a party; (2) the defendant must have a claim against the new third-party defendant; and (3) the theory of liability against the third-party defendant must be for all or part of the plaintiff's claim. These elements were all readily met in *Gross*.

■ CASE VOCABULARY

CONVERSION: The wrongful possession or disposition of another's property as if it were one's own; an act or series of acts of willful interference, without lawful justification, with an item of property in a manner inconsistent with another's right, whereby that other person is deprived of the use and possession of the property.

SUBROGATION: The principle under which an insurer that has paid a loss under an insurance policy is entitled to all the rights and remedies belonging to the insured against a third party with respect to any loss covered by the policy.

CHAPTER FOUR

Discovery

Hickman v. Taylor

Instant Facts: Hickman (P) sought disclosure of written and oral statements made to Taylor's (D) counsel by eyewitnesses before suit was filed.

Black Letter Rule: Discovery of attorney work product prepared in anticipation of litigation is not permitted under the Federal Rules of Civil Procedure when the opposing party fails to show necessity or prejudice from nondisclosure.

Hawthorne Land Co. v. Occidental Chem. Corp.

Instant Facts: Occidental Chemical Corporation (D) sought a protective order from Hawthorne Land Company's (D) requested discovery of historical leakage of the defendants' five pipelines, dating back many years.

Black Letter Rule: A party may obtain discovery regarding any unprivileged matter that is relevant to the claims or defenses of any party.

Hickman v. Taylor

(Estate of Deceased Crewmember) v. *(Tug Boat Owner)*

329 U.S. 495, 67 S.Ct. 385 (1947)

WRITTEN STATEMENTS PREPARED IN ANTICIPATION OF LITIGATION ARE NOT DISCOVERABLE

■ **INSTANT FACTS** Hickman (P) sought disclosure of written and oral statements made to Taylor's (D) counsel by eyewitnesses before suit was filed.

■ **BLACK LETTER RULE** Discovery of attorney work product prepared in anticipation of litigation is not permitted under the Federal Rules of Civil Procedure when the opposing party fails to show necessity or prejudice from nondisclosure.

■ **PROCEDURAL BASIS**

Certiorari to review a decision of the Third Circuit Court of Appeals reversing the trial court's judgment.

■ **FACTS**

While towing a railroad car float across the Delaware River, the *J.M. Taylor* tugboat sank, killing five crewmembers. The United States Steamboat Inspectors examined the four surviving crewmembers. Shortly thereafter, Taylor's (D) counsel took private statements from the survivors and witnesses in anticipation of litigation by the families of the deceased crewmembers. Nine months after the accident, the crewmembers' families brought a claim against Taylor (D). After four of the claims settled, Hickman (P) sued Taylor (D) and the railroad in federal court. While the suit proceeded, Hickman (P) served interrogatories on Taylor (D) demanding copies of all written statements taken from the surviving crewmembers and a summary of any oral statements similarly taken. In supplemental interrogatories, Hickman (P) also requested the nature of all records, reports, and statements collected by Taylor (D) in relation to the accident. In response, Taylor's (D) counsel acknowledged taking statements from the crewmembers, but refused to disclose the contents of those statements as privileged material obtained in preparation for litigation. After a hearing, the district court ordered Taylor's (D) counsel to produce the statements to the court to determine what portions should be disclosed to the plaintiff. When Taylor's (D) counsel refused, he was held in contempt of court. The Third Circuit Court of Appeals reversed the judgment, finding the statements were the work product of the lawyer and were privileged from discovery under the Federal Rules of Civil Procedure. Hickman (P) appealed.

■ **ISSUE**

May a party obtain the oral and written statements of witnesses secured by an adverse party's counsel in the course of preparation for possible litigation, after a claim arises?

■ **DECISION AND RATIONALE**

(Murphy, J.) No. Prior to the adoption of the Federal Rules of Civil Procedure, notice of the issues presented in litigation was primarily given through the pleadings. Pretrial discovery of the facts supporting those issues, however, was cumbersome and narrow in scope. The Federal Rules of Civil Procedure now provide a calculated method for further defining the legal issues and ascertaining the facts material to those issues at trial. Pretrial discovery ensures that all parties will have full access to the facts necessary to formulate their legal position. Any relevant information, not subject to privilege, must be disclosed to the opposing party in response to timely discovery requests. The liberal and broad application of the discovery rules prevents the possibility of surprise at trial by requiring full disclosure of the facts at issue before the day of trial. The discovery rules, however, do not permit extraordinary requests into the work product of an opposing attorney when the sources of the information sought are known to the party and those sources are readily available for the party's own examination.

Here, Hickman (P) was free to examine the crewmembers' testimony before the United States Steamboat Inspectors and further question them on his own. Instead, Hickman (P) sought the production of the written statements and mental impressions of Taylor's (D) counsel during the questioning of these witnesses without any showing of necessity or prejudice. The Federal Rules of Civil Procedure do not permit discovery of this kind, not because the statements are subject to privilege, but because written statements prepared or formed by opposing counsel in anticipation of litigation are not within the scope of the rules. While an attorney is an officer of the court bound to the pursuit of justice, privacy in the representation of his client is necessary to concurrently protect the legal interests of his client. His duty to his client requires him to prepare his client's case by identifying the crucial issues, important facts, and proper theories to advance his client's position. Invasion of these mental impressions through the discovery process would destroy a client's right to vigorous representation and damage the justice system.

Where, however, relevant and non-privileged documents remain exclusively in the possession of counsel and an opposing party's access to the information contained in those documents is prevented by the unavailability of the witness, discovery is permitted. Under such circumstances, the Federal Rules of Civil Procedure allow a trial judge much discretion to consider the justifications favoring disclosure. Here, the trial court was afforded no opportunity to consider those justifications, as none were offered. Hickman (P) provided no showing of a necessity for the written statements, but presented just a blanket interrogatory requesting their disclosure. Respecting oral statements made by the witnesses to Taylor's (D) counsel, there can be no showing of necessity to justify disclosure. Requiring Taylor's (D) counsel to recall the oral statements made to him in the past presents grave concerns of their accuracy and reliability. The attorney's recollection cannot be construed as the substance of what was told to him, but merely as what the attorney recalls from the encounter. While a party may not hide material, non-privileged facts from his opponent, the discovery rules require only the disclosure of those facts, not the conclusions reached by the opponent's counsel concerning the importance of the evidence. Affirmed.

■ CONCURRENCE

(Jackson, J.) A civil trial is and always has been an adversary proceeding, testing the wits of opposing attorneys in the representation of their clients' positions. The Federal Rules of Civil Procedure cannot be understood as sanctioning legal representation without wit or on the wit of opposing counsel. The integrity of the legal profession requires that each attorney formulate his own litigation strategies and draw his own conclusions from the existing facts. Pretrial statements are often used to impeach contradictory statements made on the witness stand. A statement prepared by an opposing attorney provides no assurance that the pretrial statement is more truthful than the witness's in-court statement. The inevitable situation would then require opposing counsel to take the stand to either support his own version of the witness's testimony or defend his credibility before the jury.

Analysis:

The *Hickman* rule mirrors Federal Rule of Civil Procedure 26(b)(3). Following *Hickman*, however, courts continued to struggle with the proper scope of discovery of written pretrial statements obtained or prepared by opposing counsel, as the line between factual disclosure and attorney work product is often difficult to draw. The rule is further complicated in cases involving a corporate party and when the discovery sought relates to expert opinions. In response to the latter, the Federal Rules of Civil Procedure were amended in 1970 to include Rule 26(b)(4), which permits the discovery of any "facts known or opinions held by an expert who has been retained or specially employed by another party in anticipation of litigation or preparation for trial and who is not expected to be called as a witness at trial." Some courts have construed this rule as excluding any privilege attaching to an attorney's mental impressions once they have been revealed to the expert.

■ CASE VOCABULARY

DISCOVERY: Compulsory disclosure, at a party's request, of information that relates to the litigation.

INTERROGATORIES: A written question (usually a set of questions) submitted to an opposing party in a lawsuit as part of discovery.

WORK PRODUCT: Tangible material or its intangible equivalent—in unwritten or oral form—that was either prepared by or for a lawyer or prepared for litigation, either planned or in progress.

WORK–PRODUCT RULE: The rule providing for qualified immunity of an attorney's work product from discovery or other compelled disclosure. Fed. R. Civ. P. 26(b)(3).

Hawthorne Land Co. v. Occidental Chem. Corp.

(Landowner) v. *(Pipeline Operator)*

No. Civ. A. 01–0881, 2002 WL 1976931 (E.D. La. Aug. 23, 2002)

HISTORICAL LEAKAGE FROM PIPELINES NOT ON THE PLAINTIFF'S PROPERTY IS IRRELEVANT TO THE PLAINTIFF'S CLAIMS

■ **INSTANT FACTS** Occidental Chemical Corporation (D) sought a protective order from Hawthorne Land Company's (D) requested discovery of historical leakage of the defendants' five pipelines, dating back many years.

■ **BLACK LETTER RULE** A party may obtain discovery regarding any unprivileged matter that is relevant to the claims or defenses of any party.

■ **PROCEDURAL BASIS**

Trial court consideration of the defendants' request for a protective order.

■ **FACTS**

Hawthorne Land Co. (P) owned land through which it leased a pipeline right of way to Occidental Chemical Corp. (D) and Texas Brine Company (D). Hawthorne (P) sued the defendants for contamination of its land as a result of at least twenty-nine leaks in its pipeline. The plaintiff alleged that five leaks occurred in 1985, five occurred in 1986, and the remainder occurred in 1987. The plaintiff asserted that the defendants failed to clean up the contamination when they knew or should have known it existed. Hawthorne (P) served notices of deposition on the defendants, with subpoenas to produce documents relating to leaks in any of the defendants' five pipelines dating from 1965 to the present, regardless of location. The defendants sought a protective order, arguing that the plaintiff's discovery requests were overbroad. In support of its request, the defendants cited a 1990 report demonstrating that Occidental (D) had made reasonable inspections of its pipelines from 1984 through 1989 and corrected all known leaks. The report also indicated the pipeline was stable with no unexpected leakage for the first nineteen years with a low historical rate of leakage, though some was present. The report further provided that although the defendants' corrective measures were reasonable, future leakage could occur.

■ **ISSUE**

Is the plaintiff's request for documents unrelated to the defendants' use of the plaintiff's right of way relevant to a claim or defense at issue?

■ **DECISION AND RATIONALE**

(Shushan, Magistrate J.) No. Under Rule 26(b) of the Federal Rules of Civil Procedure, a party may obtain discovery regarding any unprivileged matter that is relevant to the claims or defenses of any party. The plaintiff's claim is for damage to its property resulting from leakage from the defendants' pipeline. Accordingly, discovery of documents unrelated to its property and outside the time frame at issue is, the plaintiff argues, relevant to whether the defendant's conduct was sufficiently wanton or reckless to allow for an award of punitive damages. While leaks occurring outside the period of known leakage on the plaintiff's property are sufficiently relevant to the plaintiff's claims and, thus, are discoverable, evidence of leaks on other pipelines—not on the plaintiff's land—is not. The pipeline on the plaintiff's land is the largest and oldest pipeline the defendants operate and provides sufficient history to support the plaintiff's claims. Discovery on other pipelines falls within the exceptions to Rule 26(b), as being cumulative and duplicative. The defendant's motion for a protective order is therefore granted in part and denied in part.

Analysis:

A party can seek relief from the discovery request of an opposing party in a number of ways. As demonstrated in *Hawthorne*, a party may seek a protective order from the court. The party may also simply object to discovery as outside the scope of the Federal Rules of Civil Procedure, providing a detailed explanation of the grounds for the objection. While court involvement is not necessary under the latter method, the party seeking discovery may then request a judicial determination of its discovery requests by seeking an order to compel discovery.

■ CASE VOCABULARY

PROTECTIVE ORDER: A court order prohibiting or restricting a party from engaging in conduct (especially a legal procedure such as discovery) that unduly annoys or burdens the opposing party or a third-party witness.

SUBPOENA: A writ commanding a person to appear before a court or other tribunal, subject to a penalty for failing to comply.

MAGISTRATE: A judicial officer with strictly limited jurisdiction and authority, often on the local level and often restricted to criminal cases.

CHAPTER FIVE

THE RIGHT TO JURY TRIAL AND JUDICIAL CONTROL OF RE-SULTS

Chauffeurs, Teamsters and Helpers, Local No. 391 v. Terry

Instant Facts: Terry (P) and other union members sued the union (D) for backpay when they were laid off after the reorganization of their employer.

Black Letter Rule: Absent congressional direction, a trial by jury is afforded by the Seventh Amendment to statutory actions seeking legal relief.

Edmonson v. Leesville Concrete Co., Inc.

Instant Facts: A civil defendant exercised peremptory challenges to exclude black jurors without a race-neutral explanation.

Black Letter Rule: The Equal Protection Clause of the Fourteenth Amendment forbids the exercise of peremptory challenges in a civil trial based solely on a prospective juror's race.

J.E.B. v. Alabama

Instant Facts: In a paternity and child support suit brought by the State of Alabama (P) against J.E.B. (D), the alleged father, the State exercised its peremptory challenges to remove male jurors from the jury panel, leaving an all-female jury.

Black Letter Rule: Peremptory challenges on the basis of gender violate the Equal Protection Clause.

Adickes v. S. H. Kress & Co.

Instant Facts: Adickes (P) was denied service at the defendant's store and was subsequently arrested when she entered in the company of six black students.

Black Letter Rule: The moving party bears the burden of proving an absence of a genuine issue of material fact to sustain a motion for summary judgment.

Celotex Corp. v. Catrett

Instant Facts: Catrett (P) sued fifteen named asbestos manufacturers, including Celotex Corp. (D), alleging her husband's death was caused by the manufacturers' negligence, breach of warranty, and strict liability.

Black Letter Rule: To sustain a motion for summary judgment, the moving party must present a showing of the absence of a genuine issue of material fact through pleadings, depositions, answers to interrogatories, and admissions on file, with or without supporting affidavits.

Galloway v. United States

Instant Facts: Galloway (P) suffered from mental conditions for which he sought insurance benefits for a total and permanent disability that arose, he claimed, prior to policy termination for failure to pay premiums.

Black Letter Rule: A federal court may order a directed verdict when a party fails to provide sufficient evidence to support an issue in his case.

Brandon v. Chicago Board of Education

Instant Facts: A federal district court dismissed Brandon's (P) discrimination suit for failure to prosecute when his attorney failed to appear at status conferences due to a clerical mistake by the court clerk.

Black Letter Rule: Rule 60(b)(1) permits relief from a final judgment based upon the mistakes of judicial officers, parties, or their representatives, if sought within one year from entry of a final order.

Campolongo v. Celotex Corp.

Instant Facts: Campolongo (P) died after health complications allegedly caused by exposure to the defendant's asbestos products.

Black Letter Rule: Bifurcation is appropriate when it simplifies the fact-finding process, avoids confusion, promotes judicial economy, and results in fundamental fairness to the parties.

Chauffeurs, Teamsters and Helpers, Local No. 391 v. Terry

(Union) v. *(Employee)*
494 U.S. 558, 110 S.Ct. 1339 (1990)

A SUIT FOR BREACH OF THE DUTY OF FAIR REPRESENTATION SEEKING BACKPAY IS LEGAL IN NATURE, ALLOWING FOR TRIAL BY JURY

■ **INSTANT FACTS** Terry (P) and other union members sued the union (D) for backpay when they were laid off after the reorganization of their employer.

■ **BLACK LETTER RULE** Absent congressional direction, a trial by jury is afforded by the Seventh Amendment to statutory actions seeking legal relief.

■ **PROCEDURAL BASIS**

Certiorari to review a decision of the Fourth Circuit Court of Appeals, affirming the federal district court's denial of the union's motion to strike a jury demand.

■ **FACTS**

Terry (P) and his coworkers were members of Chauffeurs, Teamsters and Helpers, Local No. 391 (D), which entered into a collective bargaining agreement with McLean Trucking Company. McLean Trucking thereafter changed operations and transferred Terry (P) and several coworkers to a different location, promising to give them seniority rights over inactive workers. After several weeks at the new location, Terry (P) and other coworkers were laid off and recalled several times, stripping them of their seniority rights each time. The plaintiffs filed a grievance with the union over the denial of their agreed-upon seniority rights, which resulted in an order to recall any laid-off worker, the subsequent lay off of recalled inactive workers, and the reinstatement of special seniority rights. After the plaintiffs were reinstated, McLean recalled the inactive workers, allowing them to regain their original seniority rights over the plaintiffs. The plaintiffs were subsequently laid off due to their inferior seniority rights. At another grievance hearing, the grievance committee approved of McLean's practices. After further grievances were not referred to the grievance committee, Terry (P) and others sued McLean for breach of the collective bargaining agreement and the union (D) for breach of its duty of fair representation, seeking backpay. The plaintiffs requested a trial by jury in their pleading, and the union (D) moved to strike the demand as unavailable in a duty of fair representation suit. After the district court denied the motion, the Fourth Circuit Court of Appeals affirmed.

■ **ISSUE**

Does an employee seeking backpay for a union's alleged breach of its duty of fair representation have a right to trial by jury?

■ **DECISION AND RATIONALE**

(Marshall, J.) Yes. The Seventh Amendment to the United States Constitution affords all litigants the right to trial by jury in all cases in which the litigants' legal rights are to be ascertained and determined and the amount in controversy exceeds twenty dollars. To determine whether a plaintiff seeks vindication of his or her legal rights in a statutory action, the court must compare the nature of the action to those brought at law and in equity before the courts of England and examine the nature of the remedy the plaintiff seeks. Of these two considerations, the nature of the remedy most guides the court. Since a suit for the breach of the duty of fair representation was unknown to the English courts, analogous actions must be considered.

The plaintiffs' claim is not analogous to a suit to vacate an arbitration award, which was an equitable action under the laws of England, because no arbitrator has considered the suit the plaintiffs now bring. Nor is the plaintiffs' suit analogous to an action for attorney malpractice, which was historically legal in nature. Unlike in the union-employee relationship, the attorney-client relationship places control in the hands of the client, not the attorney. Similarly, the analogy to an action for breach of fiduciary duty against a trustee, traditionally an equitable action, does not render the plaintiffs' claims wholly equitable. The plaintiffs' action requires proof of more than the union's breach of duty, including also a breach of contract claim against McLean. The plaintiffs' claims, therefore, encompass both equitable and legal issues. The end result sought by the plaintiffs is primarily monetary damages, a legal remedy though back pay has at times been deemed equitable. In this case, the plaintiffs' claim for monetary damages is not based on the equitable disgorgement of money wrongfully withheld by McLean, but rather relates to the wages and benefits they would have earned but for the defendant's wrongdoing. Additionally, the plaintiffs' monetary claims are not intertwined with claims for equitable relief, such as restitution or an injunction. Notwithstanding the congressional direction that back pay is an equitable remedy under Title VII of the Civil Rights Act of 1964, Congress has made no such statement concerning a statutory action for the breach of the duty of fair representation. Absent congressional direction, the remedy sought here is different than that under Title VII. The plaintiffs' claims for back pay thus seek legal remedies, to which the Seventh Amendment affords a trial by jury.

■ **CONCURRENCE IN PART, DISSENT IN PART**

(Brennan, J.) While the plaintiffs' claim is legal in nature, the right to trial by jury under the Seventh Amendment should be determined by consideration of the legal remedy sought without a review of the historical treatment of analogous actions in England. Resort to historical treatment is often unproductive, as many statutory rights and remedies enforced today failed to exist in England. Even if the court is able to locate an analogous action through the multitude of legal precedents decided centuries ago, the court must still consider the nature of the remedy sought to determine whether it is legal or equitable in nature. Focusing exclusively on the remedy will provide judges a better framework on which to determine whether the right to trial by jury is afforded under the Seventh Amendment.

■ **DISSENT**

(Kennedy, J.) While the majority is correct that a suit for breach of the duty of fair representation is more akin to an equitable suit for breach of a trustee's fiduciary duty than a legal action for attorney malpractice, the Court's decision should stop there. The Court's rationale for treating a breach of the duty of fair representation differently than the breach of fiduciary duty is that one must view the character of the individual issues rather than the claim as a whole, as well as the significance of the remedy sought. Such a rationale, however, reads too much into recent precedent characterizing an action as equitable where it implicates both an equitable remedy, such as an injunction, and a legal remedy, such as damages for breach of contract. When a plaintiff raises primarily an equitable claim, coupled with a legal claim, the right to a jury trial should not be afforded. The Seventh Amendment requires that the Court look to the historical treatment of cases to determine their character for trial-by-jury purposes, for it cannot "preserve" the right without it. The Court is not free to fashion its own conclusions as to the wisdom of a jury trial when the Constitution requires otherwise.

Analysis:

The primary difference between the various opinions of the Justices in *Chauffeurs* centers on the value of looking back in time for analogous causes of action against which to compare the present case. Critics, siding with Justice Brennan's reasoning, argue that because the Court states that the nature of the remedy sought is the most important factor, there is no need to consider historical analogues when the relief sought is clearly equitable. Two years after the *Chauffeurs* decision, the Supreme Court did exactly that, finding that a federal suit seeking money damages under a labor statute was an action at law, without considering its analogous historical treatment.

■ CASE VOCABULARY

EQUITABLE REMEDY: A nonmonetary remedy, such as an injunction or specific performance, obtained when monetary damages cannot adequately redress the injury.

LEGAL REMEDY: A remedy available in a court of law, as distinguished from a remedy available only in a court of equity.

TRIAL BY JURY: A trial in which the factual issues are determined by a jury, not by the judge.

Edmonson v. Leesville Concrete Co., Inc.

(Injured Construction Worker) v. *(Construction Company)*

500 U.S. 614, 111 S.Ct. 2077 (1991)

THE EXCLUSION OF BLACK JURORS WITHOUT A RACE–NEUTRAL EXPLANATION VIOLATES THE EQUAL PROTECTION CLAUSE

■ **INSTANT FACTS** A civil defendant exercised peremptory challenges to exclude black jurors without a race-neutral explanation.

■ **BLACK LETTER RULE** The Equal Protection Clause of the Fourteenth Amendment forbids the exercise of peremptory challenges in a civil trial based solely on a prospective juror's race.

■ **PROCEDURAL BASIS**

Certiorari to review a decision of the Fifth Circuit Court of Appeals affirming a trial court order declining to extend *Batson v. Kentucky* to civil actions.

■ **FACTS**

Edmonson (P), a black man, sued Leesville Concrete Co., Inc. (D) in federal court for negligence after he was injured on a construction site. Edmonson (P) claimed a Leesville (D) employee negligently permitted a truck to roll, pinning him against some construction equipment. During voir dire, Leesville (D) exercised two of its three peremptory challenges to strike potential black jurors. Edmonson (P) demanded the court require a race-neutral explanation for the challenges under *Batson v. Kentucky*. The court denied Edmonson's (P) request, holding that *Batson* did not apply to civil suits. A jury comprised of eleven white persons and one black person found Edmonson (P) eighty percent negligent for his injuries. On appeal, the Fifth Circuit Court of Appeals reversed, holding that *Batson* applies to civil suits, as private parties become state actors when they exercise peremptory challenges in a civil action. The case was remanded for Leesville's (D) race-neutral explanation. On rehearing, however, the Fifth Circuit reconsidered and held private litigants do not act as state actors in the exercise of peremptory challenges, and *Batson* does not apply. Edmonson (P) appealed.

■ **ISSUE**

May a private litigant in a civil case use peremptory challenges to exclude jurors on account of their race?

■ **DECISION AND RATIONALE**

(Kennedy, J.) No. Under Court precedent, race-based peremptory challenges in a criminal prosecution violate the Equal Protection Clause and a defendant maintains third-party standing to assert the constitutional protections on behalf of the excluded jurors. Underlying this holding is the goal of eliminating racial prejudice in the jury selection process. Though the Court's past decisions have addressed only impermissible racial discrimination by prosecutors or other government officials, racial prejudice in the selection of a civil jury is no less invidious than in a criminal trial. The Equal Protection Clause, however, applies by its terms only to state action by the government. The actions of a private party constitute state action only when a claimed constitutional violation results from the exercise of a

---

H I G H   C O U R T   C A S E   S U M M A R I E S

right or privilege derived from state authority and the private party can be fairly described as a state actor.

To determine whether a particular action is governmental in character, the court must examine the extent to which the actor relies on governmental assistance, whether the actor is performing a traditional governmental function, and whether the injury caused is aggravated by the incidents of governmental authority. Here, there is no doubt that the constitutional violation arises out of the exercise of a right derived from state authority. While the exercise of state-sponsored peremptory challenges does not by itself constitute state action, state action can be found when private parties make extensive use of state procedures with the overt assistance of state officials. Peremptory challenges are useful only in the courtroom when the government, by statute or otherwise, deems it appropriate to allow private individuals to exercise them. The party exercising the challenge does so on the formal authority of the court. Without court involvement, the peremptory challenge serves no purpose. Also, the exercise of a peremptory challenge involves the performance of a traditional government function. Its use is limited to the selection of a distinctly governmental body—the jury—having no attributes of a private actor. Finally, the injury caused by a race-based peremptory challenge is aggravated because the court permits it to occur.

Race-based peremptory challenges in a civil case violate Equal Protection Clause. While the peremptory challenges deprive equal protection to the excluded juror, not the civil litigant, the litigant suffers a concrete, redressable injury in the process. Just as in a criminal trial, a party to the suit has third-party standing to challenge the constitutional violation if he can show a sufficient interest in challenging the exclusion of jurors on the basis of their race. Because the court declined to require Leesville (D) to provide a race-neutral explanation for its challenges, the case must be remanded for consideration of the plaintiff's interests. Reversed and remanded.

■ DISSENT

(O'Connor, J.) The exercise of a peremptory challenge by a private party is not state action merely because it occurs in the courtroom. The courtroom is merely a governmental platform for private individuals to litigate their private matters. The exercise of the peremptory challenge is a matter of private choice, not state action. Discretion in the use of a peremptory challenge lies solely with the litigant, not the judge. Furthermore, the reason underlying the exclusion of a juror is the litigant's, not that of the court. Although a potential juror is qualified for service by state action, the choice to exclude a qualified juror is not. The government's role in the jury selection process is the determination of who is qualified to serve, not which qualified jurors ultimately serve after voir dire. Peremptory challenges are a matter of private choice and are not a traditional government function. Because a private lawyer represents the interests of the private litigant, he cannot simultaneously represent the government under color of state law. His participation in the courtroom does not convert his status as a private actor into a state actor with the significant participation of the government. The government is not responsible for all that occurs in the courtroom.

■ DISSENT

(Scalia, J.) While the evils of race-based peremptory challenges are easily conceived, they also present a measure of protection to a minority litigant seeking to protect his legal interests. The Court's holding stands only to create additional burdens on the court system by providing yet another avenue of appeal from adverse judgments not on the basis of the merits presented, but by side issues tangentially related to the case.

Analysis:

Commentators suggest that *Edmonson* reflects a major change of emphasis by the Court regarding the use of peremptory challenges. While *Batson* protected the defendant's right to a fair trial, the application of *Batson* in the civil context shifts the protections afforded away from the defendant and toward the excluded juror. Unlike in a criminal case, the Sixth Amendment guarantee of an impartial jury does not apply to civil cases, necessitating the reliance on the Fourteenth Amendment.

■ CASE VOCABULARY

BATSON CHALLENGE: In criminal law, a defendant's objection that the prosecution has used peremptory challenges to exclude potential jurors on the basis of race, ethnicity, or gender.

EQUAL PROTECTION: The constitutional guarantee of the Fourteenth Amendment that the government must treat a person or class of person the same as it treats other person or classes in like circumstances.

PEREMPTORY CHALLENGE: One of a party's limited number of challenges that need not be supported by any reason, although a party may not use such a challenge in a way that discriminates on the basis of race, ethnicity, or gender.

STATE ACTION: Anything done by a government; especially in constitutional law, an intrusion on a person's rights (especially civil rights) either by a governmental entity or by a private requirement that can be enforced only by governmental action (such as a racially restrictive covenant, which requires judicial action for enforcement).

VOIR DIRE: A preliminary examination of a prospective juror by a judge or lawyer to decide whether the prospect is qualified and suitable to serve on a jury.

J.E.B. v. Alabama

(*Putative Father*) v. (*State Government*)

511 U.S. 127, 114 S.Ct. 1419 (1994)

THE GENDER–BASED EXCLUSION OF MEN BY PEREMPTORY CHALLENGES IS HELD UNCONSTITU-
TIONAL

■ **INSTANT FACTS** In a paternity and child support suit brought by the State of Alabama (P) against J.E.B. (D), the alleged father, the State exercised its peremptory challenges to remove male jurors from the jury panel, leaving an all-female jury.

■ **BLACK LETTER RULE** Peremptory challenges on the basis of gender violate the Equal Protection Clause.

■ **PROCEDURAL BASIS**

Certiorari to review a decision of an Alabama appeals court affirming a trial court judgment.

■ **FACTS**

The State of Alabama (P) filed suit for paternity and child support against J.E.B. (D) on behalf of the mother of a minor child. When selecting the jury, twelve of the thirty-six potential jurors were male. After three jurors were removed for cause, the State (P) exercised peremptory challenges to remove nine additional male jurors, believing a predominantly female jury would better sympathize with its case. Similarly, J.E.B. (D) used all but one of his peremptory challenges to excuse female jurors. Consequently, an all-female jury was selected. After J.E.B. (D) objected to the State's (P) peremptory challenges as unconstitutional under the Equal Protection Clause, the jury was empanelled. The jury found against J.E.B. (D) and judgment was entered. J.E.B. (D) renewed his objection that the jury was improperly selected, which objection was again overruled by the court. An Alabama state appeals court affirmed.

■ **ISSUE**

Does the Equal Protection Clause of the Fourteenth Amendment forbid intentional discrimination on the basis of gender in the exercise of a peremptory challenge?

■ **DECISION AND RATIONALE**

(Blackmun, J.) Yes. In *Batson v. Kentucky*, the Supreme Court ruled that the use of peremptory challenges to exclude jurors on the basis of race violates the Equal Protection Clause. Under the same reasoning, peremptory challenges may not be used on the basis of gender or other classifications, such as race, subject to heightened constitutional scrutiny. "Intentional discrimination by state actors violates the Equal Protection Clause, particularly where, as here, the discrimination serves to ratify and perpetuate invidious, archaic, and overbroad stereotypes about the relative abilities of men and women." While the exclusion of women from jury service has not persisted to the same extent as the exclusion of African–Americans, both groups share a long history of exclusion from juries. Because of such historical treatment, any gender-based classification must be subjected to heightened scrutiny under the Equal Protection Clause, requiring an "exceedingly persuasive justification" that substantially furthers an important government objective to pass constitutional muster. The State (P) argues that men are more likely to be sympathetic to J.E.B.'s (D) position, while women would sympathize more with the arguments it sets forth. Such a justification is not exceedingly persuasive, as it plays on the very stereotypes the law condemns. Gender-based discrimination relying on stereotype or bias ratifies and reinforces the prejudicial views of the relative abilities of men and women, threatening the confidence the public places on the judicial system. The Equal Protection Clause prohibits discrimination in jury selection on the basis of gender, or on the assumption that an individual will be biased in a particular case for no reason other than the person's gender.

Analysis:

Just as *Batson v. Kentucky* prohibits race-based peremptory challenges and *J.E.B. v. Alabama*, 511 U.S. 127 (1994), prohibits gender-based peremptory challenges, the Supreme Court has similarly prohibited peremptory challenges based on other prejudices or biases, such as ethnic origin, but not because a juror was unable to speak the English language. Other classifications, such as religion, have been prohibited under various state laws, though not addressed by the Supreme Court.

■ CASE VOCABULARY

PEREMPTORY CHALLENGE: One of a party's limited number of challenges that need not be supported by any reason, although a party may not use such a challenge in a way that discriminates on the basis of race, ethnicity, or gender.

VOIR DIRE: A preliminary examination of a prospective juror by a judge or lawyer to decide whether the prospect is qualified and suitable to serve on a jury.

Adickes v. S. H. Kress & Co.

(White School Teacher) v. *(Store Owner)*

398 U.S. 144, 90 S.Ct. 1598 (1970)

SUMMARY JUDGMENT WILL NOT BE GRANTED WHEN MATERIAL FACTS ARE AT ISSUE

■ **INSTANT FACTS** Adickes (P) was denied service at the defendant's store and was subsequently arrested when she entered in the company of six black students.

■ **BLACK LETTER RULE** The moving party bears the burden of proving an absence of a genuine issue of material fact to sustain a motion for summary judgment.

■ **PROCEDURAL BASIS**

Certiorari to review a decision of the Second Circuit Court of Appeals affirming the trial court's summary judgment and directed verdict for the defendant.

■ **FACTS**

Adickes (P), a white Northern school teacher, sued S.H. Kress & Co. (D) in federal court under 42 U.S.C. § 1983 when the defendant refused to serve her lunch in its Mississippi store and she was subsequently arrested for vagrancy. At the time, Adickes (P) was accompanied by six black students from a Mississippi school at which she was teaching for the summer. The students were offered service and were not arrested. The plaintiff alleged two counts of violation of the Equal Protection Clause of the Fourteenth Amendment because of her race. In the first count, the plaintiff alleged the defendant refused to serve her pursuant to a custom in the community to segregate the races. In the second count, the plaintiff alleged a conspiracy between the defendant and the local police. As to the first count, the court directed a verdict for the defendant because the plaintiff was unable to prove at trial that a custom of refusing service to white persons in the company of black persons existed or that such a custom was enforced. The second count was dismissed before trial on summary judgment because the plaintiff failed to allege any facts supporting a conspiracy. On appeal, the Second Circuit Court of Appeals affirmed. Adickes (P) appealed.

■ **ISSUE**

Is summary judgment appropriate when the moving party fails to demonstrate an absence of a genuine issue of material fact?

■ **DECISION AND RATIONALE**

(Harlan, J.) No. Under § 1983, the plaintiff must prove two elements to recover on a count of conspiracy. First, the plaintiff must establish that the defendant has deprived her of her constitutional rights. Second, the plaintiff must show that the defendant acted under color of law in so doing. Thus, although the defendant is a private party, the plaintiff may recover if she can prove that the defendant and the local police entered into an understanding to deny the plaintiff service or arrest her for entering in the company of blacks. The involvement of the local police satisfies the state action requirement of § 1983, and the defendant, as a private party, is liable nonetheless as if the store itself were a state actor.

In granting the defendant's motion for summary judgment on the conspiracy count, the district court held that no evidence supports a reasonable inference of a conspiracy. Kress (D) offered evidence that no employee had communicated with the local police and that its store manager refused to serve Adickes (P) only for fear of a public riot. Adickes (P), in opposing the defendant's motion, asserted that the defendant failed to account for the allegation in her complaint that a policeman was in the store at the time she was refused service and that policeman subsequently arrested her. The plaintiff contended that, although she possessed no knowledge of any prior agreement between the defendant and the policeman, his presence created a sufficient inference of conspiracy to defeat summary judgment. Additionally, the plaintiff offered evidence against the defendant's account of the situation in the store, questioning its motive for the refusal. As the moving party, the defendant had the burden of showing an absence of a genuine issue of material fact, viewing the evidence in a light most favorable to the plaintiff. Here, the defendant failed to carry that burden, as it offered no evidence to foreclose the possibility that there was a policeman in the store when the plaintiff entered, through an agreement with the defendant. While the store manager testified by deposition that no such agreement existed, affidavits from third-party witnesses and the police officers involved in the arrest failed to rebut the plaintiff's claim that the policeman was in the store by agreement with the defendant.

The defendant's evidence simply fails to prove an absence of a genuine issue of material fact as to whether a policeman was in the store when the plaintiff entered. If he had been, a jury could reasonably conclude that he was present by a mutual agreement with the defendant. Because this inference must be viewed in a light most favorable to Adickes (P), summary judgment was inappropriate. The plaintiff need not produce an affidavit in response to the defendant's motion for summary judgment to establish the existence of a material fact unless the defendant, upon whom the burden of proof initially lies, produces some evidence that would bring the material fact into question. Rule 56(e) does not shift the burden of proof from the moving party to his or her opponent. Since the defendant offered no affidavit from the policeman or otherwise that the policeman was not in the store when Adickes (P) entered, the defendant failed to meet its burden of proof. Adickes (P) need not provide any evidence in support of her position for purposes of the defendant's summary judgment motion. Reversed.

Analysis:

Adickes demonstrated the difficulty of obtaining summary judgment throughout the 1970s and early 1980s. In order to succeed on a motion for summary judgment, a party must negate all possible material fact issues with sufficient evidence. Failure to bring forth evidence on a material fact alleged in a plaintiff's complaint, such as the police officer's presence in *Adickes*, prohibited summary judgment in this case. The *Adickes* requirement, while still good law, has been reshaped by the Supreme Court's trilogy of summary judgment cases in 1986.

■ Case Vocabulary:

SUMMARY JUDGMENT: A judgment granted on a claim about which there is no genuine issue of material fact and upon which the movant is entitled to prevail as a matter of law.

Celotex Corp. v. Catrett

(Asbestos Manufacturer) v. *(Widow)*

477 U.S. 317, 106 S.Ct. 2548 (1986)

SUMMARY JUDGMENT MAY BE SUPPORTED BY PLEADINGS, DEPOSITIONS, ANSWERS TO INTERROGATORIES, ADMISSIONS ON FILE, AND AFFIDAVITS

■ **INSTANT FACTS** Catrett (P) sued fifteen named asbestos manufacturers, including Celotex Corp. (D), alleging her husband's death was caused by the manufacturers' negligence, breach of warranty, and strict liability.

■ **BLACK LETTER RULE** To sustain a motion for summary judgment, the moving party must present a showing of the absence of a genuine issue of material fact through pleadings, depositions, answers to interrogatories, and admissions on file, with or without supporting affidavits.

■ **PROCEDURAL BASIS**

Certiorari to review a decision of the U.S. Circuit Court of Appeals for the District of Columbia, reversing summary judgment entered on the behalf of the defendant.

■ **FACTS**

Catrett (P) sued Celotex Corp. (D) for the wrongful death of her husband due to exposure to asbestos products. The defendant moved for summary judgment, arguing that the plaintiff had failed to identify any of the defendant's products to which the decedent had been exposed. In response, Catrett (P) offered a transcript of the deposition of the decedent, a letter from an official of one of decedent's former employers, and a letter from an insurance company to her attorney, all tending to show that the decedent had been exposed to asbestos at his job site over a two-year period. The district court granted the defendant's motion for summary judgment because the plaintiff's evidence failed to establish that any Celotex (D) product was the proximate cause of decedent's death. The U.S. Circuit Court of Appeals for the District of Columbia reversed because the defendant had not supported its motion with any evidence to prove the absence of a genuine issue of material fact. Celotex (D) appealed.

■ **ISSUE**

Must a party moving for summary judgment support its motion with evidence affirmatively proving the absence of a genuine issue of material fact?

■ **DECISION AND RATIONALE**

(Rehnquist, J.) No. Under Rule 56(c) of the Federal Rule of Civil Procedure, summary judgment is appropriate "if the pleadings, depositions, answers to interrogatories, and admissions on file, together with the affidavits, if any," indicate the absence of a genuine issue of material fact. A party moving for summary judgment need not affirmatively negate an essential element of an opponent's claim when the opponent bears the burden of proof and fails to prove that element. No evidence, by affidavit or otherwise, is needed to support a motion for summary judgment unless the moving party bears the burden of proof at trial. Rule 56(a) and (b) explicitly provide that summary judgment may be requested "with or without affidavits." Without affidavits, a motion for summary judgment remains properly supported by the "pleadings, depositions, answers to interrogatories, and admissions on file." No additional evidence is required. As the Court held in *Adickes v. S.H. Kress Co.*, Rule 56 does not shift the initial burden of proof away from the moving party to demonstrate the absence of a genuine issue of material fact. *Adickes*, however, requires only that the moving party direct the court's attention to an absence of evidence supporting the nonmoving party's case. Rule 56(e) was adopted not to shift the moving party's burden of proof to the nonmoving party, but to require the nonmoving party to come forward with evidence beyond the pleadings to establish a genuine issue of material fact where the moving party has met its initial burden. The court of appeals failed to address whether Catrett (P) offered such evidence and whether such evidence would be sufficient to carry her burden of proof at trial. Because the court of appeals is better suited to make such a determination, the decision of the court of appeals is reversed and remanded.

■ CONCURRENCE

(White, J.) While the Court is correct that the moving party must always support its motion for summary judgment with evidence showing an absence of a genuine issue of material fact, the moving party may not support its motion by conclusory statements that the nonmoving party cannot prove her case. The nonmoving party may possess sufficient evidence to prove her case that has not been disclosed to the moving party because the moving party has failed to properly conduct discovery. Accordingly, the moving party must demonstrate with affirmative evidence that no genuine issue of material fact exists.

■ DISSENT

(Brennan, J.) The majority's decision fails to explain what is required of a moving party seeking summary judgment because the nonmoving party possesses no evidence to support her case. The party moving for summary judgment bears both the burden of production and the burden of persuasion in establishing the absence of material issues of fact. The burden of production requires a moving party to set forth prima facie evidence supporting summary judgment. If the moving party also bears the burden of persuasion at trial, it must offer credible evidence that would entitle it to a directed verdict if not contraverted at trial. If the nonmoving party bears the burden of persuasion at trial, however, the moving party may meet its burden of production by offering evidence that negates the nonmoving party's claims or proving to the court that the moving party's evidence does not support the claims brought. Either way, the moving party must make an affirmative showing, rather than unsupported conclusory assertions, to meet its burden of production. Instead, the moving party must show credible evidence, such as the deposition testimony of the nonmoving party's witnesses or the inadequacy of documentary evidence, to meet its burden of production. *Adickes* was consistent with these principles, but has often been misconstrued as requiring Kress to present affirmative evidence that there was no policeman in the store, as alleged in the plaintiff's complaint. The plaintiff, however, also provided deposition testimony alleging the policeman's presence, though the defendant offered no evidence on the issue. The defendant had failed to meet its initial burden of production. Similarly, Celotex (D) provided no affirmative evidence to discount the possibility that the decedent had been exposed to its product. Catrett (P), on the other hand, offered at least one witness who would testify at trial that the decedent had been exposed to the defendant's products. The defendant has ignored this evidence, just as Kress ignored Adickes' evidence that a policeman was present. Celotex (D) has failed to meet its burden of production on summary judgment.

Analysis:

Celotex was one of three important summary judgment cases decided by the Supreme Court in 1986. Along with *Anderson v. Liberty Lobby* and *Matsushita v. Zenith*, the three cases—known as "the trilogy cases"—reshaped summary judgment procedure and requirements. The effect of the trilogy cases has been a judicial tendency to embrace summary judgment as a means of disposing of groundless cases to promote judicial economy and the interests of the parties.

■ CASE VOCABULARY

BURDEN OF PERSUASION: A party's duty to convince the fact-finder to view the facts in a way that favors that party.

BURDEN OF PRODUCTION: A party's duty to introduce enough evidence on an issue to have that issue decided by a fact-finder, rather than decided against the party in a peremptory ruling such as a summary judgment or a directed verdict.

SUMMARY JUDGMENT: A judgment granted on a claim about which there is no genuine issue of material fact and upon which the movant is entitled to prevail as a matter of law.

Galloway v. United States

(Insane Person) v. *(Federal Government)*
319 U.S. 372, 63 S.Ct. 1077 (1943)

A DIRECTED VERDICT IS PROPER WHEN THERE IS ONLY ONE POSSIBLE CONCLUSION

■ **INSTANT FACTS** Galloway (P) suffered from mental conditions for which he sought insurance benefits for a total and permanent disability that arose, he claimed, prior to policy termination for failure to pay premiums.

■ **BLACK LETTER RULE** A federal court may order a directed verdict when a party fails to provide sufficient evidence to support an issue in his case.

■ PROCEDURAL BASIS

Certiorari to review a decision of a federal court of appeals affirming a trial court order for a directed verdict.

■ FACTS

Galloway (P) worked as a longshoreman in Philadelphia until he entered the Army in 1917. From 1917 through 1922, Galloway (P) served in the Army and Navy until he deserted his second enlistment with the Army. From April 1918 through April 1919, Galloway's (P) battalion was stationed in France as part of the war against Germany. Beginning in 1930 and extending through 1934, Galloway (P) underwent various medical evaluations by Veterans' Bureau physicians, who found Galloway (P) suffered from dementia, psychosis, and depressive insanity. Galloway's (P) wife, who was appointed the guardian of his estate, submitted a claim for insurance benefits in 1934, claiming he was entitled to benefits for his total and permanent insanity dating back to May 31, 1919, as a result of mental breakdown brought upon by the strains of active service. On that date, Galloway's insurance benefits terminated for failure to pay the necessary premium. The Board of Veterans' Appeals denied the claim in 1936. Galloway (P) thereafter filed suit against the United States (D). At trial, the plaintiff offered the testimony of five witnesses in an effort to demonstrate the onset of his total and permanent disability occurred prior to May 31, 1919. At the close of the evidence, the court granted the Government's (D) motion for directed verdict and entered judgment for the defendant. On appeal, the federal court of appeals affirmed, holding that the evidence was insufficient to sustain a verdict for the plaintiff. Galloway (P) appealed, arguing the evidence sufficiently supported his position and the entry of a directed verdict deprived him of his right to a jury trial under the Seventh Amendment.

■ ISSUE

Was the evidence introduced at trial sufficient to support a verdict for the plaintiff such that the court erred in entering a directed verdict for the defendant?

■ DECISION AND RATIONALE

(Rutledge, J.) No. At trial, the plaintiff had the burden to prove that his total and permanent disability existed on May 31, 1919, the date on which his policy lapsed for nonpayment. While the plaintiff has shown evidence of medical disability as early as 1930, the plaintiff must show by more than speculative inference that his disability existed within the policy period and extended through the years to 1930. The only evidence offered by the plaintiff to support a finding of disability prior to May 31, 1919, are two incidents of abnormal behavior while serving in the Army in France. His subsequent punishment for these two incidents does not sufficiently support the plaintiff's claim of disability. To this evidence, the plaintiff adds the vague testimony of a longtime acquaintance describing the plaintiff's change of appearance and demeanor upon his return from France. The plaintiff, however, had recently been hospitalized for influenza, and the witness's vagueness of dates, times, and specific incidents supporting his testimony renders it speculative at best. The testimony of his commanding officers from 1920 to 1922 establishes their belief that Galloway (P) suffered no insanity, and within the eight years that followed Galloway (P) married his wife, during which time no insanity can be inferred. Had Galloway (P) truly suffered continuous insanity between 1922 and 1930, the effects of his insanity would undoubtedly have shown themselves, requiring no inference to support Galloway's (P) claims. The plaintiff's burden of proof requires him to come forward with reliable evidence of his continuous disability without resort to a broad inference. Since the plaintiff offered no evidence of disability over this eight-year period, no favorable inference can be afforded to allow the plaintiff to meet his burden. While medical inference can fill gaps in the plaintiff's proof, eight years is simply too large a gap to be filled by speculation and inference without any evidence to carry the plaintiff's burden of proof.

Although the plaintiff claims that the directed verdict violates the Seventh Amendment right to trial by jury, the Amendment has no application to a suit against the government for monetary damages, as traditional common law, on which the Seventh Amendment is based, provided for no jury trial as of right. Even so, the Seventh Amendment does not prohibit the entry of a directed verdict by a federal court. Under traditional common law, as now, the court possesses broad power to exclude irrelevant and otherwise admissible facts from consideration by the jury. It often did so by consideration of demurrers and motions for a new trial. The Seventh Amendment does not require the disregard of additional procedural methods for challenging a plaintiff's proofs simply because they failed to exist at the time of its enactment. Affirmed.

■ DISSENT

(Black, J.) At the time of enactment of the Seventh Amendment, juries were often judges of fact and of law in both civil and criminal trials. The court's power to control the jury function lay exclusively in its power to order a new trial before a new jury, not weigh the facts itself to render a judgment. Alternatively, when it appears to the court that the plaintiff has offered no evidence sufficient to carry a plaintiff's burden, instructions to the jury should be issued, while preserving the jury's function to weigh the evidence and determine its effect. With the invention of the directed verdict, courts now gain control not granted with demurrers. Under a demurrer, the party invoking it admits to the facts asserted, turning the matter over to the court for a determination at law. A motion for directed verdict carries no such risk to the movant. If the motion is denied, the consequence is the consideration by the jury just as it would have been without the motion. Similarly, a directed verdict is based not on factual admissions by the movant, but on the substantial evidence rule, permitting a verdict to be entered though the plaintiff may present substantially more evidence than would be required to withstand a demurrer. Under this rule, some evidence is insufficient, for a plaintiff must demonstrate substantial evidence to withstand the directed verdict. The spirit of the Seventh Amendment requires the entry of directed verdict only when, without weighing the credibility of the witnesses, there is no room for an honest difference of opinion over the facts at issue. Here, the factual issue is whether the plaintiff sustained a total and permanent disability prior to May 31, 1919. In support of his case, the plaintiff offered direct testimony of wartime companions suggesting that his present disability existed prior to that time. This testimony was corroborated by the plaintiff's medical expert, who opined that the shock of actual combat caused the condition from which he now suffers. Without consideration of the credibility of these witnesses, the plaintiff's proof shows a healthy person when he entered the Army who was no longer healthy at a later time. Whether the plaintiff's later health condition was a result of a continuous disability brought on before May 31, 1919 is open to a reasonable difference of opinion, which should have been considered by the jury.

Analysis:

Galloway has been cited by tort reform proponents as a Supreme Court endorsement of the constitutionality of procedures and protections that further define the federal court system. Opponents point out that while the motion for directed verdict did not exist at the time the Seventh Amendment was adopted, its approval by the Court was based on its procedural resemblance to a demurrer, not any substantive constitutional rights implicated. Any tort reform measures, therefore, that are not merely modern procedural adaptations of historical methods are not affected by *Galloway*.

■ **CASE VOCABULARY**

DEMURRER: A pleading stating that although the facts alleged in a complaint may be true, they are insufficient for the plaintiff to state a claim for relief and for the defendant to frame an answer.

DIRECTED VERDICT: A ruling by a trial judge taking a case from the jury because the evidence will permit only one reasonable verdict.

MOTION FOR NEW TRIAL: A party's post-judgment request that the court vacate the judgment and order a new trial for a reason such as factually insufficient evidence, newly discovered evidence, or jury misconduct.

Brandon v. Chicago Board of Education

(Disabled Plaintiff) v. *(School Board)*
143 F.3d 293 (7th Cir. 1998)

RULE 60(B)(1) RELIEF FROM MISTAKES IS DENIED WHEN NOT SOUGHT WITHIN ONE YEAR OF ENTRY OF THE FINAL ORDER

■ **INSTANT FACTS** A federal district court dismissed Brandon's (P) discrimination suit for failure to prosecute when his attorney failed to appear at status conferences due to a clerical mistake by the court clerk.

■ **BLACK LETTER RULE** Rule 60(b)(1) permits relief from a final judgment based upon the mistakes of judicial officers, parties, or their representatives, if sought within one year from entry of a final order.

■ **PROCEDURAL BASIS**

Appeal from a district court order denying the plaintiff's Rule 60 motion to vacate.

■ **FACTS**

Brandon (P) filed suit against the Chicago Board of Education (D) under the Americans with Disabilities Act. His attorneys entered their appearance and provided the clerk of court with the address of their law firm. The clerk erroneously entered the address for another attorney of a similar name, resulting in all court notices being mailed to the wrong attorney at the wrong address. The other attorney, upon receiving the court's notices, informed the clerk that he was not counsel of record, had no connection with the case, and was returning the materials sent to him. Nonetheless, the clerk failed to correct the address and continued to use the incorrect address. After Brandon's (P) attorneys failed to appear for two status conferences, his suit was dismissed for failure to prosecute. A year and three days later, upon realizing that he had not received any notices in the case, including the notice of dismissal, Brandon's (P) attorney learned of the clerk's error and moved to vacate the judgment under Rule 60 of the Federal Rules of Civil Procedure. The motion, however, contained the incorrect case number. Upon noticing the error on the date the hearing was scheduled, Brandon's (P) attorney informed the clerk, who canceled the hearing and rescheduled it under the correct case number. Before the new hearing was held, the court issued a minute order granting the motion. Despite notifying the defendant's counsel of the minute order, the defendant's counsel appeared for the hearing and persuaded the court to vacate its order. The court ultimately denied the plaintiff's motion to vacate the dismissal. Brandon (P) appealed, arguing that the court abused its discretion in refusing to grant Rule 60 relief because of the clerical error.

■ **ISSUE**

May a party obtain Rule 60 relief from a judgment due to clerical errors by the court clerk and his attorney when such relief is sought more than one year after judgment was entered?

■ **DECISION AND RATIONALE**

(Rovner, J.) No. Rule 60(b)(1) allows the court, upon motion, to grant a party relief from a final judgment for "mistake, inadvertence, surprise, or excusable neglect." Similarly, Rules 60(b)(2) and 60(b)(3) permit relief upon newly discovered evidence and fraud by an adverse party, respectively. But each of these

---

rules requires a motion by the party seeking relief within one year after the judgment, order, or proceeding. Rule 60(b)(6), however, serves as a catchall provision, allowing relief for "any other reason justifying relief from the operation of the judgment." Rule 60(b)(6) relief need not be sought within any specified time period. The defendant contends that the only rule available to the plaintiff is Rule 60(b)(1), as the basis for the relief sought is a clerical mistake by the court clerk. Accordingly, relief is unavailable to the plaintiff because it was not sought within one year from the entry of the order. The plaintiff claims Rule 60(b)(6) permits the relief sought as he has presented a valid reason justifying relief. Rule 60(b)(6) operates exclusively of the other rules, however; in other words, a party may not incorporate within Rule 60(b)(6) those reasons specifically addressed elsewhere in the rule, thereby avoiding the time period within which relief may be sought. It is clear that Rule 60(b)(1) applies to mistakes made by judicial officers as well as parties. It also covers mistakes by a party's attorney during the course of representation. Since Brandon (P) failed to move for relief within the prescribed one-year period, the court did not abuse its discretion in denying the motion. Affirmed.

Analysis:

Rule 60(b)(6) provides a party affected by a final order or judgment one additional basis for obtaining relief. Because the most common grounds for relief are covered elsewhere in the rule, however, Rule 60(b)(6) is limited to only those rare circumstances not otherwise covered by the rule. Courts have applied Rule 60(b)(6) to relieve a party from harm caused by the fraud of the party's own attorney or other third party, where a judgment or order is entered after an opposing party fails to comply with a settlement agreement, and where a party fails to receive notice of the adverse order within the time period permitted for appeal.

Campolongo v. Celotex Corp.

(*Decedent*) v. (*Manufacturer*)

681 F.Supp. 261 (D.N.J. 1988)

BIFURCATION OF COMPENSATORY AND PUNITIVE DAMAGES CLAIMS ENSURES A JUST VERDICT BASED ON PROXIMATE CAUSE

■ **INSTANT FACTS** Campolongo (P) died after health complications allegedly caused by exposure to the defendant's asbestos products.

■ **BLACK LETTER RULE** Bifurcation is appropriate when it simplifies the fact-finding process, avoids confusion, promotes judicial economy, and results in fundamental fairness to the parties.

■ **PROCEDURAL BASIS**

Trial court consideration of the defendant's motion in limine to sever the case.

■ **FACTS**

Campolongo (P), through his executrix, filed a products liability suit against Celotex Corp. (D) for compensatory and punitive damages for his exposure to asbestos products, causing the health conditions that eventually led to his death. Immediately prior to trial, Celotex (D) filed a motion in limine to sever strict liability claims to preclude the introduction of evidence relevant to Campolongo's (P) negligence claims and plea for punitive damages. In its motion, the defendant agreed to waive its affirmative defenses of assumption of risk and superseding cause and also agreed to a jury instruction that an asbestos product without a warning is a defective product as a matter of law. Campolongo (P) objected, arguing the severance would severely prejudice his case by altering his burden to prove proximate cause and directing the focus of the case toward his conduct rather than toward the defendant. The plaintiff also contended severance was precluded by Rule 8(e)(2) of the Federal Rules of Civil Procedure. After jury selection, but before the court decided the motion in limine, the case settled. The court decided the defendant's motion nonetheless.

■ **ISSUE**

Should the defendant's motion in limine be granted to sever the plaintiff's compensatory damages claims from his punitive damages claims at trial?

■ **DECISION AND RATIONALE**

(Wolin, J.) Yes. While Rule 8(e)(2) permits a plaintiff to plead alternative theories of recovery, Rule 42(b) entrusts a federal judge with the discretionary power to separate those claims in furtherance of convenience or to avoid prejudice so long as the right to trial by jury is preserved. New Jersey courts have often separated claims for compensatory damages from punitive damages claims in order to simplify the fact-finding process, avoid confusion of the facts and issues, further judicial economy, and pursue fundamental fairness to all parties. Furthermore, severance of punitive damages claims avoids the prejudice to the defendant that may result from conduct-related proof unrelated to the actual injuries suffered by the plaintiff. Such evidence may excite the passions of the jury, resulting in punitive damages in the guise of a compensatory award.

A severance guarantees the resulting verdict will be truly compensatory without the taint and suspicion that permeates a verdict when all claims are tried together. Under New Jersey law, a manufacturer's knowledge of the dangerousness of its product is not relevant in a strict liability case for compensatory damages. Such knowledge is, however, crucial to a finding of punitive damages under a negligence theory. A jury instruction, which as been agreed to by the defendant, informing the jury that an asbestos product is a defective product as a matter of law ensures that the plaintiff will recover only those damages caused by its product without the risk that damages are awarded, not because its products proximately caused the injuries claimed, but because the jury finds that the defendant knew its products were dangerous. The jury instruction notwithstanding, introduction of evidence related to assumption of the risk would undercut the policy rationale for bifurcation of this case. Assumption of risk requires the defendant to introduce evidence of the plaintiff's voluntary choice to encounter a known risk. However, introduction of conduct-related evidence against the plaintiff without permitting such evidence against the defendant is illogical and inappropriate. The defendant's defense of superseding cause, on the other hand, requires proof of the conduct of others in causing the plaintiff's injuries. Quite different from concurrent negligence, a superseding cause defense relieves a manufacturer of liability because its products are found not to be the proximate cause of injuries, rather than one of several concurrent causes. With a superseding cause defense, it becomes incumbent upon a plaintiff to introduce conduct-related evidence against the defendant to establish that its conduct was indeed the proximate cause of the injuries claimed. In order to create a conduct-free trial, as requested by the defendants, all conduct-related evidence not attributed to co-the defendants must be eliminated along with all defenses traditionally related to a showing of proximate cause. As the elimination of conduct-related evidence will serve all the goals of a bifurcated trial, the plaintiff's claims for compensatory damages would have been severed from his punitive damages claims but for the settlement of the case.

Analysis:

The defendants in toxic torts cases often face the problem of jury sympathy for the individual plaintiff because of the often devastating effects of toxic exposure. Such cases, however, present difficult causation problems, especially when the plaintiff could have been exposed to many different defective products manufactured by different defendants. Because a finding of a particular defendant's knowledge of the defects in its products is likely to divert a jury's attention away from the ultimate issue of causation, which is required to find a defendant liable, bifurcation is commonly sought in toxic tort cases.

■ CASE VOCABULARY

BIFURCATED TRIAL: A trial that is divided into two stages, such as for guilt and punishment or for liability and damages.

MOTION IN LIMINE: A pretrial request that certain inadmissible evidence not be referred to or offered at trial.

SEVERANCE: The separation of claims, by the court, or multiple parties either to permit separate actions on each claim or to allow certain interlocutory orders to become final.

CHAPTER SEVEN

The Choice of an Appropriate Court: Personal Jurisdiction, Notice, and Venue

Pennoyer v. Neff

Instant Facts: Neff (P), who sued Pennoyer (D) to recover possession of land that had been transferred to Pennoyer (D) at a sheriff's sale after a default judgment was entered against Neff (P), claims that the default judgment was invalid because an Oregon state court did not have jurisdiction over him.

Black Letter Rule: A state court does not have jurisdiction over a nonresident defendant unless the defendant is personally served with process in the state or voluntarily appears in state court.

Harris v. Balk

Instant Facts: Balk (P) brought a suit against Harris (D) in North Carolina on a $180 debt, and Harris (D) claimed that the debt had already been satisfied in an earlier proceeding in Maryland.

Black Letter Rule: A state court may exercise jurisdiction over a debt that was incurred in another state, if the nonresident debtor is served with process while in the state.

Hess v. Pawloski

Instant Facts: Pawloski (P) sued Hess (D), a Pennsylvania resident who was driving in Massachusetts, for injuries incurred when Hess's (D) vehicle struck and injured Pawloski (P).

Black Letter Rule: A state does not violate a nonresident driver's due process rights by enacting legislation that subjects the driver to jurisdiction in the state for all actions arising from use of the state's public highways.

International Shoe Co. v. Washington

Instant Facts: The State of Washington (P) sought to recover unemployment compensation fund contributions from International Shoe Co. (D), and, even though it employed salespeople in Washington, International Shoe (D) argued that it was not subject to jurisdiction in Washington.

Black Letter Rule: A corporation is subject jurisdiction in any state with which it has "minimum contacts," so that the exercise of jurisdiction is consistent with notions of "fair play and substantial justice."

World-Wide Volkswagen Corp. v. Woodson

Instant Facts: A New York family involved in an automobile accident in Oklahoma sued Seaway Volkswagen, an automobile dealership, and World–Wide Volkswagen (P), a regional distributor, in Oklahoma state court, alleging design defects in their new Audi.

Black Letter Rule: A nonresident defendant cannot be subject to jurisdiction in a state in which the defendant has no contacts, except for a single isolated and fortuitous occurrence.

Calder v. Jones

Instant Facts: Calder (D) edited an article about Shirley Jones (P), an entertainer, that was published in *The National Enquirer*, and Jones (P) brought suit in California against *The National Enquirer* and others, including Calder (D), who argued that the California court lacked jurisdiction over him.

Black Letter Rule: Personal jurisdiction is proper over nonresident defendants who engage in conduct that is directed at and causes harm to a resident of the forum state.

Asahi Metal Industry Co., Ltd. v. Superior Court of California, Solano County

Instant Facts: Zurcher, a victim of a motorcycle accident, brought a suit in California against a Taiwanese tire-tube maker, which brought a cross-claim against the Japanese manufacturer of the tire tube valve assembly.

Black Letter Rule: To be subject to personal jurisdiction in a forum state, a non-resident defendant must do more than simply place a product into the stream of commerce in order for the fairness requirement to be met.

Burger King Corp. v. Rudzewicz

Instant Facts: Burger King (P), which is headquartered in Florida, sued Rudzewicz (D), a Michigan franchisee, in Florida federal court for default on payments due under the franchise agreement.

Black Letter Rule: While a contract alone is not enough to confer personal jurisdiction, a nonresident defendant that establishes an ongoing business relationship with a plaintiff is subject to jurisdiction in the plaintiff's state.

Shaffer v. Heitner

Instant Facts: Heitner (P) brought a shareholders' derivative action against Shaffer (D) and other officers and directors of Greyhound, Inc., filing suit in Delaware and taking advantage of a Delaware statute allowing the court to sequester the defendants' stock shares.

Black Letter Rule: Minimum contacts must exist for personal jurisdiction to exist, whether the proceeding is in personam or in rem.

Burnham v. Superior Court of California

Instant Facts: Dennis Burnham (D), a New Jersey resident who was served with process for a divorce proceeding while visiting California, contends that California jurisdiction violates his due process.

Black Letter Rule: A state may exercise personal jurisdiction over a nonresident if the nonresident is served with process while temporarily in the state, even if the suit is not related to the nonresident's presence in the state.

Helicopteros Nacionales de Colombia v. Hall

Instant Facts: Hall (P) sued Helicopteros Nacionales de Colombia (D) ("Helicol"), a Colombian company that owned a helicopter that crashed in Peru, for wrongful death, alleging that Helicol (D) had sufficient contacts to subject it to in personam jurisdiction in Texas.

Black Letter Rule: If a lawsuit does not arise from or relate to a nonresident defendant's contacts with the forum state, jurisdiction over the nonresident party is proper only if its contacts with the state are systematic and continuous.

Carnival Cruise Lines, Inc. v. Shute

Instant Facts: Shute (P), a Washington resident who was injured while on a cruise vacation, sued Carnival Cruise Lines (D) in Washington, but Carnival Cruise Lines (D) argued that a forum-selection clause in the contract limited jurisdiction to Florida.

Black Letter Rule: A fair and reasonable forum-selection clause in a contract between two parties amounts to consent to jurisdiction in a given forum.

ALS Scan, Inc. v. Digital Service Consultants, Inc.

Instant Facts: ALS Scan, Inc., (P), a Maryland company, sued Digital Service Consultants, Inc., (D), a Georgia Internet service provider for copyright infringement.

Black Letter Rule: Jurisdiction over a nonresident based on Internet activity is proper if the nonresident directs electronic activity into the state with the purpose of engaging in business in the state and, through that activity, creates a potential cause of action there.

Mullane v. Central Hanover Bank & Trust Co.

Instant Facts: Central Hanover Bank & Trust Co. (P), which petitioned to have a New York court approve its handling of a common trust fund, published notice of the petition in a local newspaper, intending to reach the beneficiaries of the various trust funds, but Mullane (D) objected to the notice by publication.

Black Letter Rule: Notice of a lawsuit must be reasonably calculated, based on all of the facts and circumstances, to inform interested parties that a lawsuit is pending.

Piper Aircraft Co. v. Reyno

Instant Facts: Reyno (P) brought suit in a state court in the United States against Piper Aircraft Co., arising from a plane crash that occurred in Scotland, and Piper Aircraft (D) moved to dismiss because the court was not a convenient forum for the litigation, which it claims should have been brought in Scotland.

Black Letter Rule: Under the doctrine of forum non conveniens, a court may dismiss a case if there is an alternate forum with jurisdiction and if proceeding in the forum would impose a heavy burden on the parties or the court.

Pennoyer v. Neff

(Current Land Occupier) v. *(Former Landowner)*

95 U.S. 714 (1877)

STATE–COURT JURISDICTION EXISTS WHEN THE DEFENDANT IS SERVED WITH PROCESS IN THE STATE OR VOLUNTARILY APPEARS

■ **INSTANT FACTS** Neff (P), who sued Pennoyer (D) to recover possession of land that had been transferred to Pennoyer (D) at a sheriff's sale after a default judgment was entered against Neff (P), claims that the default judgment was invalid because an Oregon state court did not have jurisdiction over him.

■ **BLACK LETTER RULE** A state court does not have jurisdiction over a nonresident defendant unless the defendant is personally served with process in the state or voluntarily appears in state court.

■ **PROCEDURAL BASIS**

Review on writ of error of lower court's decision holding the Oregon state court's judgment against Neff (P) was invalid.

■ **FACTS**

In a prior lawsuit, Mitchell sued Neff (P) for attorneys' fees in a state court in Oregon. Neff (P) was not an Oregon resident, was not personally served with notice of the lawsuit (which was published in a newspaper), and did not appear to defend the case. Because Neff (P) did not appear, the Oregon court entered a default judgment against him and in favor of Mitchell. Neff (P) owned land in Oregon, which was sold at a sheriff's sale in order to satisfy Mitchell's judgment against Neff (P). Pennoyer (D) bought Neff's (P) property at the sheriff's sale. Neff (P) brought a lawsuit in federal court against Pennoyer (D) to recover title to his property, arguing that the default judgment against him was invalid, so that the sale of his land to Pennoyer (D) was invalid.

■ **ISSUE**

Is a state court's judgment against a non-resident defendant valid if the defendant is not personally served with process in the state and does not appear voluntarily?

■ **DECISION AND RATIONALE**

(Field, J.) No. A state court may not exercise in personam jurisdiction over a non-resident defendant unless the defendant is personally served with process in the state or appears voluntarily. If a state court does not have in personam jurisdiction over a non-resident, any judgment rendered against that defendant is invalid and violates the party's due process rights under the Fourteenth Amendment. However, a state court may properly exercise jurisdiction over property owned by a non-resident for purposes of an in rem proceeding, even if service is by publication, because a defendant in an in rem proceeding is not personally bound by the judgment beyond the property in question. In this case, the judgment against Neff (P) was a money judgment, requiring the Oregon court to have in personam jurisdiction. The Oregon proceedings were not in rem because the court did not attach the property; rather, the court disposed of the property only to execute on a money judgment against Neff (P).

Because Neff (P) was not personally served in Oregon and did not voluntarily appear, the Oregon court lacked jurisdiction over him, and the judgment and subsequent land sale were invalid. Affirmed.

Analysis:

Neff's suit in federal court to challenge the Oregon court's jurisdiction over him was a "collateral attack" because it was a separate proceeding from the original suit brought by Mitchell. A defendant may also challenge a court's personal jurisdiction directly by bringing a motion to dismiss under Fed. R. Civ. P. 12(b)(2). By filing such a motion, the defendant is not voluntarily appearing or consenting to suit, and thus preserves the right to challenge personal jurisdiction. Although *Pennoyer* is no longer the law of the land, it is the background for all subsequent cases addressing personal jurisdiction.

■ CASE VOCABULARY

DEFAULT JUDGMENT: A judgment entered against a defendant who has failed to plead or otherwise defend against the plaintiff's claim, often by failing to appear at trial.

EX PARTE PROCEEDING: A proceeding in which not all parties are present or given the opportunity to be heard.

IN PERSONAM JURISDICTION: A court's power to bring a person into its adjudicative process; jurisdiction over a defendant's personal rights, rather than merely over property interests.

IN REM JURISDICTION: A court's power to adjudicate the rights to a given piece of property, including the power to seize and hold it.

Harris v. Balk

(Debtor) v. *(Creditor)*

198 U.S. 215, 25 S.Ct. 625 (1905)

A NONRESIDENT DEBTOR MAY BE SERVED WHILE TEMPORARILY IN THE STATE

■ **INSTANT FACTS** Balk (P) brought a suit against Harris (D) in North Carolina on a $180 debt, and Harris (D) claimed that the debt had already been satisfied in an earlier proceeding in Maryland.

■ **BLACK LETTER RULE** A state court may exercise jurisdiction over a debt that was incurred in another state, if the nonresident debtor is served with process while in the state.

■ PROCEDURAL BASIS

Certiorari to review the Supreme Court of North Carolina's affirmance of a judgment against Harris (D) for the collection of a debt.

■ FACTS

This case involves two debts: Harris (D), a North Carolina resident, owed Balk (P), also a North Carolina resident, $180; and Balk (P) owed Epstein, a Maryland resident, more than $300. While Harris (D) was in Baltimore, Epstein had a Baltimore court issue a writ of attachment to attach the debt Harris (D) owed to Balk (P), which writ was served on Harris (D) while he was still in Baltimore. Harris (D) did not challenge the garnishment, and judgment was later rendered in favor of Epstein for $180. Harris (D) paid the $180 to Epstein's attorney. Later, Balk (P) sued Harris (D) for the $180. Harris (D) argued that the Maryland judgment in favor of Epstein and his payment to Epstein barred Balk's (P) suit. The trial court entered judgment in favor of Balk (P), reasoning that the Maryland judgment was invalid because the Maryland court did not have jurisdiction to garnish the debt.

■ ISSUE

May a state court garnish a debt owed by a nonresident to a third party, if the nonresident is served while temporarily in the state, even though the debt was incurred out of state?

■ DECISION AND RATIONALE

(Peckham, J.) Yes. The Maryland judgment in favor of Epstein was valid because Harris (D), who owed Balk (P) $180, was served with process while temporarily in Maryland. In addition, Balk (P), who owed money to Epstein, had notice of the garnishment because Harris (D) raised the Maryland judgment as a defense to Balk's (P) suit. Maryland law allows a debt to be garnished as long as Maryland courts have jurisdiction over the debtor. Here, the Maryland court had jurisdiction over Harris (D) because he was served within the state. Moreover, Balk (P) could have sued Harris (D) in Maryland to recover the debt while Harris (D) was temporarily in Maryland. Thus, the Maryland judgment was valid. Reversed.

Analysis:

The decision in *Harris* turned on the notion that a debt is property, the location of which is determined by the location of the debtor. Therefore, Epstein was able to assert jurisdiction over Balk in Maryland by garnishing Balk's debtor, Harris, while Harris was in Maryland. *Harris* has been criticized because it permits jurisdiction over a defendant in a forum with which the defendant has no real connection. The Supreme Court later overruled *Harris. See Shaffer v. Heitner*, 433 U.S. 186 (1977); *Rush v. Savchuk*, 444 U.S. 320 (1980).

■ **CASE VOCABULARY**

ATTACHMENT: The seizing of a person's property to secure a judgment or to be sold in satisfaction of a judgment.

Hess v. Pawloski

(Negligent Nonresident Driver) v. *(Accident Victim)*

274 U.S. 352, 47 S.Ct. 632 (1927)

STATES HAVE JURISDICTION OVER NONRESIDENT DRIVERS BY APPOINTING A STATE REGISTRAR AS AGENT FOR SERVICE OF PROCESS

■ **INSTANT FACTS** Pawloski (P) sued Hess (D), a Pennsylvania resident who was driving in Massachusetts, for injuries incurred when Hess's (D) vehicle struck and injured Pawloski (P).

■ **BLACK LETTER RULE** A state does not violate a nonresident driver's due process rights by enacting legislation that subjects the driver to jurisdiction in the state for all actions arising from use of the state's public highways.

■ **PROCEDURAL BASIS**

Review of Massachusetts Supreme Court's decision that Hess (D) was subject to jurisdiction in Massachusetts.

■ **FACTS**

Hess (D), a Pennsylvania resident, was driving in Massachusetts, when his car struck and injured Pawloski (P). Pawloski (P) sued Hess (D) in Massachusetts to recover damages for personal injury. No personal service was made on Hess (D), and none of his property was attached. Hess (D) moved the court to dismiss the complaint for a lack of jurisdiction. The trial court denied Hess's (D) motion based on a Massachusetts jurisdictional statute which provided that operating a motor vehicle in the state amounts to an agreement by nonresidents to appoint the registrar as agent for service of process in suits arising from accidents or collisions on Massachusetts highways, as long as the nonresident received actual notice of the service from the registrar.

■ **ISSUE**

Does a state statute conferring jurisdiction over nonresident drivers violate due process by deeming the drivers consent to the appointment of a state registrar as an agent for service of process?

■ **DECISION AND RATIONALE**

(Butler, J.) No. States may make and enforce laws that are designed to promote care on the part of both residents and nonresidents who use the public highways in the state. Motor vehicles are dangerous machines that can cause serious harm to persons and property. The Massachusetts statute limits nonresidents' implied consent to proceedings arising out of accidents or collisions involving the use of motor vehicles on a highway. A state's power to regulate the use of its highways extends to both residents and nonresidents; the Massachusetts statute does not discriminate against nonresidents, but merely places them on equal footing as residents. Affirmed.

Analysis:

As society became increasingly complex and mobile, the rigid rule set forth in *Pennoyer v. Neff*, 95 U.S. 714 (1877), was no longer adequate, requiring courts to establish a broader basis for asserting jurisdiction over nonresidents. Problems arose when nonresident drivers returned home after causing an accident and injuring state residents. If the state in which the accident occurred could not exercise jurisdiction over the out-of-state driver, its injured residents would be left without an adequate remedy unless the state had expanded its jurisdiction by providing for consent to submit to the state's jurisdiction if an accident occurred. This precedent for "implied consent" jurisdiction in *Hess* led states to enact statutes addressing other activities, such as operating airplanes and watercraft, hazardous construction work, and selling securities.

■ CASE VOCABULARY

WRIT OF ERROR: A writ issued by an appellate court directing a lower court to deliver the record in the case for review.

International Shoe Co. v. Washington

(*Delinquent Taxpayer*) v. (*State Collecting Unemployment Contributions*)

326 U.S. 310, 66 S.Ct. 154 (1945)

JURISDICTION IS PROPER OVER A NONRESIDENT DEFENDANT WITH MINIMUM CONTACTS WITH THE FORUM STATE

■ **INSTANT FACTS** The State of Washington (P) sought to recover unemployment compensation fund contributions from International Shoe Co. (D), and, even though it employed salespeople in Washington, International Shoe (D) argued that it was not subject to jurisdiction in Washington.

■ **BLACK LETTER RULE** A corporation is subject jurisdiction in any state with which it has "minimum contacts," so that the exercise of jurisdiction is consistent with notions of "fair play and substantial justice."

■ **PROCEDURAL BASIS**

Certiorari to review decisions of Washington courts upholding jurisdiction over International Shoe (D).

■ **FACTS**

International Shoe (D), a manufacturer and seller of shoes, is a Delaware corporation with its principal place of business in St. Louis, Missouri. International Shoe (D) has no office in Washington and makes no contracts for sale or purchase of merchandise there. At one point, International Shoe (D) employed 11 to 13 salesmen who resided in Washington (P) but reported to sales managers in St. Louis. The salesmen solicited orders from prospective buyers, which were transmitted to St. Louis, where the orders were processed and the products were shipped. The State of Washington (P) requires employers to contribute a certain percentage of wages to its unemployment compensation fund. Because International Shoe (D) did not pay into the fund, the State of Washington (P) issued a notice of assessment, serving the notice personally on one of the salesmen and mailing a copy to International Shoe (D) at its St. Louis address. International Shoe (D) moved to set aside the notice of assessment because it was not a Washington corporation.

■ **ISSUE**

Is it consistent with due process to subject a nonresident defendant to jurisdiction in a state where the defendant is not present, but has minimum contacts?

■ **DECISION AND RATIONALE**

(Stone, C.J.) Yes. A defendant may be subject to in personam jurisdiction, even if it is not present in a particular state, if it has certain "minimum contacts" with the state, so that maintaining the suit does not offend traditional notions of fair play and substantial justice. Determining whether jurisdiction is proper depends on the nature and quality of the defendant's contacts with the forum state. A defendant's single or isolated activity in a state is not enough to subject it to suits that are not connected with those activities. Conversely, if a defendant's conduct in a state is continuous and substantial, the defendant is subject to suits that are not related to those activities. To the extent a defendant exercises the privilege of conducting activities within a state, the defendant enjoys the benefits and protections of the law of that state. In this case, International Shoe's (D) activities in Washington (P) were neither irregular nor casual. They were systematic, continuous, and gave rise to a large volume of interstate business. The obligation to pay into the unemployment compensation fund arose directly from International Shoe's (D) activities in the state. These activities created sufficient ties with Washington (P) so as to make it reasonable to subject International Shoe (D) to jurisdiction there. Affirmed.

■ CONCURRENCE

(Black, J.) The federal Constitution confers upon the states the power to tax corporations that do business in the state, and to subject those corporations to suits in the state. Although the words "fair play," "justice," and "reasonable" have emotional appeal, the constitutional power of the states to afford judicial protection to their residents does not hinge upon these notions.

Analysis:

International Shoe departed from the rule in *Pennoyer v. Neff*, 95 U.S. 714 (1877), which required actual presence in the forum state for purposes of in personam jurisdiction. After *International Shoe*, many states enacted "long-arm" statutes authorizing state courts to exert jurisdiction over nonresidents engaging in certain types of conduct. To determine if a state court has personal jurisdiction, the long-arm statute must apply and the exercising jurisdiction must not violate the constitutional principles embodied in the "minimum contacts" analysis.

■ CASE VOCABULARY

LONG–ARM STATUTE: A statute providing for jurisdiction over a nonresident defendant who has had contacts with the territory in which the statute is in effect.

World-Wide Volkswagen Corp. v. Woodson

(*Regional Vehicle Distributor*) v. (*Judge Exercising Jurisdiction*)
444 U.S. 286, 100 S.Ct. 559, 100 S.Ct. 580 (1980)

NO PERSONAL JURISDICTION ARISES FROM A SINGLE, FORTUITOUS CONTACT

■ **INSTANT FACTS** A New York family involved in an automobile accident in Oklahoma sued Seaway Volkswagen, an automobile dealership, and World–Wide Volkswagen (P), a regional distributor, in Oklahoma state court, alleging design defects in their new Audi.

■ **BLACK LETTER RULE** A nonresident defendant cannot be subject to jurisdiction in a state in which the defendant has no contacts, except for a single isolated and fortuitous occurrence.

■ **PROCEDURAL BASIS**

Certiorari to review the Oklahoma Supreme Court's decision denying a writ of prohibition to restrain the trial court judge from exercising personal jurisdiction over the plaintiffs.

■ **FACTS**

The Robinsons purchased a new Audi automobile from Seaway Volkswagen, Inc., in Massena, New York. While driving in Oklahoma, on their way to their new home in Arizona, another car rear-ended the Robinsons' car, which caught fire, resulting in serious injury. The Robinsons brought a products-liability claim in an Oklahoma state court against various parties, including Seaway Volkswagen and World–Wide Volkswagen (P). World–Wide Volkswagen (P), which is incorporated in and has its principal place of business in New York, distributes vehicles, parts, and accessories to New York, New Jersey, and Connecticut dealerships. Neither Seaway nor World–Wide Volkswagen (P) does business in Oklahoma, and neither ships or sells products in that state. Seaway and World–Wide Volkswagen (P) moved to dismiss for lack of jurisdiction and, when the motion was denied, filed a writ of prohibition to prevent Judge Woodson (D) from exercising jurisdiction over them.

■ **ISSUE**

May a state court exercise jurisdiction over a nonresident defendant if the defendant has no contacts with the state except for a single, isolated occurrence?

■ **DECISION AND RATIONALE**

(White, J.) No. Jurisdiction is not proper if the defendant's only contact with the forum state is a single, isolated occurrence. Rather, the defendant's connections with the forum state must be sufficient enough such that the defendant should reasonably anticipate being brought into court in that state. When a defendant purposefully avails itself of the privilege of conducting business in a forum state, then the defendant has clear notice that it is subject to suit in the state. However, a plaintiff's unilateral claim of some relationship with a nonresident defendant does not satisfy the contact requirement in a forum state. Here, World–Wide Volkswagen (P) and Seaway Volkswagen conducted no activity in Oklahoma and did not avail themselves of the privileges of Oklahoma law. The only contact they had with Oklahoma resulted from the Robinsons fortuitously driving their Audi into the state. Reversed.

■ **DISSENT**

(Brennan, J.) It is neither unreasonable nor unfair to subject Seaway and World–Wide Volkswagen (P) to jurisdiction in Oklahoma because of the substantial connection between the plaintiffs and the forum state, and the forum state's interest in the litigation. Moreover, automobiles are not stationary items, and a dealer intends that purchasers will travel to other states. There is no difference between goods reaching a state through a chain of distribution and a consumer taking them there.

■ **DISSENT**

(Marshall, J.) The majority construes too narrowly the connection between the defendants and Oklahoma. Contrary to the majority's view, the defendants deliberately and purposefully became part of a nationwide network for marketing and servicing automobiles. Defendants know that their automobiles will travel to other states, and they derive revenue from servicing cars that come from other states. As economic entities, defendants knowingly reach out from New York, cause certain effects, and derive revenues from other states.

■ **DISSENT**

(Blackmun, J.) A critical factor in the jurisdictional analysis is the nature of the instrumentality, the automobile. Automobiles are likely to travel far from the places where they are licensed, distributed, or sold. The automobile is intended not only for limited-area travel, but also for long-distance travel. The defendants could easily have anticipated that the Audi in question could end up in Oklahoma.

Analysis:

Note that part of the Court's decision in *World-Wide Volkswagen* hinged on notions of state sovereignty and the limitations on states' powers to reach beyond their borders. However, two years later, in *Insurance Corp. of Ireland, Ltd. v. Compagnie des Bauxites de Guinée*, 456 U.S. 694 (1982), the Court rejected the state-sovereignty rationale in favor of emphasizing that jurisdictional requirements are matters of individual liberty under the Fourteenth Amendment. The Supreme Court in *World-Wide Volkswagen* was deeply divided, showing a split concerning whether the defendant's due process rights or the forum state's interests in litigation should control the outcome.

■ **CASE VOCABULARY**

WRIT OF PROHIBITION: An extraordinary writ issued by an appellate court to prevent a lower court from exceeding its jurisdiction.

Calder v. Jones

(*Magazine Editor*) v. (*Celebrity*)

465 U.S. 783, 104 S.Ct. 1482 (1984)

PERSONAL JURISDICTION IS PROPER OVER A DEFENDANT WHO INTENTIONALLY CAUSES HARM IN THE STATE

■ **INSTANT FACTS** Calder (D) edited an article about Shirley Jones (P), an entertainer, that was published in *The National Enquirer*, and Jones (P) brought suit in California against *The National Enquirer* and others, including Calder (D), who argued that the California court lacked jurisdiction over him.

■ **BLACK LETTER RULE** Personal jurisdiction is proper over nonresident defendants who engage in conduct that is directed at and causes harm to a resident of the forum state.

■ **PROCEDURAL BASIS**

Review of a California court's decision finding that jurisdiction was proper.

■ **FACTS**

Defendant South was a reporter employed by *The National Enquirer*, a Florida corporation that publishes and distributes a national magazine. South wrote an article about Shirley Jones (P), a California resident and entertainer, alleging that Jones (P) drank so heavily that she was unable to fulfill professional obligations. The article was published in *The National Enquirer*, which has its largest circulation in California. Jones (P) sued the magazine, its distributor, South, and Calder (D), a Florida resident employed as an editor with *The National Enquirer* in California. South and Calder (D) challenged personal jurisdiction in California, claiming that they did not have sufficient minimum contacts with California for proper jurisdiction. South did most of his research for the article in Florida, but relied on phone calls to sources in California, as well as a phone call to Jones's (P) husband. Before publication of the article, Calder (D) had been to California only twice, for purposes unrelated to the article. Calder (D) reviewed and approved the subject of South's article and edited it in its final form.

■ **ISSUE**

May a state court exercise personal jurisdiction over a nonresident whose actions are directed at and cause harm to a resident of the forum state?

■ **DECISION AND RATIONALE**

(Rehnquist, J.) Yes. If a defendant engages in conduct that is directed at and causes harm to a resident of a state, that state may exercise personal jurisdiction over the defendant. The focus of a "minimum contacts" analysis for personal jurisdiction is the relationship among the defendant, the forum, and the litigation. South and Calder (D) are not charged with mere untargeted negligence. Rather, their intentional conduct was expressly aimed at a California resident when they created an article that harmed Jones (P) in California. South and Calder (D) knew both that the article would have a potentially devastating effect on Jones (P) and that Jones (P) would feel this effect in California, where she lives and works, and where *The National Enquirer* has its largest circulation. Under these facts, South and

Calder (D) could reasonably anticipate being brought into a California court to answer for the truth of the published statements. Also, Jones (P), who was injured in California, should not have to go to Florida to seek redress for her injuries. Affirmed.

Analysis:

The Supreme Court decided a similar case, *Keeton v. Hustler Magazine, Inc.*, 465 U.S. 770 (1984), on the same day as *Calder*. In *Keeton*, the Court found that *Hustler*, an Ohio corporation, was subject to personal jurisdiction in New Hampshire because the thousands of copies sold in the state amounted to sufficient purposeful contacts with the forum state. The plaintiff chose New Hampshire because of its lengthy statute of limitations for defamation suits. Some commentators have argued that *Calder* and *Keeton* expanded the ability of plaintiffs to "forum shop" in suits against media defendants by allowing plaintiffs to assert jurisdiction in states where the defendant circulates its product.

■ CASE VOCABULARY

FORUM–SHOPPING: The practice of choosing the most favorable jurisdiction or court in which a claim might be heard. A plaintiff might engage in forum-shopping, for example, by filing suit in a jurisdiction with a reputation for high jury awards or by filing several similar suits and keeping the one with the preferred judge.

LIBEL: A defamatory statement expressed in a fixed medium, especially a writing, but also a picture, sign, or electronic broadcast.

Asahi Metal Industry Co., Ltd. v. Superior Court of California, Solano County

(Japanese Tire Valve Manufacturer) v. *(California Court Exercising Jurisdiction)*

480 U.S. 102, 107 S.Ct. 1026 (1987)

PLACEMENT OF A PRODUCT INTO THE STREAM OF COMMERCE DOES NOT CONFER PERSONAL JURISDICTION

■ **INSTANT FACTS** Zurcher, a victim of a motorcycle accident, brought a suit in California against a Taiwanese tire-tube maker, which brought a cross-claim against the Japanese manufacturer of the tire tube valve assembly.

■ **BLACK LETTER RULE** To be subject to personal jurisdiction in a forum state, a non-resident defendant must do more than simply place a product into the stream of commerce in order for the fairness requirement to be met.

■ **PROCEDURAL BASIS**

Certiorari to review the California Supreme Court's decision upholding personal jurisdiction over Asahi Metal Industry (D).

■ **FACTS**

Zurcher and Moreno were involved in a motorcycle accident that injured Zurcher and killed Moreno. Zurcher brought a products-liability cause of action in a California state court against, among others, Cheng Shin Rubber Industrial Co., Ltd., the Taiwanese manufacturer of the motorcycle's tire tube. Cheng Shin Rubber filed a cross-complaint for indemnification against Asahi Metal (D), a Japanese company that manufactures valve assemblies in Japan and sells them to others for use as components in finished tire tubes. Asahi Metal's (D) sale to Cheng Shin Rubber occurred in Taiwan, and the product was shipped to Cheng Shin Rubber in Taiwan. Zurcher ultimately settled his claims with Cheng Shin Rubber and the other defendants, leaving only Cheng Shin Rubber's indemnity action against Asahi Metal (D). Asahi Metal (D) claims that the California court lacks personal jurisdiction over it.

■ **ISSUE**

Is a nonresident defendant that places its product into the stream of commerce subject to personal jurisdiction in the forum state in which the product ultimately arrives?

■ **DECISION AND RATIONALE**

(O'Connor, J.) No. Merely placing a product into the stream of commerce, without more, is insufficient to confer personal jurisdiction over a nonresident defendant. If a defendant places a product into the stream of commerce and that product eventually ends up in the forum state, the defendant has done nothing purposeful to avail itself of the forum state market. Similarly, awareness that a product may end up in the forum state is not enough. Rather, fairness requires that there must be some purposeful action on the defendant's part to avail itself of the forum state market. Examples include designing a product for the forum market, advertising in the forum market, or marketing a product in the forum state through a distributor. Here, Asahi Metal (D) did not purposefully avail itself of the California market. It does no business in California, does not advertise in California, and did not design its product in anticipation of California sales. Reversed.

■ CONCURRENCE

(Brennan, J.) Plaintiffs should not be required to show additional conduct directed towards the forum state to support a finding of personal jurisdiction. A defendant who places its product in the stream of commerce reaps economic benefit from the sale of the final product in the forum state and indirectly benefits from laws regulating commercial activity. Here, Asahi Metal (D) had minimum contacts with California; it was aware of the manner in which the final product was marketed and regularly sold its components to a manufacturer it knew was making regular sales of the final product in California. However, the Court is correct in analyzing the fairness aspect of the jurisdiction test, and it would be fundamentally unfair and unreasonable to require Asahi Metal (D) to defend the suit in California.

■ CONCURRENCE

(Stevens, J.) Because jurisdiction over Asahi Metal (D) in this case would be unreasonable, there is no need to analyze minimum contacts between the defendant and California or to articulate "purposeful direction" as necessary to the minimum contacts analysis. Even assuming that the test set forth in Justice O'Connor's opinion is necessary, Justice O'Connor misapplied it to the facts of the case. Asahi Metal's (D) dealing with Cheng Shin Rubber amount to more than merely placing its product into the stream of commerce. Whether Asahi Metal's (D) conduct rises to the level of purposeful availment depends on the volume, value, and hazardous nature of the components at issue. A regular course of delivering over 100,000 units over a period of years amounts to purposeful availment, even though the final product was marketed worldwide.

Analysis:

Although the Court unanimously held that the California state court did not have jurisdiction over Asahi Metal (D), the Justices arrived at the conclusion differently. Justice O'Connor applied the two-part test, analyzing first whether the California contacts were sufficient and then determining whether subjecting Asahi Metal to jurisdiction in California would be unfair and unreasonable because the parties to the indemnification action were residents of Taiwan and Japan. Both of the concurring justices agreed only with the plurality's conclusion regarding the fairness of jurisdiction in California. Note that, as Justice Steven points out, even where a defendant has sufficient minimum contacts with a forum state, personal jurisdiction there may not be reasonable.

■ CASE VOCABULARY

CROSS–COMPLAINT: A claim asserted by a defendant against another party to the action; a claim asserted by a defendant against a person not a party to the action for a matter relating to the subject of the action.

INDEMNITY: Reimbursement or compensation for loss, damage, or liability in tort; especially the right of a party who is secondarily liable to the recover from the party who is primarily liable for reimbursement of expenditures paid to a third party for injuries resulting from a violation of a common-law duty.

PLURALITY OPINION: An opinion lacking enough judges' votes to constitute a majority, but receiving more votes than any other opinion.

Burger King Corp. v. Rudzewicz

(Florida Restaurant Franchise Owner) v. *(Michigan Franchisee)*

471 U.S. 462, 105 S.Ct. 2174 (1985)

AN ONGOING BUSINESS RELATIONSHIP WITH PLAINTIFF SUBJECTS A DEFENDANT TO SUIT IN THE PLAINTIFF'S STATE

■ **INSTANT FACTS** Burger King (P), which is headquartered in Florida, sued Rudzewicz (D), a Michigan franchisee, in Florida federal court for default on payments due under the franchise agreement.

■ **BLACK LETTER RULE** While a contract alone is not enough to confer personal jurisdiction, a nonresident defendant that establishes an ongoing business relationship with a plaintiff is subject to jurisdiction in the plaintiff's state.

■ PROCEDURAL BASIS

Appeal from reversal of a judgment by the Eleventh Circuit finding a lack of jurisdiction.

■ FACTS

Rudzewicz (D) and MacShara were Michigan residents who entered into a franchise contract with Burger King (P), which is headquartered in Florida, to operate a restaurant in Michigan. The franchise agreement, which required Rudzewicz (D) to pay certain royalties and other fees, stated that it was deemed to have been made in Miami, Florida, and that any dispute between the parties would be construed under Florida law. Although the Michigan restaurant was initially profitable, patronage declined after a recession. MacShara and Rudzewicz (D) fell behind in their monthly payments to Burger King (P), and Burger King (P) sued MacShara and Rudzewicz (D) in a Florida federal court. Rudzewicz (D) argued that the Florida court had no jurisdiction over him.

■ ISSUE

Is personal jurisdiction proper over a nonresident defendant who has an established an ongoing business relationship with a resident of the forum state?

■ DECISION AND RATIONALE

(Brennan, J.) Yes. Although a contractual relationship alone is not enough to confer personal jurisdiction, if a nonresident establishes an ongoing business relationship with another party, the nonresident may be subject to jurisdiction in the other party's home state. If a defendant deliberately engages in significant activities in the state and creates continuing obligations between himself and residents of the forum state, he is subject to jurisdiction in that state, even if he has never been physically present in the state. A substantial amount of business is transacted by telephone and mail, which negates the need for physical presence. As long as a commercial actor's efforts are purposefully directed towards a resident of a state, he is subject to jurisdiction in that state. To determine whether a defendant in a business relationship is subject to jurisdiction in a particular state depends on the parties' prior negotiations, contemplated future obligations, the contract's terms, and the parties' actual course of dealing. Here, Rudzewicz (D) negotiated with Burger King (P) in Florida and had a regular course of dealing with the headquarters there. The choice-of-law provision in the parties' contract, while not controlling on the issue of jurisdiction, gave Rudzewicz (D) notice that a lawsuit in Florida was possible. Moreover, Rudzewicz's (D) alleged conduct caused foreseeable injuries to a Florida corporation and personal jurisdiction over the defendant in Florida is reasonable. Reversed.

■ DISSENT

(Stevens, J.) Contrary to the majority's assertion, it is unfair to require a franchisee to defend a case such as this in a forum chosen by the franchisor, Burger King (P). Rudzewicz (D) did not maintain an office, have employees, or sell any products in Florida. Nothing in the record suggests that Rudzewicz (D) purposefully availed himself of the benefits and protections of Florida law.

Analysis:

In this case, the majority stressed the forum state's interest in the litigation, and the dissent focused on the due process concerns of the defendant. The majority also emphasized that determining whether personal jurisdiction is proper in a particular forum depends on the facts and circumstances of each case. Although Burger King wanted the Court to announce a categorical rule relating to the franchise relationship, the Court declined to do so. As Justice Brennan stated, "We ... reject any talismanic jurisdictional formulas."

■ CASE VOCABULARY

CHOICE–OF–LAW CLAUSE: A contractual provision by which the parties designate the jurisdiction whose law will govern any disputes that may arise between the parties.

Shaffer v. Heitner

(Officer/Director of Company) v. *(Shareholder)*

433 U.S. 186, 97 S.Ct. 2569 (1977)

MINIMUM–CONTACTS ANALYSIS APPLIES TO ALL QUESTIONS OF PERSONAL JURISDICTION

■ **INSTANT FACTS** Heitner (P) brought a shareholders' derivative action against Shaffer (D) and other officers and directors of Greyhound, Inc., filing suit in Delaware and taking advantage of a Delaware statute allowing the court to sequester the defendants' stock shares.

■ **BLACK LETTER RULE** Minimum contacts must exist for personal jurisdiction to exist, whether the proceeding is in personam or in rem.

■ PROCEDURAL BASIS

Certiorari to review the Delaware Supreme Court's affirmance of the rejection of arguments contesting personal jurisdiction in a shareholder's derivative suit.

■ FACTS

Heitner (P), who was not a resident of Delaware, owned one share of stock in Greyhound, Inc., which was incorporated in Delaware, but had its headquarters in Arizona. Heitner (P) brought a shareholders' derivative suit in Delaware state court against Greyhound, as well as Shaffer (D) and other individual officers and directors of the company, and requested a sequestration order under a Delaware statute that allowed a court to seize property in the state in order to compel the property owner to appear in state court and defend against a suit brought there. The court granted the request and seized 82,000 shares of Greyhound stock belonging to 19 of the defendants and options belonging to two other defendants. Shaffer (D) and other defendants challenged personal jurisdiction in the Delaware court, arguing that they had no contacts with Delaware.

■ ISSUE

Is personal jurisdiction over a nonresident determined by assessing the nonresident's minimum contacts with the forum state, even if the proceeding is in rem?

■ DECISION AND RATIONALE

(Marshall, J.) Yes. The minimum contacts analysis set forth in *International Shoe Co. v. Washington*, 326 U.S. 310 (1945), applies to all questions of personal jurisdiction, regardless of the nature of the proceeding. Contrary to *Pennoyer v. Neff*, 95 U.S. 714 (1877), a proceeding against property is essentially a proceeding against the owner, and an adverse judgment in rem directly affects the property owner by divesting him of his ownership rights. The *International Shoe* analysis should also apply to quasi in rem proceedings, in which the ownership of the property is not related to the cause of action, because subjecting a defendant to jurisdiction in the forum state may result in fundamental unfairness to the defendant who has no other contacts with the forum. Shaffer (D) and the other defendants did not have sufficient contacts with Delaware to subject them to jurisdiction there. They have never been present in Delaware, and they did not take any actions there that are related to the lawsuit. Because the defendants had no ties to Delaware, other than ownership of stock deemed to be located there, they could not have foreseen being brought into court there. Reversed.

■ CONCURRENCE

(Powell, J.) The majority is correct in holding that *International Shoe* applies to assertions of in rem and in personam jurisdiction in state courts. The majority is also correct in holding that the presence of defendants' stock in Delaware and the fact that they are officers and directors of a Delaware corporation are not enough to confer jurisdiction over them in Delaware. However, it should remain open as to whether the ownership of some forms of property located in a particular state is sufficient contact to subject the defendant to jurisdiction in that state to the extent of the property's value.

■ CONCURRENCE

(Stevens, J.) The Due Process Clause protects defendants against judgment without notice. A defendant who purchases stock on the open market should not be expected to know that he is subject to a suit in a forum that is far from his residence and unrelated to the transaction. The Delaware sequestration statute creates a risk of judgment without notice and denies a defendant the opportunity to defend the merits of the case unless he subjects himself to jurisdiction in Delaware. Although the majority is correct in holding that the minimum-contacts analysis applies to in personam and in rem jurisdiction, it may go too far in applying its holding to quasi in rem proceedings involving real estate.

■ CONCURRENCE/DISSENT

(Brennan, J.) Although Brennan agrees that the minimum-contacts analysis is sensible, he dissents from the ultimate holding of the majority. The Delaware sequestration statute is an embodiment of quasi in rem jurisdiction, which the majority invalidated because the statute allowed jurisdiction on a basis other than minimum contacts. The record as to defendants' contacts with Delaware is not sufficiently developed to allow the majority to make any conclusion about whether these contacts were sufficient to confer jurisdiction under the *International Shoe* analysis, and it was unnecessary to do so once the statute was determined to be invalid. As a general rule, however, a state should have jurisdiction over shareholder derivative actions involving corporations chartered in that state.

Analysis:

Shaffer's landmark ruling saw the majority overturn the traditional approach to in rem jurisdiction by equating the in rem test with the minimum-contacts test for personal jurisdiction. After *Shaffer*, in rem jurisdiction was appropriate only if the defendant purposefully availed himself to the benefits and protections of the forum state or the action was sufficiently related to the forum state. In response to *Shaffer*, Delaware amended its long-arm statute to include nonresidents who become officers and directors of a Delaware corporation. The statute functioned similarly to the statute in *Hess v. Pawloski*, 274 U.S. 352 (1927), by deeming the officers to have appointed an in-state agent for service of process.

■ CASE VOCABULARY

DERIVATIVE ACTION: A suit by a beneficiary of a fiduciary to enforce a right belonging to the fiduciary, especially a suit asserted by a shareholder on the corporation's behalf against a third party (usually a corporate officer) because of the corporation's failure to take some action against the third party.

QUASI IN REM: Involving or determining the rights of a person having an interest in property located within the court's jurisdiction.

SEQUESTRATION: The process by which property is removed from the possessor pending the outcome of a dispute in which two or more parties contend for it.

Burnham v. Superior Court of California

(*Prospective Divorced Father*) v. (*Court Exercising Jurisdiction*)

495 U.S. 604, 110 S.Ct. 2105 (1990)

A NONRESIDENT MAY BE SERVED WITH PROCESS WHILE TEMPORARILY IN THE FORUM

WELCOME TO CALIFORNIA, MR. BURNHAM. HERE'S A MAP OF THE STATE AND A DIVORCE PETITION!

■ **INSTANT FACTS** Dennis Burnham (D), a New Jersey resident who was served with process for a divorce proceeding while visiting California, contends that California jurisdiction violates his due process.

■ **BLACK LETTER RULE** A state may exercise personal jurisdiction over a nonresident if the nonresident is served with process while temporarily in the state, even if the suit is not related to the nonresident's presence in the state.

■ **PROCEDURAL BASIS**

Certiorari to review state court's denial of mandamus relief following its denial of defendant's motion to quash service of process in the action.

■ **FACTS**

Dennis Burnham (D) and his wife decided to separate and ultimately to divorce. Although Burnham (D) filed for divorce in New Jersey, he never had his wife served with process. Burnham's wife moved to California, where she filed a petition for divorce against Burnham (D), and served him when he was in California for business and to visit his children. Burnham (D) argued that the Superior Court of California lacked jurisdiction over him.

■ **ISSUE**

Is personal jurisdiction over a nonresident proper if the nonresident was served with process while temporarily in the forum state?

■ **DECISION AND RATIONALE**

(Scalia, J.) Yes. State courts may assert jurisdiction over nonresidents who are physically present in the state. Burnham (D) improperly argues that, despite his being served with process in California, he lacks sufficient contacts with California to be subject to jurisdiction there. Nothing in *International Shoe Co. v. Washington*, 326 U.S. 310 (1945), or its progeny overruled jurisdiction based on physical presence in a state; rather, the *International Shoe* minimum-contacts analysis applies to defendants who are not present in the forum state. Moreover, obtaining jurisdiction by service of process in the forum state is a long-recognized tradition. There is no reason to find that such a procedure now violates due process or to attempt to fit the in-state-service-of-process rule into the minimum contacts analysis, as Justice Brennan's concurring opinion attempts to do. Affirmed.

■ **CONCURRENCE**

(White, J.) Because the rule allowing jurisdiction over nonresidents by personal service is so widely accepted, there is no reason to strike it down on its face or as applied to this case. If this rule were to depend on a case-by-case analysis, courts would become too bogged down with fact-specific litigation.

■ CONCURRENCE

(Brennan, J.) Although Justice Scalia reaches the right result, it is improper to base this result on history and tradition alone. Simply because a particular rule is a tradition does not mean that it remains constitutional. The in-state-service-of-process rule comports with due process because a nonresident who is served with process in the forum state avails himself of the benefits of the state while present and is on notice that he is subject to suit there.

■ CONCURRENCE

(Stevens, J.) Justice Scalia's opinion is broader than necessary to reach the correct result that in-state service of process is sufficient to confer jurisdiction over a nonresident. However, the issues raised by Justices Scalia, Brennan, and White demonstrate that the lower court's judgment should be affirmed.

Analysis:

Burnham clarified that the traditional idea of jurisdiction based on physical presence can survive even if sufficient minimum contacts did not exist between the defendant and the forum state. Note that in footnote 1 of *Burnham*, Justice Scalia excepted corporations from the analysis. Other courts have held that serving a corporate agent temporarily in the forum state is not enough to subject the corporation to jurisdiction in that state. *See, e.g., Wenche Siemer v. Learjet Acquisition Corp.*, 966 F.2d 179 (5th Cir. 1992). Also, jurisdiction will not lie if a non-resident is served as a result of being tricked into visiting the state.

■ CASE VOCABULARY

MOTION TO QUASH: A party's request that the court nullify process or an act instituted by the other party, as in seeking to nullify a subpoena.

Helicopteros Nacionales de Colombia v. Hall

(Helicopter Transportation Provider) v. *(Injured Crash Victim)*

466 U.S. 408, 104 S.Ct. 1868 (1984)

A NONRESIDENT'S CONTACTS MUST BE SYSTEMATIC AND CONTINUOUS IN ORDER FOR THERE TO BE JURISDICTION

NOW WATCH AS THE TEXAS LONG ARM STATUTE FALLS SHORT!

■ **INSTANT FACTS** Hall (P) sued Helicopteros Nacionales de Colombia (D) ("Helicol"), a Colombian company that owned a helicopter that crashed in Peru, for wrongful death, alleging that Helicol (D) had sufficient contacts to subject it to in personam jurisdiction in Texas.

■ **BLACK LETTER RULE** If a lawsuit does not arise from or relate to a nonresident defendant's contacts with the forum state, jurisdiction over the nonresident party is proper only if its contacts with the state are systematic and continuous.

■ **PROCEDURAL BASIS**

Certiorari to review the Texas Supreme Court decision reversing the dismissal of the action due to lack of in personam jurisdiction over Helicol (D).

■ **FACTS**

Helicol (D) contracted with Consorcio to provide helicopter transportation of personnel and supplies to and from a construction site for a pipeline project in Peru. Helicol's (D) president flew to Texas to negotiate the contract. Helicol (D) also purchased helicopters in Texas and sent prospective pilots to Texas for training. However, Helicol (D) was not authorized to do business in Texas, did not sell product in Texas, did not have any employees in Texas, and owned no real estate in Texas. Hall (P) and the other plaintiffs, all survivors of pipeline project employees killed in the helicopter crash, sued Helicol (D) and other defendants for wrongful death. Even though Hall (P) and the others were not Texas residents, they sued Helicol (D) in a Texas state court. Helicol (D) challenged the jurisdiction of the Texas courts, alleging lack of jurisdiction. The lower court found in favor of the plaintiffs, and a Texas appellate court reversed the judgment, finding that Texas courts had no jurisdiction over Helicol. The Texas Supreme Court reversed that judgment, finding that Texas courts could assert jurisdiction over Helicol (D). The Supreme Court granted certiorari.

■ **ISSUE**

May a state court exercise jurisdiction over a nonresident defendant if the cause of action does not arise from the nonresident's minimal activities in the forum state?

■ **DECISION AND RATIONALE**

(Blackmun, J.) No. If a lawsuit does not arise from a nonresident corporate defendant's activities in the forum state, a state court may exercise jurisdiction only if the defendant's contacts with the state are systematic and continuous. Hall's (P) lawsuit does not arise from and is not related to Helicol's (D) activities in Texas. Thus, the court must determine whether Helicol's (D) contacts with Texas amount to continuous and systematic business contacts sufficient to confer jurisdiction over a suit that is not related to those contacts. Helicol (D) engaged in a single negotiation in Texas, made some purchases there, and accepted checks drawn on a Texas bank account. These contacts are not sufficient to subject Helicol (D) to jurisdiction in a suit that does not arise from the contacts. Reversed.

■ DISSENT

(Brennan, J.) The majority is incorrectly asserts that Helicol's (D) contacts with Texas are not related to Hall's (P) cause of action, and thus are not "minimum contacts" for purposes of asserting jurisdiction. However, Helicol (D) negotiated the contract for the transportation used at the time of the crash in Texas; the helicopter involved in the crash was purchased in Texas; and the pilot whose negligence caused the crash was trained in Texas. Accordingly, this is not a case where a state court has exercised jurisdiction over a nonresident defendant in a lawsuit wholly unrelated to the defendant's contacts with the forum.

Analysis:

This decision highlighted the distinction between general and specific jurisdiction and the type of contacts a nonresident defendant must have for each type of jurisdiction to be proper. Specific jurisdiction would apply if the defendant's contacts with the forum state arise out of or relate to the cause of action. When a nonresident's contacts with the forum state are systematic and continuous, the state courts may exert general jurisdiction over the nonresident, even in cases unrelated to those contacts. Only in cases that arise from or relate to the nonresident's contacts with the forum state would a nonresident be subject to specific jurisdiction, provided it has "minimum contacts" with the forum state.

■ CASE VOCABULARY

DECEDENT: A dead person, especially a person who has died recently.

GENERAL JURISDICTION: A court's authority to hear all claims against a defendant, at the place of the defendant's domicile or the place of service, without any showing that that a connection exists between the claims and the forum state.

SPECIFIC JURISDICTION: Jurisdiction that stems from the defendant's having certain minimum contacts with the forum state so that the court may hear a case whose issues arise from those minimum contacts.

Carnival Cruise Lines, Inc. v. Shute

(*Cruise Ship Operator*) v. (*Passenger*)
499 U.S. 585, 111 S.Ct. 1522 (1991)

A REASONABLE FORUM–SELECTION CLAUSE CONSTITUTES CONSENT TO BE SUED IN THE FORUM STATE

■ **INSTANT FACTS** Shute (P), a Washington resident who was injured while on a cruise vacation, sued Carnival Cruise Lines (D) in Washington, but Carnival Cruise Lines (D) argued that a forum-selection clause in the contract limited jurisdiction to Florida.

■ **BLACK LETTER RULE** A fair and reasonable forum-selection clause in a contract between two parties amounts to consent to jurisdiction in a given forum.

■ **PROCEDURAL BASIS**

Certiorari to review the lower court's reversal of a dismissal of the action due to lack of jurisdiction.

■ **FACTS**

The Shutes (P), residents of Washington, purchased tickets for a cruise on a ship owned and operated by Carnival Cruise Lines (D), a Florida corporation. The tickets contained a forum-selection clause stating that the parties agreed that all disputes between them would be litigated exclusively in the Florida courts. The Shutes (P) boarded the ship in Los Angeles. While the ship was in international waters off the Mexican coast, Mrs. Shute (P) slipped on a deck mat and was injured. Shute (P) brought suit in Washington, alleging that Carnival Cruise Lines' (D) employees had negligently caused her injuries. Carnival Cruise Lines (D) argued that the forum-selection clause in the parties' contract required Shute (P) to bring her suit in Florida.

■ **ISSUE**

Is a forum-selection clause requiring parties to a contract to litigate their suits in a particular forum enforceable, as long as it is fair and reasonable?

■ **DECISION AND RATIONALE**

(Blackmun, J.) Yes. Including a reasonable forum-selection clause in a contract is permissible in this case because a cruise line has a special interest in avoiding being sued in many different forums, which is a risk because it carries passengers from many locales. Also, a forum-selection clause dispels confusion about where suits must be brought and defended, and passengers benefit from reduced rates resulting from savings associated with limiting the forums in which the cruise line may be sued. No fundamental unfairness is associated with the forum-selection clause at issue and no evidence indicates that Carnival Cruise Lines (D) chose Florida as a forum as a means to discourage passengers from pursuing legitimate claims or that it engaged in fraud or overreaching to persuade the Shute (P) to agree to Florida as a forum. Shute (P) had notice of the clause and could have rejected it. Reversed.

■ **DISSENT**

(Stevens, J.) Contrary to the majority's assertion, Shute (P) was not fully and fairly notified of a forum-selection clause contained in one of 25 paragraphs in the ticket's fine print. Also, Shutes (P) did not

---

have the opportunity to read the clause until after they had paid for their tickets, for which Carnival Cruise Lines (D) would not allow any refund. Most passengers would accept the risk of having to file suit in Florida rather than canceling a planned vacation at the last minute and without a refund. The forum-selection clause should be unenforceable because of the disparate bargaining power between the parties and because it lessens Shute's (P) ability to recover for injuries on the cruise ship.

Analysis:

Carnival Cruise Lines emphasized the reasonableness requirement for forum selection clauses. In addition to a fair and reasonable forum-selection clause, parties may consent to suit in a particular jurisdiction in several ways: voluntarily appearing in court to defend the merits of the suit; applying statutory schemes appointing an agent for service of process; and failing to assert a defense of lack of personal jurisdiction in a timely fashion. Note that a forum-selection clause amounts to consent before a dispute arises. The court found that this clause was reasonable because the purported advantages of a forum-selection clause outweighed its disadvantages, even though it was unlikely that a passenger would have read the fine boilerplate language on the back of the ticket and despite the vastly unequal bargaining power of the parties.

■ **CASE VOCABULARY**

FORUM–SELECTION CLAUSE: A contractual provision in which the parties establish the place (such as the country, state, or type of court) for specified litigation between them.

ALS Scan, Inc. v. Digital Service Consultants, Inc.

(*Internet Distributor*) v. (*Internet Service Provider*)

293 F.3d 707 (4th Cir. 2002)

PERSONAL JURISDICTION BASED ON INTERNET ACTIVITY DEPENDS ON THE NATURE AND QUALITY OF THE ACTIVITY

■ **INSTANT FACTS** ALS Scan, Inc., (P), a Maryland company, sued Digital Service Consultants, Inc., (D), a Georgia Internet service provider for copyright infringement.

■ **BLACK LETTER RULE** Jurisdiction over a nonresident based on Internet activity is proper if the nonresident directs electronic activity into the state with the purpose of engaging in business in the state and, through that activity, creates a potential cause of action there.

■ PROCEDURAL BASIS

Review of the district court's dismissal of the complaint for lack of personal jurisdiction.

■ FACTS

Digital Service Consultants (D), a Georgia Internet service provider, contracted with its client, Alternative Products, Inc., to provide bandwidth for Alternative's distribution of images over the Internet. ALS Scan (P), which is a Maryland corporation that distributes adult photographs over the Internet, alleged that Alternative Products appropriated copies of its photographs and distributed them over the Internet, using bandwidth provided by Digital Services (D). ALS Scan (P) sued the parties in federal district court in Maryland, alleging copyright infringement.

■ ISSUE

Is jurisdiction proper over a nonresident Internet service provider whose activities were merely passive?

■ DECISION AND RATIONALE

(Niemeyer, J.) No. An Internet service provider engages only in passive Internet activity by providing bandwidth to another party that created a website and sent information over the Internet. Whether jurisdiction is proper in cases involving the Internet depends on the nature of the conduct and activity. If a defendant knowingly and repeatedly transmits computer files over the Internet into a particular state, jurisdiction will be proper. However, jurisdiction is not appropriate in cases where a defendant has simply posted information on a website that may be viewed in a particular state. In the case of interactive websites where the user can interact and exchange information with the host computer, whether jurisdiction is proper depends on the level of interactivity and the nature of the information exchanged. Digital Service's (D) activity was, at best, passive; it did not knowingly transmit infringing photographs into Maryland. The only direct contact Digital Service (D) had with Maryland was posting its own website, which could be viewed in Maryland. It did not specifically direct its electronic activity at any Maryland target. Affirmed.

Analysis:

The court also held that merely posting a website that is viewable in a given state would not support general jurisdiction over any claim against a nonresident defendant. Interestingly, the court returned to the notion of state sovereignty as a basis of personal-jurisdiction analysis, stating that the omnipresent nature of the Internet could not authorize a scheme whereby states could routinely reach out beyond their borders to exercise jurisdiction over residents of other states.

■ **CASE VOCABULARY**

COPYRIGHT INFRINGEMENT: The act of violating any of a copyright owner's exclusive rights granted by the federal Copyright Act, 17 U.S.C.A. §§ 106, 602.

Mullane v. Central Hanover Bank & Trust Co.

(*Special Guardian of Trusts*) v. (*Trust Management Company*)

339 U.S. 306, 70 S.Ct. 652 (1950)

NOTICE OF A LAWSUIT MUST BE REASONABLY CALCULATED TO GIVE INTERESTED PARTIES NOTICE

■ **INSTANT FACTS** Central Hanover Bank & Trust Co. (P), which petitioned to have a New York court approve its handling of a common trust fund, published notice of the petition in a local newspaper, intending to reach the beneficiaries of the various trust funds, but Mullane (D) objected to the notice by publication.

■ **BLACK LETTER RULE** Notice of a lawsuit must be reasonably calculated, based on all of the facts and circumstances, to inform interested parties that a lawsuit is pending.

■ **PROCEDURAL BASIS**

Certiorari to review the New York Court of Appeals' affirmance of an order overruling due-process objections to service of process by publication.

■ **FACTS**

The Central Hanover Bank & Trust Co. (P) is a New York corporation that manages common trust funds, which pool smaller trusts together for management and investment purposes. Central Hanover (P), which was required under New York law to have a New York court periodically approve the accounting for the trusts it manages, petitioned a New York surrogate court for an order approving an accounting for 113 trusts. Mullane (D) was appointed by the Court as a special guardian to represent the trust beneficiaries, known or unknown and not otherwise appearing in court. The only notice to the trust beneficiaries was through publication in a local newspaper, which was the method of notice allowed under the New York statute pertaining to common trusts. Mullane (D) claimed that notice by publication was inadequate under the Fourteenth Amendment and that the court lacked jurisdiction to enter an order approving the accounting.

■ **ISSUE**

Is publication an adequate means to provide notice to a party to a lawsuit if that party's contact information is readily accessible?

■ **DECISION AND RATIONALE**

(Jackson, J.) No. Due process requires that notice of a lawsuit be reasonably calculated under the circumstances to apprise the parties of pending litigation and to allow them a chance to be heard. Although personal service in the forum state is always acceptable notice of a lawsuit, it is not necessary as long as the alternate form of notice is sufficient to inform the parties of the suit and to give them an opportunity to be heard. Publication is not sufficient in this case as to the known beneficiaries whose contact information was available to Central Hanover (P) because it was not reasonably calculated to reach them. The trust beneficiaries are not likely to see a publication in the back of a local newspaper that does not even name those affected by the petition, and it is not onerous to expect that notice be mailed at least by ordinary mail. However, notice by publication was reasonable as to beneficiaries whose interests in the trusts could not be ascertained or whose whereabouts were not known. Reversed.

■ DISSENT

(Burton, J.) Whether or not notice beyond the publication prescribed by the New York statute is required is within the discretion of the state.

Analysis:

Mullane, which analyzed the essential due process requirements for notice by service of a summons and a complaint, focused on the phrase "reasonably calculated under the circumstances." Courts generally do not favor notice by publication because it is not reasonably calculated to provide notice under many circumstances, although they generally permit it in situations where there is no other way to provide notice and in some in rem proceedings. After *Mullane*, most courts held that notice by U.S. mail was the constitutional minimum for defendants whose addresses can be ascertained using reasonable diligence. Fed. R. Civ. P. 4 governs notice in federal courts; that rule gives a party extra to time to respond to a complaint if it agrees to waive service of a summons.

■ CASE VOCABULARY

SPECIAL GUARDIAN: A guardian, usually a lawyer, appointed by the court to appear in a lawsuit on behalf of an incompetent or minor party.

INTER VIVOS TRUST: A trust that is created and takes effect during the settlor's lifetime.

Piper Aircraft Co. v. Reyno

(Aircraft Manufacturer) v. *(Administrator of Estates of Crash Victims)*

454 U.S. 235, 102 S.Ct. 252 (1981)

LITIGATION IN A PARTICULAR FORUM SHOULD NOT BE OVERLY BURDENSOME ON THE DEFENDANT OR THE COURT

■ **INSTANT FACTS** Reyno (P) brought suit in a state court in the United States against Piper Aircraft Co., arising from a plane crash that occurred in Scotland, and Piper Aircraft (D) moved to dismiss because the court was not a convenient forum for the litigation, which it claims should have been brought in Scotland.

■ **BLACK LETTER RULE** Under the doctrine of forum non conveniens, a court may dismiss a case if there is an alternate forum with jurisdiction and if proceeding in the forum would impose a heavy burden on the parties or the court.

■ **PROCEDURAL BASIS**

Certiorari to review Third Circuit Court of Appeals' order reversing the district court's dismissal of the case.

■ **FACTS**

A small commercial aircraft crashed in Scotland, killing the pilot and five passengers. All of the crash victims were Scottish. The plane involved was manufactured in Pennsylvania by Piper Aircraft Co. (D), a Pennsylvania corporation. Reyno (P), a California resident, was appointed the administrator of the estates of the crash victims, even though she did not know any of them. Reyno (P) filed a wrongful death action against Piper (D) and others in California state court. The case was moved to a federal court in Pennsylvania, and Piper Aircraft (D) moved to dismiss the case based on forum non conveniens.

■ **ISSUE**

May a court dismiss a case if an alternate forum has jurisdiction to hear the case and litigating in the present forum would be overly burdensome to the defendant and the court system?

■ **DECISION AND RATIONALE**

(Marshall, J.) Yes. Under the doctrine of forum non conveniens, a court may dismiss a case if trial in the plaintiff's chosen forum imposes a heavy burden on the defendant or the court, and if the plaintiff is not able to show any specific reasons why the particular forum is convenient. Although there is a heavy presumption that the plaintiff's choice of forum is appropriate, this presumption may be overcome if private and public interest factors point to trial in an alternate forum. Also, while a substantive change in the law is part of the analysis, it cannot be the sole reason to deny a dismissal on grounds of forum non conveniens. It is appropriate to accord Reyno's (P) choice of a forum less deference because she represents foreign citizens seeking to take advantage of the American courts, where there are more favorable laws regarding products liability and damages. Similarly, the private interests of the parties weigh in favor of trial in Scotland because most of the evidence and witnesses are there, and because the defendants could more easily add other parties and claims to the lawsuit, which would not be

---

feasible in Pennsylvania. Public interest factors also point to suit in Scotland because the claims involve applications of different law, which would be confusing to the jury, and because the court is not familiar with Scottish law, which would apply to some, but not all, of the claims and parties. Reversed.

Analysis:

The underlying basis of *Piper* is that the forum non conveniens doctrine applies only when venue is proper in the initial forum and there is an alternate forum available. Therefore, the common-law doctrine of forum non conveniens is closely related to the concept of venue, which, for federal courts, is a matter of statute. Generally, venue is proper in a judicial district where a defendant resides or where a substantial part of the events giving rise to the claim occurred. If the plaintiff files suit in a district where venue is not proper, the court may either dismiss the suit or transfer it to a venue that is proper.

■ CASE VOCABULARY

VENUE: The proper or a possible place for the trial of a case, usually because the place has some connection with the events that have given rise to the case.

CHAPTER EIGHT

The Choice of an Appropriate Court: Subject Matter Jurisdiction and Removal

Louisville & Nashville Railroad Company v. Mottley

Instant Facts: The Railroad (D) refused to honor a long-standing settlement agreement giving Mottley (P) free transportation on the grounds that a newly enacted federal law prevented railroads from granting free passes or reduced rates.

Black Letter Rule: Federal question subject matter jurisdiction exists only when the plaintiff's own statement of the cause of action in the complaint shows that the claim is based upon the Constitution or the laws of the United States.

United Mine Workers of America v. Gibbs

Instant Facts: Gibbs (P), a mine superintendent, sued the United Mine Workers (D) in federal court for blocking the opening of a new mine he was managing, claiming violations of both state and federal law.

Black Letter Rule: The exercise of pendent jurisdiction is within the sound discretion of the trial court.

Owen Equipment and Erection Company v. Kroger

Instant Facts: Kroger was electrocuted when a crane operated by Owen Equipment came too close to a power line owned by Omaha Public Power District (D).

Black Letter Rule: A plaintiff in a diversity case cannot rely on ancillary jurisdiction to permit an amendment to a complaint to bring a claim against a non-diverse third-party defendant.

Finley v. United States

Instant Facts: Finley's (P) husband and children were killed when the plane in which they were riding struck power lines on its approach to the San Diego airport; she sought to add state tort claims against other defendants to her federal court action against the Federal Aviation Agency for negligent operation of runway lights and air traffic control.

Black Letter Rule: Independent parties and factually related state law claims cannot be made part of a Federal Tort Claims Act action against the United States.

Burnett v. Birmingham Board of Education

Instant Facts: Burnett (P) and other employees of the Birmingham Board of Education (D) brought an action in state court for back wages under their employment contract; the plaintiffs sought remand to state court following removal to federal court.

Black Letter Rule: When state law claims predominate, a case including both state and federal law claims that has been removed to federal court can be remanded to state court.

Louisville & Nashville Railroad Company v. Mottley

(Railroad) v. *(Railroad Passengers)*

211 U.S. 149, 29 S.Ct. 42 (1908)

FEDERAL QUESTION JURISDICTION ARISES ONLY FROM A WELL–PLEADED COMPLAINT

■ **INSTANT FACTS** The Railroad (D) refused to honor a long-standing settlement agreement giving Mottley (P) free transportation on the grounds that a newly enacted federal law prevented railroads from granting free passes or reduced rates.

■ **BLACK LETTER RULE** Federal question subject matter jurisdiction exists only when the plaintiff's own statement of the cause of action in the complaint shows that the claim is based upon the Constitution or the laws of the United States.

■ PROCEDURAL BASIS

On appeal from a judgment entered for the plaintiffs. The Court on its own motion raised the issue of subject matter jurisdiction.

■ FACTS

In 1871, Mottley (P) and his wife, citizens of Kentucky, were injured by the negligence of the Louisville & Nashville Railroad Company (D), also a citizen of Kentucky. The Mottleys (P) released their claim against the railroad in exchange for free passage on the railroad for life. This agreement was honored up to January 1, 1907. The Mottleys (P) brought suit in federal court in Kentucky for specific performance of the agreement after the railroad refused to honor it because, the complaint alleged, Congress in 1906 passed a law forbidding railroads to give free passes or free transportation. The complaint further alleged that the law did not apply to passes given under these circumstances, and that even if it did, the law violated the Fifth Amendment to the Constitution because it deprived the plaintiffs of their property without due process of law. The railroad demurred to the complaint. The trial court overruled the demurrer and granted judgment to the Mottleys (P). The railroad appealed directly to the Supreme Court.

■ ISSUE

Does a federal court have federal question jurisdiction based on an allegation in a complaint that the defendant may set up a defense based on federal statutes?

■ DECISION AND RATIONALE

(Moody, J.) No. There was no diversity of citizenship, so the only ground for jurisdiction is that the suit arises under the Constitution or laws of the United States. The established interpretation of a suit "arising under" federal law is one where the plaintiff's complaint setting forth his own cause of action shows that it is based upon federal law or the Constitution. It is not enough that the plaintiff anticipates some defense based on federal law, or even if it is likely that questions of federal law will ultimately arise during the course of litigation. Here, the cause of action is for performance of the contract. The anticipated defense based on the federal statute, and the potential issue of the constitutionality of that statute, if applicable, does not create federal question jurisdiction under this interpretation of "arising under." Reversed.

Analysis:

The requirement that a plaintiff's complaint state a cause of action based on a federal law or the Constitution in order to confer federal question subject matter jurisdiction is known as the "well-pleaded complaint" rule. Commentators have suggested that the rule stems from the notion that unless the initial pleading is sufficient to confer jurisdiction on the court, the court lacks power to require a responsive pleading or take any other action in the case. The rule continues to be applied. Just as an anticipated defense or an answer cannot create federal question jurisdiction, neither can a counterclaim raising a federal question.

■ CASE VOCABULARY

FEDERAL QUESTION JURISDICTION: The exercise of federal-court power over claims arising under the U.S. Constitution, an act of Congress, or a treaty.

SUBJECT MATTER JURISDICTION: Jurisdiction over the nature of the case and the type of relief sought; the extent to which a court can rule on the conduct of persons or the status of things.

SPECIFIC PERFORMANCE: A court-ordered remedy that requires precise fulfillment of a legal or contractual obligation when monetary damages are inappropriate or inadequate, as when the sale of real estate or a rare article is involved.

WELL–PLEADED COMPLAINT: An original or initial pleading that sufficiently sets forth a claim for relief–by including the grounds for the court's jurisdiction, the basis for the relief claimed, and a demand for judgment–so that a defendant may draft an answer that is responsive to the issues presented. A well-pleaded complaint must raise a controlling issue of federal law for a federal court to have federal-question jurisdiction over the lawsuit.

United Mine Workers of America v. Gibbs

(Union) v. *(Mine Superintendent)*
383 U.S. 715, 86 S.Ct. 1130 (1966)

THE EXERCISE OF PENDENT JURISDICTION IS DISCRETIONARY

■ **INSTANT FACTS** Gibbs (P), a mine superintendent, sued the United Mine Workers (D) in federal court for blocking the opening of a new mine he was managing, claiming violations of both state and federal law.

■ **BLACK LETTER RULE** The exercise of pendent jurisdiction is within the sound discretion of the trial court.

■ **PROCEDURAL BASIS**

Certiorari to review a judgment granting damages on state law claims and dismissing federal claims.

■ **FACTS**

The case grew out of the rivalry between the United Mine Workers (D) and the Southern Labor Union over representation of mine workers in the southern Appalachians. Tennessee Consolidated Coal Company laid off 100 miners represented by Local 5881 of the United Mine Workers (D) when it closed a mine. A few months later, its wholly owned subsidiary hired Gibbs (P) as mine superintendent to open a new mine using members of the Southern Labor Union. Gibbs (P) also had a contract to haul coal from the new mine to the nearest railroad loading point. Armed members of Local 5881 prevented the new mine from opening, threatening Gibbs (P) and injuring an organizer for the Southern Labor Union. Officials of the United Mine Workers (D) were not present; when they learned of the violence, they came to the mine with instructions to establish a limited picket line, quell the violence, and keep the strike from spreading. A peaceful picket line was established and maintained for nine months; no further attempts were made to open the mine. Gibbs (P) lost his job and performed no services under the haulage contract. He claimed that he began to lose other haulage contracts and business as a result of alleged concerted union plan against him. Gibbs (P) brought suit against only the United Mine Workers (D) in federal court. Jurisdiction was premised on violation of § 303 of the Labor Management Relations Act of 1947, which permits recovery of compensatory damages for unlawful secondary boycotts. He also brought state common law claims for alleged conspiracy to interfere with his employment contract and his haulage contract.

The jury verdict found violations of both state and federal law and awarded $60,000 in compensatory damages on the employment contract, $14,000 in compensatory damages on the haulage contract, and $100,000 in punitive damages. The damage award on the haulage contract was set aside on post-verdict motions for lack of proof of damages. The Union's (D) pressure to have Gibbs (P) discharged from employment was found to be a primary boycott, not cognizable under § 303. However, the state law claims of unlawful interference with the employment contract were sustained and judgment was entered for Gibbs (P). This judgment was affirmed on appeal.

■ **ISSUE**

Did the trial court abuse its discretion in exercising pendent jurisdiction over state law claims, even though federal claims were ultimately dismissed?

■ DECISION AND RATIONALE

(Brennan, J.) No. Pendent jurisdiction is a doctrine of discretion, not a plaintiff's right. Pendent jurisdiction exists whenever there is a claim arising under federal law and the relationship between that claim and the state claims permit the conclusion that the entire action is but one case or controversy. The federal question must have sufficient substance to confer subject matter jurisdiction. If both the state and federal claims are such that a plaintiff would ordinarily be expected to try them all in one judicial proceeding, there is power in the federal courts to hear the whole. Justification for pendent jurisdiction lies in considerations of judicial economy, convenience, and fairness to litigants. Absent these considerations, the federal court should not exercise jurisdiction over the state law claims.

If the federal claims are dismissed before trial, the state claims should be dismissed as well. If it appears that the state issues will substantially predominate, then the state claims may be dismissed without prejudice and left for a state proceeding. When the state claim is closely tied to issues of federal policy, such as federal preemption, that is a factor relevant to the exercise of discretion. Other reasons, such as potential jury confusion from conflicting remedies or legal theories that might require separating state and federal claims at trial, may justify refusing to exercise jurisdiction over the state claims. While issues of jurisdiction will ordinarily be decided on the pleadings, the issue of pendent jurisdiction remains open throughout the litigation. Whenever it appears that the state claim constitutes the real body of the case, and the federal claim is only an appendage, then the state claim may be dismissed.

Here, it does not appear that the trial court abused its discretion in proceeding to judgment on the state claim. Even though the federal § 303 claim was ultimately dismissed, the claim was substantial. Although the state and federal claims provided different remedies, the claims arose from the "same nucleus of operative facts" and reflected alternative remedies. The federal issues were not so remote nor did they play such a minor role that in effect only the state claim was tried. It was only on post-verdict motions that all the federal claims were denied, and then some only for lack of proof of damages, not for lack of liability. Finally, the issue of whether the scope of state claims was limited by federal preemption was an additional reason for exercising pendent jurisdiction, because this issue is particularly appropriate for resolution by federal courts. Under the circumstances, although the trial court could have refused to exercise pendent jurisdiction, it was not error to refuse to do so. [The judgment was reversed for failing to meet the burden of proof on the state law claim of conspiracy.]

Analysis:

Congress explicitly ratified *Gibbs* when it adopted 28 U.S.C. § 1367 in 1990. The issues raised in *Gibbs* were before the Supreme Court again in *Owen Equipment & Erection Co. v. Kroger*, 437 U.S. 365 (1978), and *Finley v. United States*, 490 U.S. 545 (1989). As these two cases and passage of § 1367 demonstrate, the courts and Congress have continued to struggle with the exact scope of ancillary and pendent jurisdiction.

■ CASE VOCABULARY

PENDENT JURISDICTION: A court's jurisdiction to hear and determine a claim over which it would not otherwise have jurisdiction, based on the claim's arising from the same transaction or occurrence as another claim that is properly before the court. Pendent jurisdiction has now been codified as supplemental jurisdiction. 28 U.S.C.A. § 1367.

PRIMARY BOYCOTT: A boycott [a concerted refusal to do business with a party to express disapproval of that party's practices] by union members who stop dealing with a former employer.

SECONDARY BOYCOTT: A boycott [a concerted refusal to do business with a party to express disapproval of that party's practices] of the customers or suppliers of a business so that they will withhold their patronage from that business.

SUPPLEMENTAL JURISDICTION: Jurisdiction over a claim that is part of the same case or controversy as another claim over which the court has original jurisdiction. 28 U.S.C.A. § 1367.

Owen Equipment and Erection Company v. Kroger

(Crane Operator) v. *(Widow of Electrocuted Construction Worker)*

437 U.S. 365, 98 S.Ct. 2396 (1978)

ANCILLARY JURISDICTION DOES NOT PERMIT A CLAIM AGAINST A THIRD PARTY WHO DOES NOT HAVE COMPLETE DIVERSITY

■ **INSTANT FACTS** Kroger was electrocuted when a crane operated by Owen Equipment came too close to a power line owned by Omaha Public Power District (D).

■ **BLACK LETTER RULE** A plaintiff in a diversity case cannot rely on ancillary jurisdiction to permit an amendment to a complaint to bring a claim against a non-diverse third-party defendant.

■ **PROCEDURAL BASIS**

On writ of certiorari from a judgment for the plaintiff.

■ **FACTS**

Kroger was electrocuted when a crane he was walking near came in contact with a power line owned by Omaha Public Power District (OPPD) (D). The widow of Kroger (P), a citizen of Iowa, brought a wrongful death action against OPPD (D), a citizen of Nebraska, in federal district court in Nebraska, alleging that its construction, maintenance and operation of the power line caused Kroger's death. Federal jurisdiction was based on diversity of citizenship; there was no federal question. OPPD (D) filed a third-party complaint against Owen Equipment and Erection Company, alleging that Owen owned and operated the crane and that Owen's negligence caused Kroger's death. OPPD (D) moved for summary judgment. While this motion was pending, Kroger (P) was granted leave to amend her complaint naming Owen as an additional defendant. OPPD's (D) motion for summary judgment was granted and trial between Kroger (P) and Owen (now D) followed.

The amended complaint alleged that Owen (D) was a Nebraska corporation with its principal place of business in Nebraska. Owen's (D) answer admitted that it was a Nebraska corporation. At trial, it was disclosed that Owen's (D) principal place of business was in Iowa, which meant that it was also a citizen of Iowa. Owen (D) moved to dismiss for lack of jurisdiction because both Kroger (P) and Owen (D) were citizens of Iowa. The trial court deferred ruling on the motion, and the jury returned a verdict in favor of Kroger (P). The trial court then denied the motion to dismiss. The judgment for Kroger (P) was affirmed on appeal.

■ **ISSUE**

Using a court's ancillary jurisdiction in a case based on diversity of citizenship, can a plaintiff assert a claim against a third-party defendant who does not have complete diversity of citizenship from the plaintiff?

■ **DECISION AND RATIONALE**

(Stewart, J.) No. The relevant statute, 28 U.S.C. § 1332(a)(1), creates diversity jurisdiction. This statute has been consistently held to require complete diversity of citizenship: each defendant must be a citizen of a different state from each plaintiff. Kroger (P) could not have originally brought suit against both

OPPD (D) and Owen (D) because citizens of Iowa would have been on both sides. Her amendment resulted in the same effect; complete diversity was destroyed just as surely as if she had sued Owen (D) initially. The Court of Appeals, relying on *United Mine Workers v. Gibbs*, held that the district court had discretion to adjudicate Kroger's (P) claim against Owen (D) because the claim arose from the same core of operative facts as Kroger's (P) claim against OPPD (D). But *Gibbs* involved pendent jurisdiction, the resolution of state and federal law claims against a single defendant in one action. In contrast, here there is no federal law claim; there are state law claims against two different defendants. *Gibbs* defined the constitutional limits of a federal court's jurisdiction to hear state law claims. However, in additional to these constitutional limits, statutory limits on jurisdiction must also be considered. Here, the statutory limits on diversity jurisdiction require complete diversity. If the reasoning of the court of appeals were accepted, a plaintiff could defeat the statutory requirement of complete diversity simply by suing only those defendants who were diverse and waiting for those defendants to implead the non-diverse defendants. Similarly, if a common nucleus of operative facts were the only basis for ancillary jurisdiction, then there would be no principled basis for not permitting the plaintiff from joining her cause of action against Owen (D) in her original complaint. The statutory requirement of complete diversity would be eviscerated.

Permitting the exercise of ancillary jurisdiction in situations involving impleader, cross-claims, or counterclaims is not inconsistent with this decision. A third-party complaint is factually and logically dependent on resolution of the primary dispute; here, the plaintiff's claim against Owen (D) is new and independent of her claim against OPPD (D). Second, ancillary jurisdiction typically involves claims by a defending party brought into court against its will or by another person whose rights might be lost unless he or she could assert them in an ongoing action in federal court. Here, the plaintiff voluntarily chose to bring suit upon state law claim in federal court. The plaintiff cannot complain if all claims cannot be heard in one action, since the plaintiff is the one who chose federal rather than state court, which could have heard all claims. Reversed.

Analysis:

Note that the Court, in footnote 3, raised, but did not answer, the question of whether the third-party complaint was properly permitted. The third-party complaint did not allege the basis of Owen's (D) liability to OPPD (D); it only alleged that Owen's (D) negligence caused Kroger's death, a problematic basis for a third-party complaint. Note, as does the Court in *Owen Equipment*, that ancillary jurisdiction permits a court to grant the impleading of a third-party defendant even if the addition of that party defeats complete diversity. Congress specifically preserved *Owen Equipment* when it adopted 28 U.S.C. § 1367(b) in 1990.

■ CASE VOCABULARY

ANCILLARY JURISDICTION: A court's jurisdiction to adjudicate claims and proceedings that arise out of a claim that is properly before the court. The concept of ancillary jurisdiction has now been codified, along with the concept of pendent jurisdiction, in the supplemental-jurisdiction statute. 28 U.S.C.A. § 1367.

COMPLETE DIVERSITY: In a multiparty case, diversity between both sides to the lawsuit so that all plaintiffs have different citizenship from all defendants.

DIVERSITY JURISDICTION: A federal court's exercise of authority over a case involving parties from different states and an amount in controversy greater than a statutory minimum (now $75,000). 28 U.S.C.A. § 1332.

Finley v. United States

(Widow) v. *(United States)*

490 U.S. 545, 109 S.Ct. 2003 (1989)

PENDENT JURISDICTION DOES NOT APPLY TO STATE LAW CLAIMS AGAINST INDEPENDENT PARTIES IN A TORT CASE AGAINST THE U.S.

■ **INSTANT FACTS** Finley's (P) husband and children were killed when the plane in which they were riding struck power lines on its approach to the San Diego airport; she sought to add state tort claims against other defendants to her federal court action against the Federal Aviation Agency for negligent operation of runway lights and air traffic control.

■ **BLACK LETTER RULE** Independent parties and factually related state law claims cannot be made part of a Federal Tort Claims Act action against the United States.

■ PROCEDURAL BASIS

On writ of certiorari. The trial court granted the plaintiff's motion to amend her Federal Tort Claim Act complaint to include state tort claims against independent defendants, and the court of appeals reversed.

■ FACTS

Finley's (P) husband and children were killed when the plane in which they were riding struck power lines on its approach to the San Diego airport. Finley (P) brought a state tort action against the San Diego Gas and Electric Company for negligently positioning and illuminating of the power lines and against the City of San Diego for negligent maintenance of the runway lights, which were not operating the night of the crash. When Finley (P) discovered that the Federal Aviation Administration was responsible for the runway lights, she brought a Federal Tort Claims Act action against the United States (D) in federal court. Finley (P) later moved to amend her federal complaint to include state tort claims against San Diego Gas and the City of San Diego. No independent basis for federal jurisdiction over these defendants or claims existed. The trial court granted the motion under *United Mine Workers v. Gibbs* because the claims arose from a common nucleus of operative facts. On an interlocutory appeal, the court of appeals summarily reversed.

■ ISSUE

Does the Federal Tort Claims Act permit an assertion of pendent party jurisdiction over additional parties?

■ DECISION AND RATIONALE:

(Scalia, J.) No. The Federal Tort Claims Act (FTCA) requirement that federal courts have exclusive jurisdiction over claims against the United means that FTCA actions can be brought against the United States and no one else. Parties to related claims cannot be brought into federal courts in FTCA actions. *Gibbs* stands for the proposition that pendent jurisdiction–jurisdiction over nonfederal claims between parties litigating other matters properly before the court–exists whenever the federal and nonfederal claims "derive from a common nucleus of operative facts" and the plaintiff would ordinarily be expected to try them in one proceeding. This case is different, because it involves an issue of jurisdiction over parties not named in any claim that is independently cognizable by the federal court. With respect to the addition of parties, the jurisdictional statutes will be read narrowly.

The *Gibbs* test of a common nucleus of facts was not extended to confer jurisdiction in a diversity action over a different, nondiverse defendant, as in *Owen Equipment & Erection Co. v. Kroger*, 437 U.S. 365 (1978). As in *Kroger,* there must be an examination of the procedural and statutory context in which the nonfederal claim is asserted. Here, the added claims involve added parties over whom no independent basis of jurisdiction exists. Mere factual similarity is inadequate to confer jurisdiction, because neither convenience of the litigants nor consideration of judicial economy can justify extension of ancillary jurisdiction. Moreover, the text of the FTCA conferring jurisdiction over claims "against the United States" means against the United States and no one else. The statute, therefore, defines jurisdiction in a manner that does not reach defendants other than the United States. Affirmed.

■ **DISSENT**

(Blackmun, J.) In the FTCA, Congress has made the federal forum the only forum in which the whole case may be heard. In these circumstances, the sensible result is to permit exercise of pendent-party jurisdiction.

■ **DISSENT**

(Stevens, J.) The court's decision is inconsistent with precedent and sixteen years of federal court experience applying *United Mine Workers v. Gibbs*, 383 U.S. 715 (1966). Following *Gibbs,* courts have recognized that its reasoning applied to cases in which it was necessary to add an additional party on a pendent, nonfederal claim in order to grant complete relief. The FTCA grant of jurisdiction for claims "against the United States" should be read to authorize federal courts to hear state-law claims against a pendent party. The fact that FTCA claims are within exclusive federal jurisdiction and Congressional acceptance of the intervening decisions applying pendent-party jurisdiction to FTCA cases provides a sufficient justification for applying *Gibbs* in this case. Forcing a party to litigate in both federal and state forums impairs the power of federal courts to grant complete relief and creates a bias against the use of federal courts because, if chosen, duplicative litigation will be required. When Congress has indicated its intent that the federal right be litigated in a federal forum, there is no reason to believe that Congress intended that the federal right be diminished by increased costs of litigation in two forums. This is distinct from *Kroger*, where no such federal interest was at stake in a diversity action and all state law claims could be litigated in a state forum.

Analysis:

Finley was essentially reversed by Congress with the passage of 28 U.S.C. § 1367, which defines "supplemental jurisdiction" to include both ancillary and pendent jurisdiction. Section 1367(a) generally authorizes a district court to exercise jurisdiction over a supplemental claim whenever it arises from the same nucleus of facts as the claims that confer the court's original jurisdiction, including authorizing supplemental jurisdiction over claims involving additional parties. In effect, § 1367(a) codifies the scope of supplemental jurisdiction set forth in *Gibbs* for actions that arise from a common nucleus of operative facts. Section 1367(b) implements the rationale of *Owen Equipment*.

■ **CASE VOCABULARY**

FEDERAL TORT CLAIMS ACT: A statute that limits federal sovereign immunity and allows recovery in federal court for tort damages caused by federal employees, but only if the law of the state where the injury occurred would hold a private person liable for the injury. 28 U.S.C.A. §§ 2671—2680.

PENDENT–PARTY JURISDICTION: A court's jurisdiction to adjudicate a claim against a party who is not otherwise subject to the court's jurisdiction, because the claim by or against that party arises from the same transaction or occurrence as another claim that is properly before the court.

Burnett v. Birmingham Board of Education

(Employee) v. *(School Board)*

861 F.Supp. 1036 (N.D. Ala. 1994)

BOTH FEDERAL AND STATE LAW CLAIMS CAN BE REMANDED TO STATE COURT WHEN STATE LAW CLAIMS PREDOMINATE

■ **INSTANT FACTS** Burnett (P) and other employees of the Birmingham Board of Education (D) brought an action in state court for back wages under their employment contract; the plaintiffs sought remand to state court following removal to federal court.

■ **BLACK LETTER RULE** When state law claims predominate, a case including both state and federal law claims that has been removed to federal court can be remanded to state court.

■ **PROCEDURAL BASIS**

Hearing on the plaintiffs' motion to remand the action to state court following removal to federal court by the defendants.

■ **FACTS**

Burnett and others (P) were employees of the Birmingham Board of Education (D). They brought a state court action seeking a writ of mandamus requiring the defendants to pay them in accord with the pay scale in their contract. In addition to breach of contract claims, they "threw in" a claim that they were in some way deprived of constitutional due process and entitled to relief under 42 U.S.C. § 1983. The defendants removed the action to federal court pursuant to 28 U.S.C. §§ 1331 and 1343 on the ground that a federal question under § 1983 was presented. The plaintiffs filed a motion to remand the entire matter to state court under 28 U.S.C. § 1441(c), asserting that because state law predominated the entire case should be remanded.

■ **ISSUE**

Does 28 U.S.C. § 1441(c) permit a remand of both state and federal claims when the state law claims predominate?

■ **DECISION AND RATIONALE**

(Acker, J.) Yes. Remand under 28 U.S.C. § 1441(c) is not available only to cases removed solely pursuant to § 1331. Section 1441(c) provides that a district court can remove "an entire case" when a separate claim is within the jurisdiction conferred by § 1331 "or, in its discretion, may remand all matters in which State law predominates." The language of § 1441(c) cannot be interpreted to create an exception prohibiting remand for any cases that also contain a claim under § 1983 (and jurisdiction under § 1343) as to which state courts have concurrent jurisdiction. In the present case, removal by the defendant was invoked under both § 1331 and § 1343, so remand under § 1441(c) was proper, even under the defendants' argument that remand is only proper when solely § 1331 is invoked. The fact that the plaintiffs invoked redundant jurisdiction under both § 1331 and § 1343 does not defeat remand. The clear trend among courts is to remand both state and federal claims when state law predominates. Here, the federal law claim was tacked onto the state law claims, so clearly the state law claims predominate. The state law claims are not pendent to the federal claims. Therefore, remand of the entire matter is proper.

Analysis:

The court in *Burnett* noted that the plaintiffs could have easily defeated the initial motion to remove the matter to federal court by attacking the defendants' procedural defect of failing to include a copy of the summons served on the board with their notice of removal. This omission was a fatal defect, but by failing to raise it within thirty days as required by 28 U.S.C. § 1447(c), the plaintiffs waived the defect. Note also that, if the plaintiffs had not used the "kitchen sink" approach to pleading, as described by the court, and had not thrown in the § 1983 claim, there would have been no basis for removal in the first place.

■ CASE VOCABULARY

MANDAMUS: A writ issued by a superior court to compel a lower court or a government officer to perform mandatory or purely ministerial duties correctly.

REMAND: To send (a case or claim) back to the court or tribunal from which it came for some further action.

REMOVAL: The transfer of an action from state to federal court.

CHAPTER NINE

Choice of Federal or State Law—The Erie Doctrine

Erie Railroad Co. v. Tompkins

Instant Facts: Tompkins (P), alleging that federal general common law should govern, brought a negligence action against Erie (D) in federal court for injuries suffered.

Black Letter Rule: Federal courts must apply the substantive common law of the state to diversity cases.

Guaranty Trust Co. v. York

Instant Facts: York (P) sued Guaranty Trust (D) in federal court in order to avoid the application of the state's statute of limitations, which would have barred the claim.

Black Letter Rule: Federal courts with diversity jurisdiction must apply the state's statute of limitations or other procedural rules if they have a significant effect on the outcome of the case.

Byrd v. Blue Ridge Rural Electric Cooperative, Inc.

Instant Facts: Byrd (P), who sued Blue Ridge Rural Electric Cooperative, Inc. (D) for negligence, appealed a court of appeals decision that he was not entitled to a jury trial in federal court because he would not have been entitled to a jury trial under state law.

Black Letter Rule: A state rule that requires a judge to make a factual determination does not prevent federal courts from having a jury make the determination if federal policy in enacting the federal rule outweighs the state policy for the state rule.

Hanna v. Plumer

Instant Facts: Hanna (P), who sued in Massachusetts district court for negligence arising out of an automobile accident, appealed a court of appeals ruling that her substituted service of process under the Federal Rules of Civil Procedure was not sufficient in a federal court diversity case.

Black Letter Rule: The Federal Rules of Civil Procedure regarding service of process apply to federal diversity cases, even if a state rule conflicts.

Walker v. Armco Steel Corp.

Instant Facts: Walker (P), a carpenter injured by a faulty nail, brought suit in a federal district court within the state limitations period, but failed to serve process within the time period required by the state statute.

Black Letter Rule: State law controls tolling of the state statute of limitations in a state law action filed in federal court under diversity jurisdiction.

Gasperini v. Center for Humanities, Inc.

Instant Facts: Gasperini (P), a photographer whose slides were lost by Center for Humanities, Inc. (D), challenged the federal court of appeals vacation of a judgment in his favor because the lower court used the state's standard of review.

Black Letter Rule: A federal appellate court can give effect to state statutes regarding the reexamination of jury awards without violating the Seventh Amendment's reexamination clause.

Erie Railroad Co. v. Tompkins

(Railroad) v. *(Injured Pedestrian)*

304 U.S. 64, 58 S.Ct. 817 (1938)

FEDERAL COURTS MUST APPLY STATE SUBSTANTIVE LAW

■ **INSTANT FACTS** Tompkins (P), alleging that federal general common law should govern, brought a negligence action against Erie (D) in federal court for injuries suffered.

■ **BLACK LETTER RULE** Federal courts must apply the substantive common law of the state to diversity cases.

■ PROCEDURAL BASIS

Certiorari to review an affirmance of a damage award recovered against a railroad based on federal general common law.

■ FACTS

Tompkins (P) brought a negligence action against Erie Railroad (D) for injuries he suffered when a door from the defendant's train hit him while he was walking along the railroad right-of-way. The circuit court affirmed the judgment in favor of Tompkins, holding that Erie Railroad was liable under the general law that allowed federal courts to make decisions independent of state law. The railroad argued that is was not liable under state common law and that state common law should have been applied to the case.

■ ISSUE

Should general federal common law be applied to cases in federal court involving parties from different states?

■ DECISION AND RATIONALE

(Brandeis, J.) No. There is no federal general common law. Except in matters governed by the federal Constitution or Congressional acts, a federal court must apply the law of the state. No clause in the Constitution gives Congress the right to impose substantive common law rules on a state, and *Swift v. Tyson*, which held that federal courts could exercise an independent judgment, is unconstitutional. By applying a general federal common law, courts invaded rights that the Constitution reserves for the states. Reversed.

■ CONCURRENCE

(Reed, J.) The court should not have declared *Swift v. Tyson* to be unconstitutional. In disapproving *Swift v. Tyson*, the court needed only note that "the laws" include state court decisions, in which case the court could simply say that the course previously pursued was erroneous, rather than unconstitutional.

■ DISSENT

(Butler, J.) The issue of whether there is a federal general common law, a constitutional question, need not have been considered. Pursuant to the common law of Pennsylvania and other states throughout the country, the evidence required a finding that plaintiff was guilty of contributory negligence, so that the judgment should be reversed on that ground.

Analysis:

The *Erie* case overturned *Swift v. Tyson*, which held that federal courts exercising diversity jurisdiction in matters of general jurisprudence need not apply the unwritten law of the state as declared by the state's highest court, but that they were free to exercise their independent judgment regarding what the state's common law is or should be. *Erie* held that the *Swift* doctrine was an unconstitutional assumption of state powers by the federal courts. The *Erie* holding is often considered one of the most important in American law, and the majority decision has far-reaching implications. Not only does *Erie* affirm the concepts of state sovereignty and autonomy, but it also eliminates forum-shopping because the same law applies whether the case is brought in federal or state court.

■ CASE VOCABULARY

GENERAL FEDERAL COMMON LAW: In the period before *Erie v. Tompkins*, judge-made law developed by federal courts decided disputes in diversity cases. Since *Erie* was announced in 1938, a federal court has been bound to apply, as a general matter, the law of the state in which it sits. Thus, although there is a "federal common law," there is no *general* federal common law applicable to all disputes heard in federal court.

DIVERSITY: A federal court's exercise of authority over a case involving parties from different states and an amount in controversy greater than the statutory minimum ($75,000). 28 U.S.C.A. § 1332.

Guaranty Trust Co. v. York

(Bond Trustee) v. *(Victim Note–Holder)*
326 U.S. 99, 65 S.Ct. 1464 (1945)

FEDERAL COURTS MUST APPLY STATE PROCEDURAL RULES IF THE RULES DETERMINE THE OUTCOME OF THE CASE

■ **INSTANT FACTS** York (P) sued Guaranty Trust (D) in federal court in order to avoid the application of the state's statute of limitations, which would have barred the claim.

■ **BLACK LETTER RULE** Federal courts with diversity jurisdiction must apply the state's statute of limitations or other procedural rules if they have a significant effect on the outcome of the case.

■ **PROCEDURAL BASIS**

Certiorari to review the reversal of summary judgment based upon a state statute of limitations in federal court diversity-of-jurisdiction case.

■ **FACTS**

York (P) sued Guaranty Trust (D) in a federal diversity action for breach of fiduciary duty, allegedly arising out Guaranty Trust's failure to protect the plaintiff's interest in the trust. Guaranty Trust (D) appealed the reversal of summary judgment that barred York (P) from bringing a breach of trust action against Guaranty Trust (D). The court of appeals held that the suit could be brought on the equity side of a federal district court because the federal court was not required to apply the state statute of limitations that would govern the suit had it been filed in state court. Guaranty Trust (D) argued that because the suit was time barred under state law, York should not be able to use diversity jurisdiction to circumvent the state statute of limitations and obtain a result that would not be available under the applicable state law.

■ **ISSUE**

Are federal courts bound by the state statute of limitations in an equity suit based on state law and diversity of citizenship?

■ **DECISION AND RATIONALE**

(Frankfurter, J.) Yes. If substantive state-created rights are the basis for an equity action in the federal courts, the federal courts are bound to follow the law of the state. However, the question of whether a state statute of limitations is substantive or procedural is immaterial because the policy that underlies *Erie Railroad Co. v. Tompkins* requires that the outcome of litigation in a federal court exercising diversity jurisdiction should provide the same outcome as if the case were tried in a state court. The fact that one party is from a different state should not allow the other party the advantage of not being subject to a state law that would time-bar the claim. Reversed.

■ **DISSENT**

(Rutledge, J.) The Court should not have addressed the broad constitutional issue. Instead, it should have sent the case back to the court of appeals to decide the simple question of whether the cause of action was time-barred under the applicable state law. Also, the statute of limitations is a remedial right, not a substantive right, and *Erie Railroad Co. v. Tompkins* applies to substantive rights. Congress, not the Court, should expand *Erie* to encompass remedial rights.

Analysis:

Guaranty Trust expanded *Erie* to provide that if the federal court's jurisdiction is based on diversity, a federal court should reach the same outcome as a state court, regardless of whether the remedy sought was of law or equity. The case also addresses the issue of whether a state statute of limitations is effectively substantive, so that it should be controlling in federal court. However, the court did not rely on the terms "substantive" and "procedural" because of their different meanings in different contexts. Instead, the court established what is now known as the "outcome-determination" test, so that a federal court should follow a state rule that is outcome-determinative whether it is labeled procedural or substantive.

■ CASE VOCABULARY

DIVERSITY OF CITIZENSHIP: A basis for federal-court jurisdiction that exists when (1) a case is between citizens of different states, or between a citizen of a state and an alien, and (2) the matter in controversy exceeds a specific value (now $75,000). 28 U.S.C.A. § 1332. For purposes of diversity jurisdiction, a corporation is considered a citizen of both the state of incorporation and the state of its principal place of business. An unincorporated association, such as a partnership, is considered a citizen of each state where at least one of its members is a citizen.

EQUITABLE REMEDY: A nonmonetary remedy, such as an injunction or specific performance, obtained when monetary damages cannot adequately redress the injury.

Byrd v. Blue Ridge Rural Electric Cooperative, Inc.

(Injured Construction Worker) v. *(Contracting Electric Company)*

356 U.S. 525, 78 S.Ct. 893 (1958)

FEDERAL COURTS USE A BALANCING TEST TO DETERMINE WHETHER FEDERAL LAW APPLIES

■ **INSTANT FACTS** Byrd (P), who sued Blue Ridge Rural Electric Cooperative, Inc. (D) for negligence, appealed a court of appeals decision that he was not entitled to a jury trial in federal court because he would not have been entitled to a jury trial under state law.

■ **BLACK LETTER RULE** A state rule that requires a judge to make a factual determination does not prevent federal courts from having a jury make the determination if federal policy in enacting the federal rule outweighs the state policy for the state rule.

■ **PROCEDURAL BASIS**

Certiorari granted to determine whether it was error for the court of appeals to direct judgment in favor of Blue Ridge in a negligence action.

■ **FACTS**

Byrd (P) was employed by a construction company that had a contract with Blue Ridge Electric Cooperative (D) to build power stations and power lines. While working as a lineman, Byrd (P) was injured and sued for damages. A jury returned a judgment in Byrd's favor. However, the court of appeals reversed and directed a verdict in favor of Blue Ridge Electric Cooperative. Blue Ridge (D) claimed that Byrd's exclusive remedy under state law was through the South Carolina Workmen's Compensation Act, and that he was not entitled to a jury trial under state law.

■ **ISSUE**

Must the federal court in a diversity action apply the state rule that would have prevented the petitioner from having a jury trial in state court?

■ **DECISION AND RATIONALE**

(Brennan, J.) No. Federal policy favoring jury decisions of disputed fact questions should not yield to a state rule solely to further the objective of having the same outcome whether in federal or state court. State rules should not disrupt the judge-jury relationship in federal courts. In addition, there is no certainty that there would be a different result in a federal court simply because a jury decided the factual issue. The likelihood of a different result is not so strong as to require the federal practice of jury determination to yield to the state rule of court determination in the interest of uniformity of outcome.

■ **DISSENT**

(Whitaker, J.) South Carolina law requires courts, not juries, to determine a factual issue in this case, and it follows that in a diversity case, a judge must decide the issue. The result of a federal court with diversity jurisdiction may not be substantially different than the result would be in the state court. A federal court should not substantially affect the enforcement of a right that is granted by a state.

■ DISSENT

(Frankfurter, J.) The court of appeals should not be reversed because the decision to enter judgment for the defendant is amply sustained as to whether or not the issue was one for a court to decide. If the question was for the court, the court of appeals resolved it in accordance with state law and, if the issue was such that it would have to be submitted to a jury, the court of appeals found that the evidence would have required the court to grant a directed verdict in favor of the defendant.

■ DISSENT

(Harlan, J.) Agreeing with Justice Frankfurter, Justice Harlan notes that petitioner would not be able to produce any evidence that would change the directed verdict.

Analysis:

The Supreme Court found that federal policy favors juries making determinations of disputed fact questions. The *Guaranty Trust* policy that federal courts hearing a diversity case must reach the same outcome as a state court does not take precedence over federal policy favoring jury determination of factual questions. *Byrd* effectively expands *Guaranty Trust's* outcome-determination test by adding a balancing approach. The court also notes that several factors must be balanced in deciding whether to apply federal or state rules to federal diversity cases, including the relationship between the state rule and the underlying state rights.

■ CASE VOCABULARY

DIRECTED VERDICT: A ruling by a trial judge taking a case from the jury because the evidence will permit only one reasonable verdict.

AFFIRMATIVE DEFENSE: A defendant's assertion raising new facts and arguments that, if true, will defeat the plaintiff's or prosecution's claim, even if all allegations in the complaint are true. Examples of affirmative defenses include duress and contributory negligence (in a civil case) and insanity and self-defense (in a criminal case).

Hanna v. Plumer

(Injured Person) v. *(Executor of Deceased Driver's Estate)*

380 U.S. 460, 85 S.Ct. 1136 (1965)

FEDERAL RULES OF CIVIL PROCEDURE APPLY OVER STATE RULES IN A FEDERAL DIVERSITY ACTION

■ **INSTANT FACTS** Hanna (P), who sued in Massachusetts district court for negligence arising out of an automobile accident, appealed a court of appeals ruling that her substituted service of process under the Federal Rules of Civil Procedure was not sufficient in a federal court diversity case.

■ **BLACK LETTER RULE** The Federal Rules of Civil Procedure regarding service of process apply to federal diversity cases, even if a state rule conflicts.

■ **PROCEDURAL BASIS**

Certiorari to review the court of appeals' affirmance of the trial court's decision to grant summary judgment because Hanna's (P) service of process did not comply with state law requirements.

■ **FACTS**

Hanna (P), who was injured in an automobile accident, brought a personal injury suit against Plumer (D), the executor of the negligent driver's estate. Hanna made service of process in compliance with the Federal Rules of Civil Procedure, by leaving a copy with Plumer's (D) wife at their residence. Under Massachusetts law, the plaintiff was required to make service of process personally, in-hand to the defendant. The court of appeals affirmed the trial court's decision that service of process had not been properly made under state law, and that Plumer (D) was entitled to summary judgment. Hanna argued that the Federal Rules of Civil Procedure, not state law, governed service of process for cases before federal courts, including diversity cases.

■ **ISSUE**

In a civil action where federal court jurisdiction is based upon diversity, must service of process be made in compliance with state law?

■ **DECISION AND RATIONALE**

(Warren, J.) No. The Federal Rules of Civil Procedure may govern the method of service of process in diversity actions, even if the state law conflicts. Although the *Erie* doctrine requires a federal court to apply certain state laws to a diversity case, it does not invalidate or void a federal rule. Applying the Federal Rules of Civil Procedure is appropriate even though it is outcome-determinative because it causes the litigation to continue, whereas holding that the state service of process rule applied would end the litigation. One of the purposes of the Federal Rules of Civil Procedure was to bring uniformity to the federal court. The federal rules must not cease to function every time the Court alters the enforcement of state-created rights. Reversed.

■ CONCURRENCE

(Harlan, J.) The correct approach in determining whether to apply a state or federal rule is to determine whether the choice of rule would substantially affect the decisions that are left to state regulation. The majority opinion goes too far: the state had a strong policy interest in its service of process requirements, and the state rule should apply. However, in this case, applying federal rules for service of process instead of the state rules did not undermine the state's underlying policy concerns.

Analysis:

Pursuant to *Hanna*, the *Erie* doctrine does not obligate federal courts in diversity cases to invalidate its rules because they conflict with state rules. The Constitution provides for a federal court system, and Congress is empowered to make rules governing its operation (28 U.S.C. § 2072). The outcome-determinative test is not meant to determine the validity of the Federal Rules of Civil Procedure, and it should be applied only in those situations in which the rule would encourage forum shopping or cause inequitable application of law.

■ CASE VOCABULARY

SERVICE OF PROCESS: The formal delivery of a writ, summons, or other legal process.

OUTCOME–DETERMINATIVE TEST: A test used to determine whether an issue is substantive for purposes of the *Erie* doctrine by examining the issue's potential effect on the outcome of litigation.

Walker v. Armco Steel Corp.

(Injured Carpenter) v. *(Nail Manufacturer)*

446 U.S. 740, 100 S.Ct. 1978 (1980)

FEDERAL RULES OF CIVIL PROCEDURE CANNOT BE USED TO TOLL THE STATE STATUTE OF LIMITATIONS

■ **INSTANT FACTS** Walker (P), a carpenter injured by a faulty nail, brought suit in a federal district court within the state limitations period, but failed to serve process within the time period required by the state statute.

■ **BLACK LETTER RULE** State law controls tolling of the state statute of limitations in a state law action filed in federal court under diversity jurisdiction.

■ **PROCEDURAL BASIS**

Certiorari to review the court of appeals' decision, which found that a federal court should follow state law rather than the Federal Rules of Civil Procedure in determining whether to toll the state statute of limitations.

■ **FACTS**

Walker (P), a carpenter who was struck in the eye when a nail manufactured by Armco Steel (D) shattered, filed suit against Armco Steel within the state statute of limitations, but did not make service of process until after the statute of limitations had expired. The state law required service of process to be made within sixty days after the expiration of the statute of limitations as long as the suit was timely filed. Service was late under state law, but would not have been late under the Federal Rules of Civil Procedure. The district court dismissed the complaint because the statute of limitations had expired. The court of appeals affirmed, holding that the sixty-day tolling provision was an integral part of the state statute of limitations. Walker argued that the Federal Rules of Civil Procedure governed for all purposes regarding the manner in which an action is commenced in federal court, including the tolling of the statute of limitations.

■ **ISSUE**

Should the federal court in a diversity action follow state law, instead of the Federal Rules of Civil Procedure, in determining when a statute of limitations period is tolled?

■ **DECISION AND RATIONALE**

(Marshall, J.) Yes. The state statute is a statement of the state's substantive decision that actual service and notice are an integral part of its statute of limitations. The ending of the limitation period establishes a deadline after which the defendant may have peace of mind. Thus, the service rule is a policy determination that is inseparable from the statute of limitations. Also, there is no direct conflict between the federal and state law, and the Federal Rules of Civil Procedure do not replace policy determinations under state law. In the absence of a federal rule directly on point, state service requirements that are an integral part of the state statute of limitations should control in a federal diversity action based on state law. Affirmed.

Analysis:

Walker presents another step in the analysis that a federal court must conduct when applying a federal rule and a state rule would provide differing results. *Walker* holds that unless there is a direct conflict between a federal rule and state law in a diversity case, the state law will apply. The Walker court reaffirmed its decision in *Ragan v. Merchants Transfer & Warehouse Co.*, 337 U.S. 530 (1949), which held that a Kansas statute requiring service of process to commence an action, not Rule 3 of the Federal Rules of Civil Procedure, controlled in a diversity action.

■ **CASE VOCABULARY**

TOLLING STATUTE: A law that interrupts the running of the statute of limitations in certain situations, as when the defendant cannot be served with process in the forum jurisdiction.

ACTUAL NOTICE: Notice given directly to, or received personally by, a party.

Gasperini v. Center for Humanities, Inc.

(*Photographer*) v. (*Slide User*)

518 U.S. 415, 116 S.Ct. 2211 (1996)

STATE LAW GOVERNING JURY–AWARD STANDARDS OF REVIEW SURVIVES NOTWITHSTANDING THE SEVENTH AMENDMENT

■ **INSTANT FACTS** Gasperini (P), a photographer whose slides were lost by Center for Humanities, Inc. (D), challenged the federal court of appeals vacation of a judgment in his favor because the lower court used the state's standard of review.

■ **BLACK LETTER RULE** A federal appellate court can give effect to state statutes regarding the reexamination of jury awards without violating the Seventh Amendment's reexamination clause.

■ **PROCEDURAL BASIS**

Certiorari to review the court of appeals' affirmance of the decision setting aside a jury verdict as excessive.

■ **FACTS**

A federal court awarded Gasperini (P), a photojournalist, $450,000 in compensatory damages because Center for Humanities (D) lost 300 slides that Gasperini (P) had taken during the seven years he worked in Central America. The petitioner alleged several state-law claims for relief in a suit commenced in the federal court under diversity jurisdiction. At trial, witnesses testified that the value of each lost slide was $1500. The court of appeals vacated the jury's verdict because the testimony on the industry standard as to the worth of the slides was not sufficient to justify the verdict. The court of appeals held that $450,000 materially deviated from an amount that could be considered reasonable compensation. The court of appeals relied on a New York rule of civil procedure that allowed New York appellate courts to review the size of jury verdicts and to order new trials in the event a damages award was unreasonable.

■ **ISSUE**

Should a federal court apply the New York law controlling review of damage awards that are excessive or inadequate?

■ **DECISION AND RATIONALE**

(Ginsberg, J.) Yes. New York rules for review of excessive or inadequate jury awards provide that a judicial check must determine if the award "deviates materially" from tolerable awards. The federal standard provides that an award will be overturned if it "shocks the court's conscience." In *Gasperini*, the court found that New York law governed. New York's standard of review for jury awards was enacted with substantive objectives. If the federal court were to use a "shocks the conscience" standard of review, there would be substantial differences in the variations between state and federal monetary judgments. Although the Seventh Amendment governs proceedings in federal court and bears on the trial functions of the judge and jury, confining federal review to an abuse-of-discretion standard in a case involving state law rights is reconcilable with the Seventh Amendment. New York's interest in having its substantive law guide damages can be respected without disrupting the federal court system. Vacated and remanded.

■ DISSENT

(Scalia, J.) The majority did not give enough effect to the Seventh Amendment's reexamination clause or to Rule 59(a) of the Federal Rules of Civil Procedure, which governs new trials. The Seventh Amendment bars federal appellate courts from reviewing a jury's determination of damages or any other factual determination made by a jury in a federal diversity case.

Analysis:

The Court also held that the Seventh Amendment's guarantee of a trial by jury prohibited federal courts from vacating jury verdicts in federal diversity cases, even when they applied state standards. The Court found that New York's "deviates materially" standard is both procedural and substantive—procedural in that it assigns decision-making authority to the state appellate courts, and substantive in that it controls how much a plaintiff can be awarded. By characterizing the state law as substantive, the majority is able to justify its holding that the Second Circuit appellate court should have applied New York's standard to review the jury verdict. Commentators disagree on whether this holding is adequately justified, and many find Scalia's dissent compelling.

■ CASE VOCABULARY

EXCESSIVE VERDICT: A verdict that results from the jury's passion or prejudice and thereby shocks the court's conscience.

ABUSE OF DISCRETION: An adjudicator's failure to exercise sound, reasonable, and legal decision-making. An appellate court's standard for reviewing a decision that is asserted to be grossly unsound, unreasonable, or illegal.

CHAPTER TEN

Finality and Preclusion

Car Carriers, Inc. v. Ford Motor Company

Instant Facts: Car Carriers, Inc. (P) brought an action accusing Ford Motor Company (D) of violating antitrust laws, and, after its claim was dismissed, brought an action under the Racketeer Influenced and Corrupt Organizations Act (RICO) and the Interstate Commerce Act.

Black Letter Rule: Under the doctrine of res judicata, once a transaction has caused an injury, all claims arising from the transaction must be brought in one suit or they are lost.

Gonzalez v. Banco Central Corp.

Instant Facts: The Gonzalez plaintiffs (P), who believed they were misled by real estate developers and lenders, sued the lenders and sellers, alleging that their interests were not represented by an earlier group of similar plaintiffs who sued the defendants on the basis of the same set of facts and causes of action.

Black Letter Rule: Res judicata does not apply to preclude an action by a second set of plaintiffs who were not parties to the original suit, were not in privity with the parties of the original suit, did not have the opportunity to exercise substantial control of the original suit and were not virtually represented by the parties in the original suit.

Hoult v. Hoult

Instant Facts: Father, after an earlier trial in which he was required to pay damages to his daughter, brought an action alleging that his adult daughter defamed him by stating in letters that he had raped her.

Black Letter Rule: An issue not explicitly decided in an earlier trial may be decided for collateral estoppel purposes if it constituted a logical, practical and necessary part of the decision reached.

Jarosz v. Palmer

Instant Facts: Jarosz (P), a minority shareholder of several corporations who brought suit against Palmer (D), an attorney who had been involved in forming the corporations, asserted claims for breach of contract and fiduciary duty, malpractice, and violations of consumer protection statutes.

Black Letter Rule: A prior decision has an issue-preclusion effect only if the issue had a bearing on the outcome of the earlier case.

Parklane Hosiery Co., Inc. v. Shore

Instant Facts: Shore (P), a shareholder in Parklane Hosiery Co. (D), brought a class action against the corporation, alleging that Parklane Hosiery (D) had issued a materially false and misleading proxy statement involving a merger.

Black Letter Rule: Defendants who receive a full and fair opportunity to litigate the claims against it are collaterally estopped to relitigate the issues, even when they are sued by a different plaintiff, unless a second plaintiff could have easily joined in the original suit or it would be unfair to the defendant.

Federated Department Stores, Inc. v. Moitie

Instant Facts: Moitie (P) and others brought private antitrust suits against Federated Department Stores (D), alleging price fixing of women's clothing.

Black Letter Rule: The doctrine of res judicata does not include an equitable exception.

Allen v. McCurry

Instant Facts: McCurry (P), who had been found guilty of drug possession and sued Allen (D) and other police officers for alleged violation of McCurry's constitution rights against unlawful search and seizure, sought to have his claims heard in federal court.

Black Letter Rule: Collateral estoppel applies to 42 U.S.C. § 1983 claims if the issues involved have been fully heard in a state court.

Car Carriers, Inc. v. Ford Motor Company

(*Car Transporter*) v. (*Car Manufacturer*)

789 F.2d 589 (7th Cir. 1986)

A FINAL JUDGMENT ON THE MERITS PROHIBITS FURTHER CLAIMS BY PARTIES BASED ON THE SAME CAUSE OF ACTION

■ **INSTANT FACTS** Car Carriers, Inc. (P) brought an action accusing Ford Motor Company (D) of violating antitrust laws, and, after its claim was dismissed, brought an action under the Racketeer Influenced and Corrupt Organizations Act (RICO) and the Interstate Commerce Act.

■ **BLACK LETTER RULE** Under the doctrine of res judicata, once a transaction has caused an injury, all claims arising from the transaction must be brought in one suit or they are lost.

■ **PROCEDURAL BASIS**

Car Carriers, Inc. (P) sought review of a decision that dismissed its RICO action against defendants as barred by res judicata.

■ **FACTS**

Car Carriers, Inc. (P) brought an action against Ford Motor Company (D) under the Sherman Act, which action was dismissed for the plaintiffs' failure to suffer that type of harm addressed by the act. Later, the appellants brought an action under the Racketeer Influenced and Corrupt Organizations Act (RICO) and the Interstate Commerce Act. The district court dismissed the RICO action as barred by res judicata because the claims were based on the same set of facts as the earlier action that had been dismissed. Car Carriers, Inc. (P) argued that the RICO action contained additional facts that were not discoverable when the first cause of action was filed, and that the court's fact-based test for res judicata should be set aside in favor of an analysis that would differentiate causes of action based on the rights, duties and injuries allegedly addressed by each claim.

■ **ISSUE**

Is the present litigation barred by an earlier lawsuit under the doctrine of res judicata?

■ **DECISION AND RATIONALE**

(Ripple, J.) Yes. Under res judicata, a final judgment on the merits bars further claims by the parties or their privies based on the same cause of action. Prior litigation bars issues that were raised and decided in the earlier litigation and issues that could have been raised in the earlier litigation. Res judicata should be defined broadly enough to encourage parties to present all related claims at one time. The fundamental policy behind res judicata is that those who have contested an issue must be bound by the results and that matters are forever settled once they have been tried. The RICO and Interstate Commerce actions could have been brought with the original action based on The Sherman Act. All of the plaintiffs' claims were part of the same cause of action and arose from a single core of operable facts. It would undermine the basic policy of res judicata to allow appellants to access the courts again on this matter. Affirmed.

Analysis:

Res judicata applies not only to issues that were raised in the initial cause of action, but also to any issues that could have been raised in the first cause of action. A change in legal theory does not create a new cause of action. Also, federal rules regarding dismissal apply to dismissals in federal courts for failure to state a cause of action upon which relief can be granted. Therefore, a motion to dismiss for failure to state a claim is deemed to be an adjudication on the merits for res judicata purposes unless the judge states that the claim is dismissed without prejudice.

CASE VOCABULARY

RES JUDICATA: An issue that has been definitely settled by judicial decision. An affirmative defense barring the same parties from litigating a second lawsuit on the same claim, or any other claim arising from the same transaction or series of transactions and that could have been—but was not—raised in the first suit. The three essential elements are (1) an earlier decision on the same issue, (2) a final judgment on the merits, and (3) the involvement of the same parties in privity with the original parties.

PENDENT JURISDICTION: A court's jurisdiction to hear and determine a claim over which it would not otherwise have jurisdiction, based on the claim arising from the same transaction or occurrence as another claim that is properly before the court. Pendant jurisdiction has now been codified as supplemental jurisdiction. 28 U.S.C. § 1367.

Gonzalez v. Banco Central Corp.

(Purchasers) v. *(Financing Bank)*

27 F.3d 751 (1st Cir. 1994)

RES JUDICATA DOES NOT APPLY TO PLAINTIFFS WHO WERE NOT PARTIES OR IN PRIVITY WITH PARTIES IN THE INITIAL SUIT

■ **INSTANT FACTS** The Gonzalez plaintiffs (P), who believed they were misled by real estate developers and lenders, sued the lenders and sellers, alleging that their interests were not represented by an earlier group of similar plaintiffs who sued the defendants on the basis of the same set of facts and causes of action.

■ **BLACK LETTER RULE** Res judicata does not apply to preclude an action by a second set of plaintiffs who were not parties to the original suit, were not in privity with the parties of the original suit, did not have the opportunity to exercise substantial control of the original suit and were not virtually represented by the parties in the original suit.

■ **PROCEDURAL BASIS**

Appeal from a district court decision dismissing the plaintiffs' suit against the defendants on the ground that res judicata barred the action.

■ **FACTS**

The Gonzalez plaintiffs (P), a group of land purchasers, sued Banco Central Corp. (D) and others claiming they had been duped in a land deal. Because they were not permitted to join the initial suit filed by another group of plaintiffs (the Rodriguez plaintiffs), they filed a later action alleging the same facts and claims. The Rodriguez plaintiffs' case was mishandled, and the plaintiffs ultimately lost. The Gonzalez plaintiffs were represented by the same attorneys who handled the Rodriguez plaintiffs' case and alleged the same issues that the Rodriguez plaintiffs had already lost. The district court dismissed their action in its entirety on the basis of res judicata. The Gonzalez plaintiffs alleged that the Rodriquez plaintiffs did not represent their interests because the Gonzalez plaintiffs were not a party to the suit and because they were not in privity with the Rodriguez plaintiffs.

■ **ISSUE**

When the plaintiffs were neither parties to, nor in privity with the plaintiffs in an earlier action, may their claims be dismissed under the principles of res judicata?

■ **DECISION AND RATIONALE**

(Selya, J.) No. The earlier case resulted in a final judgment. The second case involves claims that arise from the same series of transactions and are sufficiently identical to that cause of action. However, the third test for res judicata is whether the parties are identical. Res judicata would bar the same parties or parties in privity from relitigating the same claim. Although res judicata can sometimes operate to bar an

---

action by persons who were technically not parties to the initial action, a court must be careful when applying res judicata to nonparties. For res judicata to apply, the litigants must have had a full and fair opportunity to litigate their claim. If a nonparty had the chance to participate vicariously in the earlier litigation by exercising substantial control or having the opportunity to exercise some control, the court could impute the status of the original parties to the nonparty and preclude its claims. In this case, the plaintiffs did not have the opportunity to exercise substantial control over the earlier litigation, and they were not virtually represented by the Rodriguez plaintiffs in the earlier suit. As a result, res judicata does not apply to the Gonzalez plaintiffs. Reversed.

Analysis:

There is no bright-line test for determining when res judicata bars a later claim. In applying the doctrine of res judicata, a court must review all three components: (1) a final judgment on the merits in an earlier suit, (2) sufficiently identical causes of action asserted in the earlier and later suits, and (3) sufficiently identical parties in the two suits. The particular fact situation in each case will determine the outcome.

■ CASE VOCABULARY

PRIVITY: The connection or relationship between two parties, each having a legally recognized interest in the same subject matter (such as a transaction, proceeding, or piece of property); mutuality of interest.

VIRTUAL REPRESENTATION: A party's maintenance of an action on behalf of others with a similar interest, as a class does in a class action.

Hoult v. Hoult

(Father) v. *(Daughter)*

157 F.3d 29 (1st Cir. 1998)

AN ISSUE MAY BE DECIDED FOR COLLATERAL ESTOPPEL PURPOSES EVEN IF IT WAS NOT EXPLICITLY DECIDED

■ **INSTANT FACTS** Father, after an earlier trial in which he was required to pay damages to his daughter, brought an action alleging that his adult daughter defamed him by stating in letters that he had raped her.

■ **BLACK LETTER RULE** An issue not explicitly decided in an earlier trial may be decided for collateral estoppel purposes if it constituted a logical, practical and necessary part of the decision reached.

■ **PROCEDURAL BASIS**

Appellant challenged a district court decision dismissing a defamation action against his daughter because the doctrine of collateral estoppel barred relitigation the issue of whether he had raped her.

■ **FACTS**

A jury awarded damages to the daughter (D) in her earlier suit against her father (P) for assault and battery where she alleged that he had raped her and sexually abused her when she was twelve years old. The father's (P) appeal was dismissed for lack of prosecution. The father (P) then brought this action for defamation after his daughter (D) repeated her rape charges in letters to several professional associations. The trial court dismissed the father's claim for defamation, finding that it was barred by the doctrine of collateral estoppel. The father (P) argued that there was no proof that the initial jury had ever determined that he had committed rape.

■ **ISSUE**

Must a jury have previously reached an explicit determination of an issue for collateral estoppel to bar litigation of the issue in a subsequent lawsuit?

■ **DECISION AND RATIONALE**

(Boudin, J.) No. The threshold question is how clear it must be that a jury previously answered the question. Confronted with a general verdict in the case, the court must determine whether finding that the appellant committed rape is a logical and practical part of the decision reached. The only plausible explanation for the jury's verdict in the first trial was that they found the father (P) had raped his daughter (D), in part because that was the central issue of the case and the jury awarded damages to the daughter (D). Thus, the father was collaterally estopped to relitigate the issue. Affirmed.

Analysis:

An issue may be decided for collateral estoppel purposes even if is not explicitly decided. However, courts must be certain that an issue has been previously decided in another case before applying the doctrine of collateral estoppel. Whether the jury rightfully or wrongfully decided the issue, its decision is not open to relitigation in a subsequent separate action. The burden of proving collateral estoppel is on the party invoking the doctrine to establish that the jury made the required determination in an earlier action.

■ **CASE VOCABULARY**

COLLATERAL ESTOPPEL: An affirmative defense barring a party from relitigating an issue determined against that party in an earlier action, even if the second action differs significantly from the first one.

GENERAL VERDICT: A verdict by which the jury finds in favor of one party or the other, as opposed to resolving specific fact questions.

Jarosz v. Palmer

(*Client*) v. (*Attorney*)
766 N.E.2d 482 (Mass. 2002)

ISSUE PRECLUSION DOES NOT APPLY IF THE OUTCOME OF AN EARLIER CASE DID NOT DEPEND ON SAME ISSUE

■ **INSTANT FACTS** Jarosz (P), a minority share-holder of several corporations who brought suit against Palmer (D), an attorney who had been involved in forming the corporations, asserted claims for breach of contract and fiduciary duty, malpractice, and violations of consumer protection statutes.

■ **BLACK LETTER RULE** A prior decision has an issue-preclusion effect only if the issue had a bearing on the outcome of the earlier case.

■ **PROCEDURAL BASIS**

The superior court dismissed Jarosz's (P) claims against Palmer (D), the appeals court reversed the dismissal, and the state supreme court granted Palmer's (D) application for further appellate review.

■ **FACTS**

Jarosz (P) filed claims against Palmer (D) and his law firm, claiming that the defendant had represented him individually in his acquisition of a corporation. The trial court granted the defendant's motion for judgment on the pleadings after determining that the plaintiff was precluded from arguing that the defendant represented him individually because another judge in a separate action concluded that Jarosz (P) and Palmer (D) did not have an attorney-client relationship. The appellate court reversed and determined that the requirements for issue preclusion had not been met. Jarosz (P) alleged that the issue had not actually been litigated, was not the subject of a final judgment, and was not essential to the earlier decision.

■ **ISSUE**

Was the issue precluded because it was previously litigated, determined by a valid and final judgment, and essential to the prior judgment?

■ **DECISION AND RATIONALE**

(Cowin, J.) No. The issue of whether an attorney-client relationship existed was not an essential part underlying the original claim. If the earlier judgment does not depend on the determinations made in the earlier case, relitigation of the issues in a subsequent action between the parties is not precluded. The plaintiff could have prevailed on his claims of breach of fiduciary duty and wrongful termination without the issue of attorney-client relationship being addressed. Because the nature of plaintiff's attorney-client relationship with defendant was not essential to a determination on the merits of the earlier claim, the issue was not essential to the judgment, and issue preclusion cannot apply. Reversed.

Analysis:

Issue preclusion prevents the relitigation of an issue determined in an earlier action if the issue arises again in another action based on a different claim between the same parties. However, in *Jarosz*, the

---

decision in the prior case did not have the requisite level of finality because the judge's determination was not subject to appellate review. Also, the nature of Jarosz's (P) attorney-client relationship with the defendant was not essential to determining the merits of the earlier claim, so it was not essential to the judgment, so that issue preclusion does not apply. Although the determination of an issue in a prior proceeding does not have a preclusive effect if the party against whom preclusion is sought had a significantly heavier burden of persuasion on the issue in the prior action, the plaintiff here had the same burden in both cases, so that factor is not determinative.

■ CASE VOCABULARY

INTERLOCUTORY: Interim or temporary, not constituting a final resolution of the whole controversy.

JUDICIAL NOTICE: A court's acceptance, for purposes of convenience and without requiring a party's proof, of a well-known and indisputable fact; the court's power to accept such a fact.

Parklane Hosiery Co., Inc. v. Shore

(*Corporation*) v. (*Shareholder*)

439 U.S. 322, 99 S.Ct. 645 (1979)

THE DOCTRINE OF MUTUALITY IS STRUCK DOWN AND OFFENSIVE COLLATERAL ESTOPPEL IS ALLOWED

■ **INSTANT FACTS** Shore (P), a shareholder in Parklane Hosiery Co. (D), brought a class action against the corporation, alleging that Parklane Hosiery (D) had issued a materially false and misleading proxy statement involving a merger.

■ **BLACK LETTER RULE** Defendants who receive a full and fair opportunity to litigate the claims against it are collaterally estopped to relitigate the issues, even when they are sued by a different plaintiff, unless a second plaintiff could have easily joined in the original suit or it would be unfair to the defendant.

■ PROCEDURAL BASIS

Certiorari granted to review the reversal of a denial of a partial summary judgment motion in which Shore sought to apply the doctrine of collateral estoppel to prevent Parklane Hosiery (D) from relitigating an issue.

■ FACTS

Shore (P), a shareholder in Parklane Hosiery (D), brought a class action suit alleging that Parklane Hosiery (D) made material and misleading misrepresentations in a proxy statement in connection with a merger. Before the suit came to trial, the Securities and Exchange Commission (SEC) also filed suit against Parklane Hosiery (D), making the same allegations. After a nonjury trial, the district court ruled in favor of the SEC. Shore (P) then moved the district court for partial summary judgment against Parklane Hosiery (D), claiming that Parklane Hosiery (D) was collaterally estopped to relitgate the issues that had been resolved against it during the SEC suit. The district court denied the motion on the ground that to estop Parklane Hosiery (D) would deny the defendant its Seventh Amendment right to a jury trial. The court of appeals reversed and found that Parklane Hosiery (D) had a full and fair opportunity to litigate the issue in the SEC action and that the mutuality doctrine, under which neither party could use a prior judgment against the other unless both parties were bound by the judgment, no longer applied. Parklane Hosiery (D) argued that they were entitled to a jury trial under the Seventh Amendment and that collateral estoppel applied only where there was mutuality of parties.

■ ISSUE

May a party who had fact issues adjudicated adversely in an equitable action be collaterally estopped to relitigate the same issues before a jury in a subsequent legal action brought against it by a new party?

■ DECISION AND RATIONALE

(Stewart, J.) Yes. Offensive collateral estoppel does not further judicial economy in the same way that defensive collateral estoppel does. However, rather than preclude offensive collateral estoppel in the federal courts, trial courts should be given broad discretion on when to apply it. If a plaintiff could have easily joined the earlier suit or when the application of offensive collateral estoppel would be unfair to a defendant, it should not be used. In the present case, Shore (P) could not have joined the original SEC suit and there is no unfairness to Parklane Hosiery Co. (D) which had every incentive to litigate the SEC suit vigorously. Because the defendant received a full and fair opportunity to litigate the claims against it, it is collaterally estopped to relitigate the question of whether the proxy statement was materially false and misleading. Affirmed.

■ DISSENT

(Rehnquist, J.) Parklane Hosiery Co. (D) was denied its Seventh Amendment rights to a jury trial. The development of nonmutual estoppel is a substantial departure from common law. Using offensive collateral estoppel runs counter to a strong federal policy of favoring jury trials. Also, the opportunity for a jury trial in the subsequent action could lead to a different result than in the first action.

Analysis:

Traditionally, a party could use collateral estoppel only if that party was bound by the earlier judgment. *Parklane Hosiery* allows a litigant who was not a party to a prior judgment to use the earlier judgment offensively to prevent a defendant from relitigating issues resolved in a prior proceeding. Therefore, the court again asserts that the doctrine of mutuality, requiring the same parties to be involved in both cases, is bad law. However, only the estopped party is bound by the prior holding because due process requires that all parties have the opportunity to litigate the issue fully.

■ CASE VOCABULARY

MUTUALITY DOCTRINE: The collateral-estoppel requirement that, to bar a party from relitigating an issue determined against that party in an earlier action, both parties must have been in privity with one another in the earlier proceeding.

OFFENSIVE COLLATERAL ESTOPPEL: Estoppel asserted by a plaintiff to prevent a defendant from relitigating an issue previously decided against the defendant and for another plaintiff.

Federated Department Stores, Inc. v. Moitie

(Large Retail Corporation) v. *(Consumer)*

452 U.S. 394, 101 S.Ct. 2424 (1981)

THERE IS NO EQUITABLE EXCEPTION TO THE DOCTRINE OF RES JUDICATA

■ **INSTANT FACTS** Moitie (P) and others brought private antitrust suits against Federated Department Stores (D), alleging price fixing of women's clothing.

■ **BLACK LETTER RULE** The doctrine of res judicata does not include an equitable exception.

■ **PROCEDURAL BASIS**

Certiorari to review an order dismissing Moitie's (P) action on the ground of res judicata.

■ **FACTS**

In a prior antitrust suit, the federal district court dismissed the plaintiffs' claims for failure to state a claim. Moitie (P) then brought an antitrust claim in state court against Federated Department Stores, Inc. (D). The other original plaintiffs appealed the decision to dismiss. Federated Department Stores, Inc. (D) removed the case to federal court and moved to have it dismissed on the basis of res judicata. The district court dismissed the complaint, but the court of appeals reversed when the actions of other private litigants were reinstated on appeal. The court of appeals found that, although Moitie's action was technically barred by res judicata, an exception to the doctrine was necessary to promote public policy and fairness. Federated Department Stores, Inc. (D) argued that there was no equitable exception to the doctrine of res judicata.

■ **ISSUE**

Does res judicata bar relitigation of an unappealed, adverse judgment in a situation in which other plaintiffs, in similar actions against the common defendants, successfully appealed the judgment?

■ **DECISION AND RATIONALE**

(Rehnquist, J.) Yes. The decision of the court of appeals to decline a case because it viewed it as so closely interwoven with the successfully appealing parties' case is an unprecedented departure from accepted principles of res judicata. The doctrine of res judicata serves vital public interests beyond a court's determination of the equities of a particular case. Moitie (P) finds herself in a predicament of her own making. She could have appealed the decision, but she made a calculated decision to forego the opportunity to appeal. Therefore, she does not deserve to be the windfall beneficiary of the other original plaintiffs' reversal. Reversed.

■ **CONCURRENCE**

(Blackmun, J.) In some cases, the doctrine of res judicata must give way to overriding concerns of public policy and simple justice. But this case is not one in which equity requires the doctrine of res judicata to give way. Because Moitie (P) made a deliberate tactical decision not to appeal the original decision, a strict application of res judicata is necessary in multiple party actions to prevent break-away litigation. In addition, Moitie's state party claims were simply disguised federal claims.

■ DISSENT

(Brennan, J.) If a plaintiff has a right to relief under federal or state law, a federal court, on a removal proceeding, should not look beyond the pleading in the state action to determine whether a federal question is presented. In this case, federal laws have not displaced the antitrust laws involved. Therefore, this case arises without reference to federal law. Yet, the majority sustains removal because at least some of the claims had a federal character to support removal. The majority is wrong in deciding that an unqualified dismissal on the merits of a substantial federal antitrust claim precludes relitigation of the same claim on a state-law theory.

Analysis:

Even a dismissal in federal court on an overruled case that was never actually argued on the merits is given a preclusive effect here, barring the plaintiff from relitigating the case under state law. The fact that other plaintiffs chose to successfully appeal the dismissal in federal court, instead of refiling the case in state court, does not require that equity allow the party that refiled to avoid the consequences of res judicata.

■ CASE VOCABULARY

FINAL JUDGMENT: A court's last action that settles the rights of the parties and disposes of all issues in controversy, except for the award of costs (and, sometimes, attorney's fees) and enforcement of the judgment.

REMOVAL: The transfer or moving of a person or thing from one location, position, or residence to another. The transfer of an action from state to federal court.

Allen v. McCurry

(Police Officer) v. *(Drug Dealer)*

449 U.S. 90, 101 S.Ct. 411 (1980)

COLLATERAL ESTOPPEL APPLIES TO CIVIL RIGHTS SUITS

■ **INSTANT FACTS** McCurry (P), who had been found guilty of drug possession and sued Allen (D) and other police officers for alleged violation of McCurry's constitution rights against unlawful search and seizure, sought to have his claims heard in federal court.

■ **BLACK LETTER RULE** Collateral estoppel applies to 42 U.S.C. § 1983 claims if the issues involved have been fully heard in a state court.

■ PROCEDURAL BASIS

Certiorari to review decision holding that the defendant's inability to obtain federal habeas corpus relief in state court rendered the doctrine of collateral estoppel inapplicable to his Fourth Amendment and § 1983 federal civil rights suit.

■ FACTS

McCurry (P) was convicted in state court of possession of heroin after his motion to suppress evidence was rejected in part. McCurry (P) failed to claim in state court that he had been denied the opportunity to litigate constitutional claims and sought to have his constitutional claims under 42 U.S.C. § 1983 heard in federal court. The court of appeals held that McCurry's (P) constitutional claims could be heard only in a federal forum. Therefore, he was not estopped to relitigate his civil rights claim. Allen (D) argued that McCurry (P) was collaterally estopped to seek relief in federal court on his civil rights claim.

■ ISSUE

Must federal courts give a preclusive effect to state court judgments if federal civil rights are at issue?

■ DECISION AND RATIONALE

(Stewart, J.) Yes. Federal courts must give preclusive effect to state court judgments even if federal civil rights are involved. Therefore, the common law doctrine of collateral estoppel applies to § 1983 suits, and the state court's decision on a federal constitutional claim is assertable as a collateral estoppel defense to a later damage action. "Full faith and credit" requires federal courts to apply collateral estoppel principles to § 1983 suits. Section 1983 is not similar to the federal habeas corpus statute that expressly renders null and void any state proceeding inconsistent with the decision of a federal habeas corpus court. Also, Congress gave no suggestion when it enacted § 1983 that it intended to allow defendants unrestricted opportunity to relitigate claims in federal court that had been previously decided in state court. Thus, the doctrine of collateral estoppel applies to a § 1983 action, even if federal habeas corpus relief is unavailable. Reversed and remanded.

■ DISSENT

(Blackmun, J.) By allowing collateral estoppel with full force to suits brought under § 1983, the Court disregards the history and policies that underlie the statute. McCurry (P) is an involuntary litigant in the state criminal proceeding. To force him to choose between foregoing a potential defense or a federal forum is fundamentally unfair.

Analysis:

The opportunity to appeal a motion to suppress evidence in state court after a conviction makes such a motion subject to collateral estoppel treatment in federal courts under § 1983. In some states such motions are not appealable and, thus, are not final judgments for purposes of collateral estoppel. However, as long as an individual had the full and fair opportunity to litigate the issues and claims against him, the earlier judgment can be used against him—even if the earlier judgment emerged from a state court and is used later by a federal court. Therefore, if McCurry (P) had not argued illegal search and seizure under the Fourth Amendment, the issue would not have been subject to defensive collateral estoppel in his federal court action.

■ CASE VOCABULARY

SUPPRESSION OF EVIDENCE: A trial judge's ruling that evidence should be excluded because it was illegally acquired. The destruction of evidence or the refusal to give evidence at a criminal proceeding. This is usually considered a crime. The prosecutor's withholding from the defense of evidence that is favorable to the defendant.

HABEAS CORPUS: A writ employed to bring a person before the court, most frequently to ensure that a party's imprisonment or detention is not illegal (habeas corpus as subjiciendum). In addition to being used to test the legality of an arrest or commitment, the writ may be used to obtain a review of (1) the regularity of the extradition process, (2) the right to or amount of bail, or (3) the jurisdiction of a court that has imposed a criminal sentence.

CHAPTER ELEVEN

Complexity: It All Comes Together

Temple v. Synthes Corp., Ltd.

Instant Facts: Temple (P) sued Synthes Corp. (D) for injuries sustained when a plate and screw device that was manufactured by Synthes Corp. (D) and surgically inserted into Temple's (P) lower spine malfunctioned.

Black Letter Rule: In a case involving damages, all permissive parties need not be named in a single lawsuit under Rule 19(b) of the Federal Rules of Civil Procedure.

Daynard v. Ness, Motley, Loadholt, Richardson & Poole, P.A.

Instant Facts: Daynard (P), who is a law professor claiming that he entered into an oral contract to assist Ness, Motley, Loadholt, Richardson & Poole, P.A. (D), a South Carolina law firm, and a Mississippi law firm in litigation against the tobacco companies, accuses the defendants of reneging on an agreement to share fees in exchange for his expertise.

Black Letter Rule: In examining whether a party to a contract dispute is "necessary and indispensable" under Fed. R. Civ. P. 19, the court must find the party to be both "necessary" because their involvement is needed to affect a just adjudication and "indispensable" because they must participate in order for the case to proceed.

United States v. Northern Indiana Public Service Co.

Instant Facts: United States (P) sought to condemn property owned by Northern Indiana Public Service Co. ("NIPSCO") (D), and the Saves the Dunes Council ("Council") sought to intervene.

Black Letter Rule: In order to intervene under Rule 24 of the Federal Rules of Civil Procedure, a prospective intervenor must move to intervene as soon as it knows or should know that its interest may be adversely affected by the outcome, and it must show that it has an interest relating to the property or transaction, that the disposition may impair or impede its ability to protect that interest, and that its interest is not adequately represented by the existing parties.

N.J. Sports Productions, Inc. v. Don King Productions, Inc.

Instant Facts: A boxing promoter who withheld a boxer's purse because of the boxer's conduct during a fight moved to bring an interpleader action to resolve disputed claims to the purse.

Black Letter Rule: Interpleader is permitted if two or more claimants to disputed funds are adverse to each other.

Hansberry v. Lee

Instant Facts: Hansberry (D), a Black homebuyer, purchased a house in a Chicago neighborhood that was subject to racially restrictive covenants.

Black Letter Rule: Due process is violated if a court gives res judicata effect to a class action judgment in which the procedures and prerequisites for class actions were not satisfied.

In The Matter of Rhone–Poulenc Rorer, Inc.

Instant Facts: Drug companies that manufacture blood solids are the defendants in a class action brought on behalf of hemophiliacs infected with the AIDS virus, which had found its way into the blood supply and the defendants' blood products.

Black Letter Rule: Class certification will not be granted if individual prosecutions are feasible and do not waste judicial resources.

General Telephone Co. v. Falcon

Instant Facts: Falcon (P), a Mexican–American, who worked for General Telephone Co. (P) and was passed over for a promotion, brought a class action on behalf of all Mexican–American employees and applicants who were denied promotions or employment, alleging race-based employment discrimination.

Black Letter Rule: In order to serve as a class representative in a case of racial discrimination, common questions of law or fact beyond race must be established to show typicality.

Martin v. Wilks

Instant Facts: After a consent decree in another action, a group of white firefighters sued the City of Birmingham ("City") and the Jefferson County Personnel Board ("Board") alleging reverse discrimination.

Black Letter Rule: A party is not bound by a judgment in which he or she was not designated as a party or has not been made a party by joinder, intervention, or other procedural device.

Temple v. Synthes Corp., Ltd.

(Injured Patient) v. *(Implant Manufacturer)*

498 U.S. 1042, 111 S.Ct. 715 (1991)

ALL PERMISSIVE PARTIES NEED NOT BE NAMED IN THE SAME LAWSUIT

■ **INSTANT FACTS** Temple (P) sued Synthes Corp. (D) for injuries sustained when a plate and screw device that was manufactured by Synthes Corp. (D) and surgically inserted into Temple's (P) lower spine malfunctioned.

■ **BLACK LETTER RULE** In a case involving damages, all permissive parties need not be named in a single lawsuit under Rule 19(b) of the Federal Rules of Civil Procedure.

■ **PROCEDURAL BASIS**

Certiorari granted to review affirmance of dismissal of claim for failure to join necessary parties in the federal diversity suit brought against Synthes Corp. (D).

■ **FACTS**

Temple (P) underwent back surgery in which a plate and screw device manufactured by Synthes (D) was inserted into his lower spine. After the surgery, the device's screws broke, causing further injury. Temple (P) sued Synthes Corp. (D) in a Louisiana federal district court based on diversity jurisdiction, claiming defective design and manufacture of the device. Temple (P) initiated a state administrative proceeding against the surgeon and the hospital in which the surgery was performed. At the end of the administrative proceeding, Temple (P) sued the doctor and hospital in a Louisiana state court. Synthes Corp. (D) filed a motion to dismiss the claim for failure to join the doctor and hospital in the federal suit. The District Court ordered Temple (P) to join the doctor and the hospital, but Temple (P) refused. The District Court dismissed the action with prejudice. The Fifth Circuit affirmed the dismissal on the grounds that Synthes Corp. (D) was prejudiced by not having the doctor and the hospital present in the litigation because one of the manufacturer's defenses might be that the doctor and the hospital were negligent.

■ **FACTS**

Must all interested parties be joined in a single lawsuit under Rule 19(b)?

■ **DECISION AND RATIONALE**

(Per curiam.) No. Pursuant to Rule 19(b), it is not necessary for all joint tortfeasors to be named as defendants in a single lawsuit. Where there is joint and several liability, the defendant is a permissive party to an action against another who may also be liable. Synthes Corp. (D), the doctor who performed the surgery, and the hospital where the surgery was performed are permissive parties under the Rule 19(b) threshold. The District Court abused its discretion and the U.S. Court of Appeals for the Fifth Circuit erred in affirming that decision. Reversed and remanded.

Analysis

Temple shows that joint, negligent parties are not always necessary parties. However, necessary party status is often conferred if the absent party would be prejudiced from the adverse effects of a judgment rendered in the party's absence. If litigation would have a preclusive effect against an absent party in later litigation, joinder may be deemed compulsory under Rule 19(a)(2)(i). This basic rule accomplishes an overriding goal of judicial efficiency, but, in this case, the policy consideration is balanced by Temple's (P) right to bring the cases in different courts.

■ CASE VOCABULARY

JOINT AND SEVERAL LIABILITY: Liability apportionable either among two or more parties or to only one or a few select members of the group, at the adversary's discretion; together and in separation.

PERMISSIVE JOINDER: The optional joinder of parties if (1) their claims or the claims asserted against them are asserted jointly, severally, or in respect of the same transaction or occurrence, and (2) any legal or factual question common to all of them will arise. Fed. R. Civ. P. 20.

Daynard v. Ness, Motley, Loadholt, Richardson & Poole, P.A.

(Law Professor) v. *(Law Firm)*

184 F.Supp.2d 55 (D. Mass. 2001)

OUT–OF–STATE LAWYER WAS NOT A NECESSARY OR INDISPENSIBLE PARTY TO A BREACH OF CONTRACT SUIT

■ **INSTANT FACTS** Daynard (P), who is a law professor claiming that he entered into an oral contract to assist Ness, Motley, Loadholt, Richardson & Poole, P.A. (D), a South Carolina law firm, and a Mississippi law firm in litigation against the tobacco companies, accuses the defendants of reneging on an agreement to share fees in exchange for his expertise.

■ **BLACK LETTER RULE** In examining whether a party to a contract dispute is "necessary and indispensable" under Fed. R. Civ. P. 19, the court must find the party to be both "necessary" because their involvement is needed to affect a just adjudication and "indispensable" because they must participate in order for the case to proceed.

■ **PROCEDURAL BASIS**

The case had been removed to a federal District Court, which, after ruling at three hearings involving jurisdiction, explained its rulings in this opinion.

■ **FACTS**

Daynard (P), who is a law professor at Northeastern University School of Law, has years of study and expertise on defeating the tobacco industry. Ness, Motley, Loadholt, Richardson & Poole, P.A. (D) and another law firm from Mississippi were involved in tobacco litigation representing the government. For four years, Daynard (P) provided advice to the defendants. He alleges that, even though there was no written contract, he shook hands with Scruggs, of the Mississippi law firm, on an agreement that Daynard (P) would receive 5% of the attorneys' fees paid to the South Carolina and Mississippi law firms as a result of the tobacco litigation. The litigation settled for billions of dollars and the law firms received attorneys' fees, but Daynard (P) received no payment. The South Carolina defendants (D) argue that, because Daynard (P) shook hands with Scruggs of the Mississippi law firm, Scruggs is a necessary and indispensable party. Although Daynard (P) brought suit against the South Carolina defendants (D) and the Mississippi defendants, the Mississippi law firm successfully moved to dismiss for lack of personal jurisdiction. (At the time of the opinion, the dismissal by the Mississippi defendants was on appeal; it was ultimately reversed.)

■ **FACTS**

Is Scruggs a necessary and indispensable party under Fed. R. Civ. P. 19(a)?

■ **DECISION AND RATIONALE**

(Young, C.J.) No. Under the criteria established by Fed. R. Civ. P. 19(a) and through precedent, Scruggs is not a necessary and indispensable party. Precedent dictates that such questions must be handled on a case-by-case basis. However, the rule of thumb is that a "necessary" party is one that should be joined in the interest of justice. An "indispensable" party is one that is required for the suit to continue. In order for a party to be "indispensable," its involvement must first be found to be

---

"necessary." Scruggs is not "necessary" because: (1) Scruggs and the South Carolina defendants are jointly and severally liable, and, therefore, are permissive parties and need not be named in a single lawsuit for the suit to continue; (2) the theory of "persuasive precedent" is rejected; (3) even though the South Carolina defendants may have to pay the entire amount owed to Daynard (P), they can pursue contribution by the Mississippi defendants based on the theory of joint and several liability; (4) as co-obligors, Scruggs and the Mississippi law firm are not necessary parties; and (5) because this is a case for damages in contract, not equity, all parties to the contract need not be joined. The fact that the continuance of this case may result in a later suit between the defendants is not relevant to Daynard (P), and, even if the case is dismissed for nonjoinder, Daynard (P) can simply bring the suit in Mississippi involving all defendants. In weighing the factors, Scruggs is not "indispensable" to this suit. Motion denied.

Analysis

The three rules of thumb that are used to determine if a party is necessary, are nicely laid out early in the opinion. First, joint tortfeasors are not necessary parties and may not be indispensable. Second, co-obligors to a contract may be necessary parties, but generally are not indispensable. Finally, as a general rule, an action to set aside a contract requires the joinder of all parties to the contract.

■ CASE VOCABULARY

NECESSARY PARTY: A party who, being closely connected to a lawsuit, should be included in the case if feasible, but whose absence will not require dismissal of the proceedings.

INDISPENSIBLE PARTY: A party who, having interests that would inevitably be affected by a court's judgment, must be included in the case.

United States v. Northern Indiana Public Service Co.

(Sovereignty Pursuing Condemnation) v. *(Property Owner)*

100 F.R.D. 78 (N.D. Ind. 1983)

A PARTY MAY NOT INTERVENE UNLESS IT HAS A PROTECTABLE INTEREST

■ **INSTANT FACTS** United States (P) sought to condemn property owned by Northern Indiana Public Service Co. ("NIPSCO") (D), and the Saves the Dunes Council ("Council") sought to intervene.

■ **BLACK LETTER RULE** In order to intervene under Rule 24 of the Federal Rules of Civil Procedure, a prospective intervenor must move to intervene as soon as it knows or should know that its interest may be adversely affected by the outcome, and it must show that it has an interest relating to the property or transaction, that the disposition may impair or impede its ability to protect that interest, and that its interest is not adequately represented by the existing parties.

■ PROCEDURAL BASIS

The case is before the court on the Save the Dunes Council's motion to intervene under Rule 24 of the Federal Rules of Civil Procedure.

■ FACTS

The United States (P) sought to condemn 36.95 acres of land owned by NIPSCO (D). The land was part of the Indiana Dunes, which are used for public recreation. Because Congress was in the process of enacting legislation to protect much of the Lake Michigan shoreline, including the land in question, the Council did not react immediately, assuming that the legislation would protect the defendant's land. When it appeared that the parties would settle and the land would not be protected, the Council filed a motion to intervene as a plaintiff under Rule 24. A pretrial conference was held and arguments were presented regarding the intervention issue. The Council filed a complaint for mandamus.

■ ISSUE

Can the Council intervene as a matter of right under Rule 24?

■ DECISION AND RATIONALE

(Sharp, C.J.) No. The Council does not have a protectable interest in the land and cannot intervene. Timeliness is the threshold question under Rule 24(a)(2), and the prospective intervenor must move to intervene as soon as it knows or should know that their interest may be adversely affected by the outcome. While the defendant argues that the Council did not file for an intervention in a timely manner, for several months the land would have been protected by a series of National Lakeshore expansion bills. Additionally, Council had no reason to believe it would need to intervene until the motion to dismiss, based on the settlement by the parties, was filed. However, an intervenor must have an interest relating to the property or transaction that is the subject of the action. While Council argues that they have an environmental interest and have protected the Indiana Dunes for public use, the court finds that Council has no protectable interest in the property. Therefore, the court denies intervention because Council is only a private citizen with no legal interest in the land and permitting intervention would cause undue delay and prejudice the parties' rights. Intervention denied.

Analysis:

Council, essentially a private citizen, does not have a protectable interest in the land and cannot intervene under Rule 24. In comparing Rule 19 to Rule 24, Rule 19 is typically used by a defendant to force the plaintiff to add a party, while Rule 24 is used by an absentee party to become part of a suit. Rule 24(b) uses a more lenient test for participation than Rule 24(a), allowing judges to expand the possibility of intervention.

■ CASE VOCABULARY

MANDAMUS: A writ issued by a superior court to compel a lower court or government officer to perform mandatory or purely ministerial duties correctly.

N.J. Sports Productions, Inc. v. Don King Productions, Inc.

(*Boxing Promoter*) v. (*Boxing Manager*)

15 F.Supp.2d 534 (D.N.J. 1998)

INTERPLEADER IS ALLOWED IF THERE ARE TWO OR MORE ADVERSE CLAIMS TO THE SAME PROPERTY

■ **INSTANT FACTS** A boxing promoter who withheld a boxer's purse because of the boxer's conduct during a fight moved to bring an interpleader action to resolve disputed claims to the purse.

■ **BLACK LETTER RULE** Interpleader is permitted if two or more claimants to disputed funds are adverse to each other.

■ PROCEDURAL BASIS

N.J. Sports Productions, Inc., d/b/a Main Events ("Main Events") (P), moves from an order permitting it to pay into the Court the amount in connection with an interpleader action, restraining any other actions affecting the funds, and directing that claims on the fund be filed.

■ FACTS

Main Events (P) was the promoter of a boxing match between Lewis and McCall. During the bout, McCall stopped boxing after the third round. McCall's purse for the fight was to be $3,075,500. The two contracts McCall entered into with Main Event (P) required McCall to present an honest exhibition of his skill and to fight in good faith. The contract also provided that if he or his manager did not present an honest fight, they would forfeit the purse. The Nevada Athletic Commission ("NAC") would decide if the fight had been an honest presentation and, if not, how the forfeited purse would be used. Shortly after the fight, the NAC notified Main Event (P) that McCall had breached the contract and that he was not to receive the purse. Ten days after the fight, the Nevada Attorney General initiated a disciplinary action before the NAC, which was settled with a $250,000 fine. The Attorney General recommended that the settlement be approved and that McCall receive the money minus the $250,000 fine. Several parties, including the defendant, claimed they were entitled to some amount of the purse. Time Warner filed a cross claim stating that Main Event breached their contract by not providing a competitive bout and by cashing a letter of credit over their objections, and that Time Warner was entitled to the funds. Main Event (P) wanted to interplead, claiming that they were cut out of the settlement negotiations, even though they had a protectable interest in the outcome.

■ ISSUE

Does Main Event have the right to interplead?

■ DECISION AND RATIONALE

(Bassler, J.) Yes. In order to interplead, there must be two or more claimants who are adverse to each other, creating possible double liability for the prospective stakeholder. Because Main Event (P) has shown that they are in a position of double liability arising from obligations owing to McCall and Time Warner, they have satisfied the existence of two or more adverse claim to the funds. Don King Productions (D) also argues that venue is improper in this district. However, venue is proper in the district where the stakeholder resides, and Main Event is located in this district. While there is no precedent as to whether a plaintiff-stakeholder could be construed as a "claimant" for purposes of the statutory interpleader, the plain language interpretation allows Main Event to be considered a "claimant" because they could assert a claim on the funds. Main Event, residing in New Jersey, brings its interpleader action in the correct venue.

Analysis:

"Rule interpleader" venue is proper in the district in which the plaintiff resides, all the claimants reside, or the claim arose. "Statutory interpleader" venue restricts venue to any district in which one or more of the claimants reside. In this case, although the court may enjoin parallel proceedings in connection with rule interpleader, the scope of the injunction is narrower than that of an injunction issued under statutory interpleader.

■ CASE VOCABULARY

NUNC PRO TUNC: Having retroactive legal effect through a court's inherent power.

STAKEHOLDER: A person who has an interest or concern in a business or enterprise, though not necessarily as an owner.

INTERPLEAD: To assert one's own claim regarding the court; to institute an interpleader action, usually by depositing disputed property into the court's registry to abide the court's decision about who is entitled to the property.

Hansberry v. Lee

(Minority Home Buyer) v. *(Covenantor)*

311 U.S. 32, 61 S.Ct. 115 (1940)

CLASS REPRESENTATIVES MUST ADEQUATELY REPRESENT THE INTERESTS OF THE CLASS MEMBERS

■ **INSTANT FACTS** Hansberry (D), a Black homebuyer, purchased a house in a Chicago neighborhood that was subject to racially restrictive covenants.

■ **BLACK LETTER RULE** Due process is violated if a court gives res judicata effect to a class action judgment in which the procedures and prerequisites for class actions were not satisfied.

■ **PROCEDURAL BASIS**

Writ of certiorari from an order affirming the res judicata effect of the prior class action decree.

■ **FACTS**

The class-action suit was brought in an Illinois state court to enforce a racially restrictive convenant on land that Hansberry (D) purchased. Lee (P) brought suit against Hansberry (D) to enforce a racially restrictive covenant and to evict Hansberry from a home in a white neighborhood. Lee prevailed at the lower court, which ordered Hansberry (D) to vacate. Hansberry (D) appealed to the Illinois Supreme Court, arguing that the requisite number of signatures had not been obtained on the covenant. Because the parties had stipulated to this fact in the lower court, the issue was considered res judicata and the decision was affirmed. The court found that the case was a class or representative suit and that the class members were the homeowners who signed the covenants and any subsequent purchasers. As a result, all matters that might have been raised were res judicata, including the validity and constitutionality of the covenants. Hansberry (D) petitioned the Supreme Court, arguing the constitutionality of racially restrictive covenants and the proprietary of the class action in this case.

■ **ISSUE**

Is the question of validity and enforceability of the racially restrictive covenant res judicata to the original signers and subsequent purchasers of the homes under the covenants?

■ **DECISION AND RATIONALE**

(Stone, J.) No. The lower court erred in finding the issue res judicata, and the parties are not bound by the earlier decisions. The Illinois Supreme Court wrongly determined that the signers of the covenants and any subsequent purchasers were members of a class. Because some may wish to enforce the racially restrictive covenants and others may wish to deny the obligation, they do not share a similar interest in enforcement or validity. Therefore, because their interests are dual and potentially conflicting, putative parties to the covenants cannot be members of a class and Lee (P) cannot represent the group without jeopardizing the interests of those who wish to challenge the covenants. No class exists, the court's decision to prohibit individual litigation on the subject denied due process, and the question of validity and enforceability of the racially restrictive covenants is not res judicata.

Analysis

Here, the plaintiffs in the so-called class action, who sought to enforce the covenants, did not act to enforce the covenants against anyone other than the named defendants. Therefore, not only were they not a class, but they did not treat all other potential black homeowners as a class, reinforcing the court's conclusion. Before *Hansberry*, much of Chicago's real property was governed by racially restrictive covenants, which prevented white homeowners in white neighborhoods from selling their property to blacks. The courts regularly enforced those covenants through court orders to vacate or face contempt charges.

■ CASE VOCABULARY

RES JUDICATA: An issue that has been definitively settled by judicial decision; an affirmative defense barring the same parties from litigating a second lawsuit on the same claim, or any other claim arising from the same transaction or series of transactions and that could have been—but was not—raised in the first suit.

CLASS: A group of people who have a common legal position, so that all their claims can be efficiently adjudicated in a single proceeding.

In the Matter of Rhone–Poulenc Rorer, Inc.

(Drug Company)

51 F.3d 1293 (7th Cir. 1995)

CLASSES MAY BE DECERTIFIED WHEN LAWSUITS ARE FEASIBLE AND WOULD NOT WASTE JUDICIAL RESOURCES

■ **INSTANT FACTS** Drug companies that manufacture blood solids are the defendants in a class action brought on behalf of hemophiliacs infected with the AIDS virus, which had found its way into the blood supply and the defendants' blood products.

■ **BLACK LETTER RULE** Class certification will not be granted if individual prosecutions are feasible and do not waste judicial resources.

■ **PROCEDURAL BASIS**

Petition for writ of mandamus instructing the district judge to rescind its order certifying the case as a class action.

■ **FACTS**

During the 1980s, the blood supply was unknowingly contaminated with the AIDS virus. Consequently, solid blood products manufactured by Rhone–Poulenc Rorer, Inc., and other drug companies (D) became contaminated, and many hemophiliacs who depended on them were infected with HIV. At the time of the suit, over 300 actions for negligence, involving 400 plaintiffs, had been filed against the defendants in state and federal courts. In *Wadleigh v. Rhone–Poulenc Rorer, Inc.*, 157 F.R.D. 410 (N.D. Ill. 1994), the suit to which this petition for mandamus relates, the district court judge allowed class certification on some issues, as allowed by Fed. R. Civ. P. 23(b)(3). Prior to the case, there had been thirteen individual cases in which the defendants won all but one.

■ **ISSUE**

Should certification be denied when the number of individual suits that are likely to be successful are not so numerous as to waste judicial resources?

■ **DECISION AND RATIONALE**

(Posner, C.J.) Yes. The district court erred in allowing class certification. His intention was to streamline a new "mass tort." He expected to obtain a special verdict that, if in favor of the defendants, would end this type of suit and, if favoring the plaintiffs, would allow members of the class to file individual suits. Although well intentioned, the decision overstepped his judicial authority. Because a special verdict certifying class is not a final decision, it is not appealable. Therefore, the court cannot intervene until after a final judgment is reached, which may be too late for the defendants in this class action lawsuit. Also, the statute of limitations will limit the number of individual lawsuits facing the defendants, reducing the need to develop a streamlined system for dealing with this type of case. If certification is allowed, the defendants will face thousands of plaintiffs and a blackmail settlement is likely, forcing the defendants to settle to limit the financial losses, which could be devastating nevertheless. Allowing class certification could cause irreversible harm to the defendants. While the awards in individual claims are likely to be sizable, because the defendants have prevailed in twelve of thirteen suits, chances are that they will continue to prevail. Also, allowing one jury to decide the fate of the industry is risky; individuals who prevail against the defendants will likely be facing awards in the millions. Such use of judicial resources is not wasteful. Weighing the benefits of the class action against its detriments, individual suits better serve the interests of the parties and those affected by the rulings. Petition decertifying the class granted.

Analysis

Certification was denied primarily because the number of individual suits that were likely to be successful would not waste judicial resources, whereas allowing the class action could risk the health of an industry that is generally beneficial to society. Decertifying the class accomplished many goals. In addition to preserving individual due process rights, it avoided the potential for disastrous results on the blood product industry because of a single trial. Reliance on societal interests as justification of a decision is common in cases presenting difficult issues with little precedence.

■ CASE VOCABULARY

SPECIAL VERDICT: A verdict in which the jury makes findings only on factual issues submitted by the judge, who then decides the legal effect of the jury's verdict.

WRIT OF MANDAMUS: A writ issued by a superior court to compel a lower court or a government officer to perform mandatory or purely ministerial duties correctly.

General Telephone Co. v. Falcon

(Employer) v. *(Employee)*

457 U.S. 147, 102 S.Ct. 2364 (1982)

CLASS REPRESENTATIVES MUST HAVE QUESTIONS OF LAW OR FACT AND CLAIMS IN COMMON WITH THE REST OF THE CLASS

■ **INSTANT FACTS** Falcon (P), a Mexican–American, who worked for General Telephone Co. (P) and was passed over for a promotion, brought a class action on behalf of all Mexican–American employees and applicants who were denied promotions or employment, alleging race-based employment discrimination.

■ **BLACK LETTER RULE** In order to serve as a class representative in a case of racial discrimination, common questions of law or fact beyond race must be established to show typicality.

■ **PROCEDURAL BASIS**

Writ of certiorari granted to review affirmance of class certification.

■ **FACTS**

Falcon (P) was hired as a groundsman through General Telephone Co.'s (D) special recruitment program aimed at hiring minorities. He was promoted twice within a year and turned down a third promotion. He later applied for a field inspector position and was denied. Promotions were given to several white employees with less seniority. Falcon (P) filed a charge with the EEOC and received a right-to-sue letter from them. Falcon (P) commenced his suit under Title VII of the Civil Rights Act of 1964, seeking to certify a class. The District Court certified a class including all Mexican–American employees and Mexican–American applicants in the company's division. At trial on the liability issues, the District Court found that Falcon (P) had been the victim of discrimination in promotion practices of General Telephone (D), but not in its hiring practices. With regard to the class, the court found the opposite was true—General Telephone had been guilty of discrimination in its hiring practices. Potential members of the class were notified and back pay was awarded to thirteen persons, including Falcon (P). The Fifth Circuit upheld the class certification and Falcon's (P) individual claim of disparate treatment in promotion, but reversed the holding that the company discriminated against the class in hiring. The disparate treatment in hiring was insufficient to support recovery on behalf of the class. The Supreme Court granted certiorari.

■ **ISSUE**

In a case of racial discrimination, can it be assumed that a purported representative is adequate simply because he or she is of the same race as the other class members?

■ **DECISION AND RATIONALE**

(Stevens, J.) No. While race is a significant factor in establishing commonality, the potential class representative must establish common questions of law or fact beyond race to show that his or her case is typical of the other class members. Falcon sought to define the class as "composed of Mexican–American persons who are employed, or who might be employed, by General Telephone at its place of business located in Irving, Texas, who have been and who continue to be or might be adversely affected by the practices complained herein." He relies on a Fifth Circuit decision that supports the contention that any victim of racial discrimination in employment may maintain an "across the board" attack on all unequal employment practices alleged to have been committed by the employer pursuant to their discriminatory policy. This approach, in effect, states that racial discrimination is, by definition, class discrimination. However, a potential representative must still show that his claim and the class claims share common questions of law or fact and that his claim is typical of the class. Although Falcon (P) was found to have been discriminated against in promotion, he was not the victim of disparate treatment with regard to hiring. Because the District Court rejected the class certification related to promotion discrimination but allowed certification related to hiring practices, Falcon (P) does not share common questions of law or fact with the other members of the class. Reversed and remanded.

■ CONCURRENCE IN PART, DISSENT IN PART

(Burger, C.J.) While the decision to decertify is correct, there is no point in remanding for further consideration. Falcon is not an adequate representative of the class. Additionally, the statistical evidence presented and accepted at trial showed that General Telephone (D) hired Mexican–Americans at a rate higher than their percentage in the labor force. This alone shows that a suit of disparate treatment in hiring cannot succeed. The class should be decertified and the case dismissed in the interest of judicial economy.

Analysis

The basis of the decision, that pleadings must show a clear link between the representative's claim and the class claims, is fundamental. Therefore, it is not surprising that the Supreme Court reversed the certification order, given that Falcon (P) suffered only discrimination in promotion whereas other members of the class suffered from discrimination in hiring. Other than the general common issue of discrimination, there is no factual relationship between the representative's claims and other class members' claims. In proving his individual case of intentional discrimination, Falcon (P) used statistics related to promotion and hiring which, in effect, destroyed his chance to stand as an adequate representative.

■ CASE VOCABULARY

NEXUS: A connection or link, often a causal one.

BIFURCATED TRIAL: A trial that is divided into two stages, such as for guilt and punishment or for liability and damages.

Martin v. Wilks

(*Intervening Black Firefighters*) v. (*White Firefighters*)

490 U.S. 755, 109 S.Ct. 2180 (1989)

UNNAMED PARTIES AFFECTED BY THE TERMS OF A JUDGMENT BETWEEN OTHER LITIGANTS ARE NOT BOUND THEREBY

■ **INSTANT FACTS** After a consent decree in another action, a group of white firefighters sued the City of Birmingham ("City") and the Jefferson County Personnel Board ("Board") alleging reverse discrimination.

■ **BLACK LETTER RULE** A party is not bound by a judgment in which he or she was not designated as a party or has not been made a party by joinder, intervention, or other procedural device.

■ PROCEDURAL BASIS

Appeal on certiorari from Eleventh Circuit Court of Appeals decision reversing a District Court decision granting the defendants' motion to dismiss.

■ FACTS

The City of Birmingham ("City") and the Jefferson County Personnel Board ("Board") (D) entered into a consent judgment with black firefighters for discrimination. Those consent decrees were put in place to rectify an earlier policy of racial discrimination against blacks. Wilks (P) and other white firefighters brought an action against the City and the Board (D) alleging that the promotions violated federal law because they were based on race. The City and the Board (D) defended on the ground that the consent judgment precluded the current suit. Martin and a group of black individuals, intervened to defend the consent decrees. The District Court found that the consent judgment was a defense to the white firefighters' (P) claim. The Eleventh Circuit Court of Appeals reversed on the ground that the consent judgment did not preclude the current suit because the white firefighters (P) were not parties to the previous judgment. The Supreme Court granted certiorari.

■ ISSUE

Are the original decrees subsequently binding on individuals who were not parties to the original suit but have a similar interest?

■ DECISION AND RATIONALE

(Rehnquist, C.J.) No. The decrees settled the issues between the parties who were involved in the lawsuit. Strangers to that proceeding are not bound. The Martin group (the intervenors) argues that the current challenges to actions consistent with the consent decrees are a collateral attack. They argue that, because the Wilks group (P) did not intervene in the initial proceedings, knowing that the result could affect them, they should not be permitted to litigate the issues in a new action. The City and the Board (D) argue that, because the white firefighters (P) failed to intervene voluntarily in the earlier action, their suit is not permissible, especially because they knew that the consent judgment would affect them. However, the Wilks group was not obligated to intervene. Because the parties to a lawsuit are more likely to know who will be affected by its outcome, the courts have traditionally placed the burden of mandatory joinder on existing parties. Additionally, mandatory intervention would not contribute to the

---

efficient use of judicial resources and everyone should have his day in court. A system of mandatory intervention would jeopardize that philosophy. Affirmed.

■ DISSENT

(Stevens, J.) The history of this case is long and complex. While the majority reaches the conclusion that the consent decrees do not "bind" the current litigants, preserving their day in court, there are more issues at play. The record does not state that subsequent litigants to the original action are bound by the consent decrees. Additionally, a "collateral attack" is treated as undesirable, but a collateral attack is an acceptable method of dealing with a prior judgment when those affected by that judgment have standing but do not have the ability to appeal, such as in this case. The collateral attack is aimed at the settlement and the consent decree, which cannot be appealed in court. The court failed to examine the validity of the consent decree. The lower court was correct in finding that the consent decree is not fraudulent, collusive, transparently invalid or lacking for want of jurisdiction. Such a finding is important because it directed the City to make conscious choices based on race. In doing so, there was, unavoidably, reverse discrimination. If the District Court had not affirmed the enforceability and validity of the consent decree, the City and other employers would be subject to an endless cycle of litigation to resolve cases of employment discrimination. The Court of Appeals judgment should be vacated and the case should be remanded based on the rule that compliance with the terms of a valid decree remedying violations of Title VII cannot itself violate that statute or the Equal Protection Clause.

Analysis

The general rule to come out of this case is that even if a party's rights may be affected, the party is not obligated to intervene, but if a party wants to make the judgment binding on a nonparty, that party must join the nonparty under the mandatory joinder rules. Cases decided after *Martin* have cast a negative light on its validity. Also, *Martin* was subsequently overruled by a federal statute that prohibits challenges to employment consent decrees by individuals with actual notice and a reasonable opportunity to intervene, or those whose interests were adequately represented. Nevertheless, *Martin* is a good example of the court's desire to preserve an individual's "day in court."

■ CASE VOCABULARY

CONSENT DECREE: A court decree that all parties agree to.

COLLATERAL ATTACK: An attack on a judgment entered in a different proceeding.

AMICUS CURIAE: A person who is not a party to a lawsuit but who petitions the court or is requested by the court to file a brief in the action because that person has a strong interest in the subject matter.